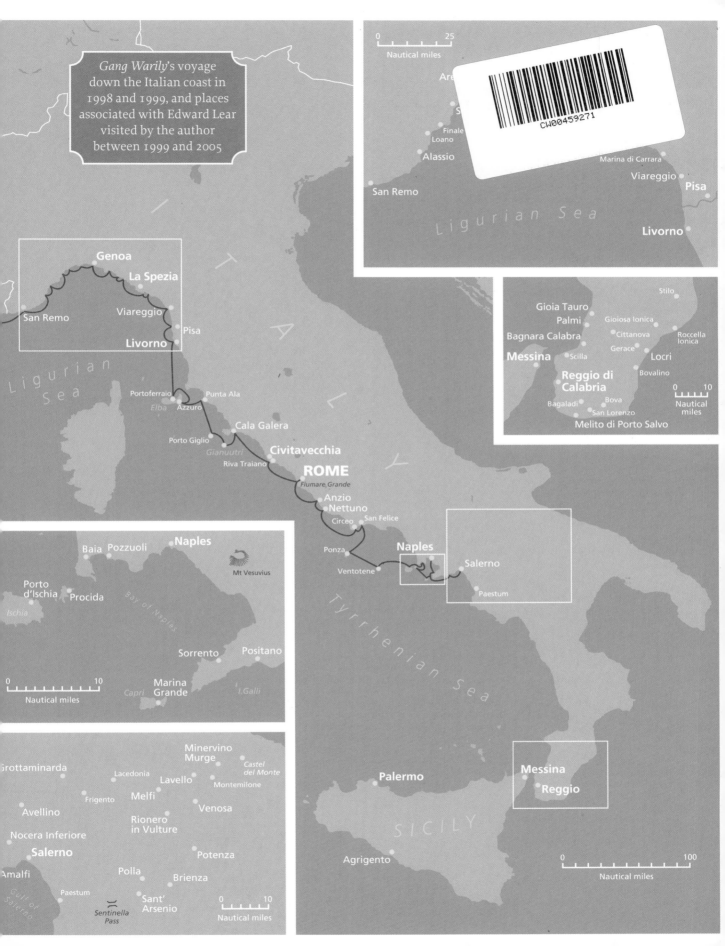

Gang Warily's voyage down the Italian coast in 1998 and 1999, and places associated with Edward Lear visited by the author between 1999 and 2005

Inset map (top right — Ligurian coast):

0 — 25
Nautical miles

Are...
S...
Finale
Loano
Alassio
San Remo
Marina di Carrara
Viareggio
Pisa
Livorno

Ligurian Sea

Main map (west coast):

Genoa
La Spezia
Viareggio
San Remo
Pisa
Livorno

Ligurian Sea

I T A L Y

Portoferraio
Elba
Azzuro
Punta Ala
Cala Galera
Porto Giglio
Gianuutri
Riva Traiano
Civitavecchia

ROME
Fiumare Grande
Anzio
Nettuno
Circeo
San Felice
Ponza
Naples
Salerno
Ventotene
Paestum

Tyrrhenian Sea

Inset map (right — Calabria):

Stilo
Gioia Tauro
Palmi
Gioiosa Ionica
Cittanova
Bagnara Calabra
Gerace
Roccella Ionica
Messina
Scilla
Locri
Bovalino
Reggio di Calabria
Bagaladi
Bova
San Lorenzo
Melito di Porto Salvo

0 — 10
Nautical miles

Inset map (left — Bay of Naples):

Baia
Pozzuoli
Naples
Mt Vesuvius
Porto d'Ischia
Procida
Ischia
Bay of Naples
Sorrento
Positano
Capri
Marina Grande
I.Galli

0 — 10
Nautical miles

Inset map (bottom left — Basilicata):

Grottaminarda
Minervino Murge
Castel del Monte
Lacedonia
Lavello
Frigento
Melfi
Montemilone
Avellino
Venosa
Rionero in Vulture
Nocera Inferiore
Salerno
Potenza
Amalfi
Polla
Brienza
Gulf of Salerno
Paestum
Sentinella Pass
Sant' Arsenio

0 — 10
Nautical miles

Inset map (bottom centre — Sicily/Messina Strait):

Palermo
Messina
Reggio
SICILY
Agrigento

0 — 100
Nautical miles

After You, Mr Lear

Maldwin Drummond

Copy number **513** of a limited edition of 1,000

To Gilly, Giovanni and Nucci

Edward Lear, showing the name written in his hat, silences
a fellow traveller who has just insisted to two ladies
that no such person as Edward Lear exists

Maldwin Drummond

After You, Mr Lear

In the wake of Edward Lear in Italy

The story of a voyage to rediscover
the ways of Edward Lear, artist and author,
through his paintings, diaries
and letters

SEAFARER BOOKS

© Maldwin Drummond 2007

Published in the UK by
Seafarer Books · 102 Redwald Road · Rendlesham · Suffolk IP12 2TE · England
www.seafarerbooks.com
ISBN-13 978-0-9550243-7-5 paperback
ISBN-13 978-0-9550243-8-2 hardback limited edition

British Library Cataloguing in Publication Data

Drummond, Maldwin
  After you Mr Lear : in the wake of Edward Lear in Italy
  1. Drummond, Maldwin - Travel - Italy, Southern
  2. Lear, Edward, 1812-1888 - Themes, motives
  3. Yachting - Mediterranean Coast (Italy)
  4. Italy, Southern - Description and travel
  5. Italy, Southern - In art
  I. Title
  797.1'246'092

  ISBN-13: 9780955024375 (pbk) – ISBN-13: 9780955024382 (hbk)

Front cover main image: *Amalfi, 1838*. Drawing in black chalk heightened with white on blue paper, by Edward Lear, by permission of the Victoria & Albert Museum, London. Front cover photograph of Edward Lear from Cadland archives. Photograph of Maldwin Drummond by Gilly Drummond. Back cover main image: Melfi, from a lithograph by Edward Lear in his *Journals of a Landscape Painter in Southern Calabria, etc,* 1852 (private collection). The harbour at Procida, photographed from *Gang Warily* by the author. Drawing of *Gang Warily* by Louis Mackay.

References and call numbers for landscape drawings by Edward Lear reproduced by permission of the Department of Printing and Graphic Arts, Houghton Library, Harvard College Library:
Alassio 16 December 1864 (45) NI.L16; *Chiavari 22 May 1860* NI.L15;
Finale 16/17 December 1864 (939), MS Typ 55.26 Oversize Box 2; *Lerici 15 May 1860* (9) NI.L15;
Rapallo 22 May 1860 (43) NI.L15; *Sestri di Levante May 21 1860* MS Typ 55.26 NI.L15 (38);
Spezia: Fort Fezzina 16 May 1860 (20) NI.L14

Photographs and incidental sketches not otherwise credited in the captions are by the author.
Illustrations by Edward Lear not otherwise credited in the captions are reproduced from works by Edward Lear in the possession of the author.

Copy-editing: Hugh Brazier

Design and typesetting: Louis Mackay
Text set digitally in Proforma

Printed in China by 1010 Printing International Ltd.
via MBC Print Consultancy

Contents

Preface –
a voyage of discovery

'What about Albania?' suggested my neighbour at lunch in London. I had asked him whether he could name a coastline that had been described in an amusing and entertaining way around a hundred and fifty years ago. He responded in one word – 'Albania' – but pronounced the name as if the first syllable was used for pricking holes in wood or tough sail cloth, adding that before the War that country's name was pronounced 'Awl-bania'. I expect he thought mine an odd question, so I ought to explain my reasons for asking. I had been reminded by his words, a minute or two before, that he had been a Parliamentary Private Secretary in the Foreign Office and had travelled extensively. For my part, I was looking for a coastline to examine in some detail, not aimlessly, but driven by the wish to follow in the wake of a diarist or an author who had recorded his experiences during the last two centuries. I could remember the pleasure and interest of a couple of similar expeditions I had undertaken in the past.

I had sailed to the Finnish Åland Islands to try and find the graves of three British sailors – George Privett, Thomas Barber and Lord Wrottesley – killed during the attack on Bomarsund during the Baltic Excursion in the Crimean War. I succeeded in another quest in 1982, when cruising under sail behind the north German Frisian Islands in an attempt to discover the truth behind Erskine Childers' novel, *The Riddle of the Sands*, first published in 1903. I had asked myself if there was really a plan to invade the United Kingdom from North Friesland in 1898, the year that Childers had sailed his cutter *Vixen* through those shallow and tricky waters. Did he really gather all that damning evidence then or was it just fiction beautifully written? After all, the Kaiser was sailing at Cowes against his uncle the Prince of Wales around that time. I had found out that eighty per cent of the story was true (Maldwin Drummond, *The Riddle*; Nautical Books, London, 1985).

Cruising under sail is given an added dimension if there is a purpose, rather than just floating about, following a salt-water desire line. The research, the anticipation and eventual success – or perhaps even failure – adds immeasurably to both the days at sea and the memory of the voyage of discovery afterward.

For the biographer, or for those who would reach back into the past, the approach of a coast or a port from the sea provides unexpected dividends. The land, from five miles out, comes complete with an understanding of the setting and the topography. The long view is missed when winding through suburbs or just following a road stained by evidence of recent years. The scene from seaward on the deck of a small boat is often not that different from the view enjoyed a hundred and more years ago.

Edward Lear.
Cadland collection

On my way home on the train, I remembered that my grandfather had kept a bundle of letters from the nonsense writer, author and artist Edward Lear (1812–88). Lear had been to Albania and fitted the requirements I had rolled off at lunch perfectly. Lear was writing and recording his experiences about a hundred and fifty years ago, he had an amusing turn of phrase and his pictures were wonderfully descriptive. I could remember my father telling me of Lear's correspondence with my grandfather and his sense of humour. Lear wrote to Edgar Drummond that he was thinking of applying for the crown of Greece, as he liked the idea of being called 'King Lear'. He had written *Journals of a Landscape Painter in Albania, etc.* in 1851.

Even the rumble and lurch of the old-style carriage operated by South West Trains that day could not dull my thrill of anticipation of the forthcoming research and the

Edgar Drummond.
Cadland collection

voyage to re-discover the ways of Mr Lear, artist and author, by comparing his pictures, diaries and letters with the scene today. I would get inside Lear and his works by sailing to the scenes described in paint and words. I would write of the experience. These were my first thoughts. However, Albania was a mysterious land then and the train wasn't the only thing that was rumbling. Albania was on the point of upheaval.

In my mind, as we rattled on, I remembered that the voyage to Albania would have to pass Italy. Edward Lear had spent a third of his life there and had managed to capture the landscape, particularly the coast, in his drawings in a way that clearly showed his admiration for Italian scenery and demonstrated his ability as a topographical artist.

Italy could provide a new insight into the man and his work. *Gang Warily*, my small boat, would be the vehicle for reaching the view from the sea into the past and would provide an unadulterated eye.

Acknowledgements

The towering scholarship of Vivien Noakes is an inspiration to all who wish to understand the world of Edward Lear. Her biography, *The Life of a Wanderer*, and her Royal Academy of Arts catalogue of 1985 were the foundation for a new understanding of the nonsense poet, artist and author. The late Sir Stephen Runciman led me round his pictures and rekindled my admiration for Lear as an artist, first excited by my grandfather, Edgar Drummond, and his collection of Lear's letters and pictures. The staff of the Houghton Library, Harvard University, made research there a joy. Roger Stoddart, Dr Ann Anniger and Eleanor Garvey were most helpful.

I would like to pay tribute to the crew who joined Gilly and me aboard *Gang Warily*. They included our son Aldred, Maurice and Jessica Hochschild, and Roly Franks. I am grateful to my daughter Frederica Templer, who has made a start on translating my text into Italian, and to Sir Mark Lennox-Boyd who, by suggesting a cruise to Albania, put the idea of Edward Lear and Italy in my mind. I would like to thank Lord Braybrooke, who arranged for my visit to Knowsley to see Lord and Lady Derby's collection of Lears. I was shown round by Dr Brendon Cole, former Curator at Knowsley. Guy Peppiatt of Guy Peppiatt Fine Arts provided me with a disk containing Edward Lear's view of La Spezia. Lord Stanley of Alderley lent me the sketchbooks of Captain Owen Stanley of HMS *Rattlesnake*.

I would like to thank all those who helped me with information and other forms of encouragement, particularly Martin Banham of Islington Borough Council; Nicholas de Rothschild; Mesiano Domenico; Nicholas and Roberta Drummond; Professor Gaetano Fierro, Mayor of Potenza; Nanette Godfrey of Tudor Hall School, Banbury; Peter Holmes; Michael Hughes; Tim Hughes; Sir Brian McGrath; Robert Neumann, Greene County Archives & Records Center, Missouri, USA; Richard Newsom; Sir William Proby; Edward Reynolds, the Fund for Epilepsy; Raffaella Rinaldis; John Rousmaniere, New York Yacht Club;

Gang Warily

Giovanni Sfara; David Standing, Wakes Museum; George Warrington; Lara Webb, Bank of England; Ursula, Lady Westbury; Philip Winterbottom, Archivist, Royal Bank of Scotland Group Archives; Suzanne Zack, Phillips Auctioneers; and Colin, Rosemary and Max Mudie. I am also grateful to Harriet Drummond of Christies and Henry Wemyss of Sotheby's.

My grateful thanks go to Patricia Eve of Seafarer Books, my publisher; Hugh Brazier, my editor; and Louis Mackay, who has designed the book and picture settings.

I would like especially to thank Brian Tillman, who photographed my collection of drawings and polished the photographs, and Mark Frost, who undertook research on the Lear family. I am also very grateful to my guides to the coast of Italy: Giovanni and Nucci Novi of the Yacht Club of Italy; Pippo della Vecchia of the Reale Yacht Club, Canottieri Savoia Napoli; Dr Antonio Scocozza, President of the Circola Canottieri Irno; Dr Mauro Scarlato; Captain Esposito, Harbourmaster, Amalfi; Paolo Luise of J Luise & Sons, Naples. My gratitude goes to the Royal Yacht Squadron and the Royal Cruising Club for their smiling assistance.

Finally I must thank Rosalie Hendey, who has processed all these words, and without whom the book would have been written with difficulty.

PART I

How pleasant
to know Mr Lear

Queen Victoria's royal yacht *Fairy*, built in 1844

I
Royal recognition

Edward Lear knocked on the door of old Osborne House on the north shore of the Isle of Wight on 14 July 1846. Lear's first volume of *Illustrated Excursions in Italy*, published that year by Thomas McLean, was to lead to a second volume. However, Queen Victoria was much impressed by the first and invited Edward Lear to Osborne, to give her drawing lessons.

Prince Albert and Queen Victoria bought the Osborne (originally Oysterborne) Estate in 1845 to house their growing family and to provide a little peace for themselves, which Windsor, Buckingham Palace and Brighton Pavilion failed to do.

On 3 April 1845, the Queen wrote to Lord Melbourne:

> The Queen ... thinks it is impossible to imagine a prettier spot – valleys and woods which would be beautiful anywhere but all this near the sea (the woods grow into the sea). It is quite perfection; we have a charming beach quite to ourselves. The sea was so blue and calm that the Prince said it was like Naples. And then we can walk out anywhere by ourselves without fear of being followed and mobbed.[1]

There was a Young Lady of Ryde, whose shoe-strings were seldom untied.
She purchased some clogs, and some small spotted dogs,
And frequently walked about Ryde.

Osborne House from the
sea in 1846, with the old
house behind.
Cadland Archives

Indeed, Osborne was a place of their own. That July the Queen and Prince were camped in the old Osborne House, purchased from Lady Isabella Blatchford. Queen Victoria had written in her diary of 1844, 'I am delighted with the house, all over which we went, and which is so complete and snug.'

This snugness did not appeal to the Queen's ministers or those who were granted an audience, as they all had to be crammed into the hall awaiting their turn. By the end of 1844, Thomas Cubitt, creator of streets and suburbs in London and the builder of the elegant Fishmongers' Hall on London Bridge in 1833, was approached to join the Prince in planning the enlargement of Osborne. Cubitt was clear – the old building would have to go. The new building was designed in the Italianate style, as the view across Spithead toward Gosport reminded the Prince of Naples.[2] The sixteen-bedroom old Osborne House was pulled down. The classical portico of the front door that Edward Lear probably saw but would not have passed through, as he would have entered by the back door, was re-used as the entrance to the walled garden.

Edward Lear would have seen the construction of the Pavilion, and it may have reminded him of his own views of Naples, a city he had visited in 1838 and which had overpowered him with its noise and turmoil.

Lear was not the only person to visit Osborne during the construction of the Pavilion. Charles Greville, who had an acid way with words, wrote, 'we walked about looking at the new house the Queen is building; it is very ugly and the whole concern wretched enough. They will spend first and last a great deal of money there, but it is her own money and not the nation's.' Greville had travelled to Gosport from London in a special train in two and a quarter hours, and then to East Cowes in the *Black Eagle* steamer.

As the Queen's guest, Edward Lear may have travelled to the island aboard the Royal Yacht *Fairy*, a 161-foot screw-propelled iron vessel, built by Messrs Ditchburn & Mare in 1844 as a tender to the royal paddler, the first *Victoria & Albert*, which had been completed several years earlier. *Fairy* also served Osborne, carrying mail, dispatches, guests and staff to the house, either landing in Osborne Bay or at East

Cowes. In other words, *Fairy* was a royal 'taxi' to the Isle of Wight.

Queen Victoria recorded in her diary of 18 July 1846: 'Osborne – Had a drawing lesson from Mr Lear, who sketched before me and teaches remarkably well, in landscape painting in watercolours.' Marina Warner, in her book *Queen Victoria's Sketchbook*, describes the Queen's picture of the Pavilion at Osborne and notes the Queen added to the sketch that it was 'only partly copied from Lear'.[3] She was obviously pleased with the results.

Osborne was not the first house the royal couple considered on the Solent shore. Eaglehurst, near Calshot on the mainland, was seriously thought about. This house also gazes at the sea toward the Isle of Wight. Osborne's soaring Italianate towers, surmounted with a flag, can be seen today from Eaglehurst when the leaves are off the trees. However, the view is divided by the 130-foot Luttrell's Tower, an elegant folly designed by Thomas Sandby, which rises from a 30-foot cliff on the edge of Stanswood Bay. The tower was built to the order of Temple Simon Luttrell and acted as a smuggling hideout. The small gravel cliff was ideal for creating caves for the temporary storage of brandy and other contraband. Luttrell died in prison in Paris in 1803 and his small estate was bought by the Earl of Cavan, who had been the second in command to Sir Ralph Abercromby (1734–1801) in the Egyptian campaign. Cavan erected his tent behind the tower, which inspired Eaglehurst.

The royal inspection of Eaglehurst arose because the purchaser of the estate, on the death of Lord Cavan, wanted to achieve an early sale and turn a quick profit. Eaglehurst was too small for courtiers, ambassadors and the royal family in the 'tent'. A royal landing could have been achieved at Calshot, as Henry VIII's tower there remained in the hands of her Coastal Artillery. An additional disadvantage of the property may have been the smuggling reputation of Luttrell's Tower. In any event, the royal couple plumped for Osborne. Eaglehurst was purchased by the Drummonds of Cadland to round up their holdings. Edward Lear would have walked the shores of Stanswood Bay with his banker and friend, Edgar Atheling Drummond, who owned Bournehill or The Cottage further west.

Lear's own drawing of Osborne House.
The Royal Collection
© *HM Queen Elizabeth II*

When Prince Albert died in 1861, Lear recalled in a letter to his friend, Chichester Fortescue (later Lord Carlingford) that 'Prince Albert showed me the model of the house (then being built only) and particularly the terrace, saying, this is what I like to think of – because when we are old we shall hope to walk up

Bournehill Cottage.
Cadland Archives

and down this terrace with our children, grown up into men and women.' Vivien Noakes, Lear's biographer, unearthed this snippet.[4]

In Lady Strachey's collection of letters from Edward Lear to Chichester Fortescue and to Frances, Countess of Waldegrave, she remembers the drawing lessons that the artist gave Queen Victoria. She cites two stories that Lear told about his experiences with the Queen:

Edgar Atheling Drummond, sketched at Cadland by Sir Edwin Landseer RA (1802–73).
Cadland collection

Lear had a habit of standing on the hearth rug. When at Windsor he was in the room with the Queen and as was his wont, he had somehow managed to migrate to his favourite place. He observed that whenever he took up this position, the Lord-in-Waiting or Private Secretary who was in attendance kept luring him away, either under the pretext of looking at a picture or some object of interest. After each interlude, he made again to the hearth rug and the same thing was repeated. It was only afterward that he discovered that to stand where he had done was not etiquette.

On another occasion the Queen, with great kindness was showing him some priceless treasures in the cabinets either at Windsor Castle or Buckingham Palace, I do not know which, and explaining their history to him. Mr Lear, entirely carried away by the wonderful beauty and interest of what he saw, became totally oblivious of all other facts and in the excitement and forgetfulness of the moment exclaimed, 'Oh! how did you get all these beautiful things?' Her Majesty's answer, as Mr Lear said, was an excellent one, so kind, yet so terse and full of the dignity of a Queen: 'I inherited them, Mr Lear.'[5]

Edward Lear was not the only tutor in watercolours to the Queen. She had the benefit of instruction from others. William Leighton Leitch, who executed some sensitive views of Osborne, was introduced to the Court by Lady Canning. She was the Queen's painting companion in the Highlands of Scotland. Charlotte Canning was a Lady-in-Waiting to the Queen and later Vicereine of India. Her talent as a watercolourist was considerable and the two often painted together. Lear first met Sir Stratford Canning, British

Ambassador to Turkey, in Rome. The Cannings invited Lear to join them on their way to Constantinople in June 1848.

Another royal instructor was the celebrated animal artist and recorder of Highland scenes, Sir Edwin Landseer, who had painted for the young Queen before she met Albert. He disclosed the secrets of painting in oils, which the Queen tried, but she preferred watercolour and pastel.

There is no doubt that the efforts of these three artists did much to provide solace to the Queen after Albert's death. The three L's – Landseer, Leitch and Lear – had talents that the Queen absorbed and made her own. Later, Lear was somewhat critical of Landseer. In 1854, when Lear's pictures *Marathon* and *Sparta* were hung at the Royal Academy's Summer Exhibition, he wrote to Holman Hunt in Jerusalem:

> The Academy Exhibition is unusually bad. Frith's Ramsgate Sands is his best ... the Queen has bought it. Landseer has a huge canvas full of slosh – melancholy to see when one thinks of what he could do if he liked.

But to return to 1846, a turning point for Lear. All but two of his Rome years were behind him and he had confidence in his own ability. The letter inviting him to Osborne to teach the Queen was a confirmation of this progress.

Teaching friends and acquaintances became an activity that provided a thin red line throughout Lear's life and helped him finance his painting expeditions. One of his first pupils was Captain Owen Stanley, Royal Navy. Stanley was the son

A sketch of Bahia, by Lear's pupil, Captain Owen Stanley.
Lord Stanley of Alderley

of the Bishop of Norwich and grandson of Lord Stanley of Alderley. These Stanleys were related to Lear's patrons, the Derbys, through the first Earl.

Captain Stanley was given command of Her Majesty's surveying ship *Rattlesnake* and ordered by Admiral Sir Francis Beaufort (1774–1857) to survey the Coral Sea, with particular attention to the treacherous waters of the Torres Strait.

The Bishop, Owen's father, was President of the Linnean Society, of which Lear was elected an Associate in 1831. *Gleanings from the Menagerie and Aviary at Knowsley Hall*, illustrated by Edward Lear, was published by Lord Derby, his patron, in 1846. This was in addition to his two volumes illustrating his Italian travels published in the same year. If this was not enough, 1846 also stands out as Lear's red-letter year, for he concluded his considerable achievements with the publication of his first *Book of Nonsense*, under the pseudonym of Derry Down Derry. This departure, which did more than anything else to make his name, will be highlighted later.

2

Gang Warily sets sail

In the summer of 1996, 150 years to the month after Lear's first visit to Osborne and the subsequent twelve drawing lessons for Victoria, he was remembered in the Royal Yacht Squadron after the Royal toast to the present Queen. It was drunk in port, not marsala, which Lear preferred, according to *How Pleasant to Know Mr Lear*. He celebrates his palate, and perhaps his excursions in Sicily, in the fourth verse:

> He sits in a beautiful parlour,
> With hundreds of books on the wall;
> He drinks a great deal of marsala
> But never gets tipsy at all.

On Wednesday 19 June 1996, the yacht *Gang Warily*, with its crew of three – myself, my wife Gilly, and nephew Maurice – left the celebrated port of Cowes at 6.15 a.m., bound for Saint-Vaast, on the east side of the Cherbourg peninsula. The morning was overcast and what wind there was was on the nose. As I looked back, a description of Cowes written a few years after Lear's visit came to mind. 'Nothing like its aspect,' remembers a writer,

There was an Old Man of Spithead, who opened the window, and said,—
"Fil-jomble, fil-jumble, fil-rumble-come-tumble!"
That doubtful Old Man of Spithead.

was ever seen out of a box of Dutch toys. From the sea it looked like heap of superior dog-kennels which have been rolled down from the hill on which it lies and brought up full on the edge of the water; the in-and-outness of its waterside premises seems incredible, and the rooms of its houses on the shore are built on that model of yacht cabins which is the highest flight of the Cowes imagination. Longing eyes have been cast by many an agent on the Ward Estate, which happily closes in the houses between itself and the sea, and every kind of plan has been made for cutting it up into desirable villas of the Cockney type.[6]

I could not leave Cowes astern without thinking of J M W Turner's (1775–1851) great picture of *East Cowes Castle: the Regatta Beating to Windward.* The picture was painted for the architect John Nash in 1827, along with another called *The Regatta Starting for their Moorings.* Nash's house, East Cowes Castle, was a neighbour to Osborne, but looked over Cowes Roads. The title should read 'starting *from* their moorings', as in 1827 yachts started races from anchor and did not gill up and down on the start line, waiting for the gun, as now.

The author at *Gang Warily's* helm.
Photo: Gilly Drummond

Turner was a hero to Edward Lear. He met him at least once and was enthralled by his works. *The Regatta* and *Shipping off East Cowes Headland, 1827* were probably hanging as a pair in East Cowes Castle while Lear was at Osborne.

We passed through the Forts at 7.30. The day was still grey, with the sky like corduroy. As the land receded until it became a faint, blue line astern, our world became 32 feet long, or 38 feet, with the bowsprit and stern davits. This shrinking world is one of the great pleasures of cruising under sail, for everything on board becomes of great moment, while the world, its troubles and responsibilities disappear. What matters now is confined to the vessel. If she is well built, well found and well maintained, the onboard worries are few.

Gang Warily was constructed at Woodbridge, Suffolk, by Whisstocks in 1971, under the all-seeing eye of Claude Whisstock and his son George. Claude had lost a finger in a band saw. He told me that all inexperienced boat builders or craftsmen in wood were in imminent danger of this sort of injury. He forgot to push the work through the flashing band with another piece of wood and so used – and lost – a finger. It seemed to me that he regarded this as a badge of honour, rather than a disability. Claude Whisstock was a legend. He had worked on fitting out Alan Villiers' full-rigged ship *Joseph Conrad.*

Jack Francis Jones, FRSA, MSIA, ARIMA, was chosen as the naval architect for two good reasons. The first was that his office was in Woodbridge, alongside the yard in which the yacht was to be built, and this is always of good advantage. The other was that he would respond readily and enthusiastically to the wishes of the owner, rather than persuade the client to accept a bigger or smaller yacht of his own distinctive design. Many yacht designers have really created only one design, and those that follow are longer or shorter editions, with profile and sheer recognisably the same. Sometimes this focus produces a magic result. William Fife II always held that a yacht should be 'eye sweet', and with Captain Nathaniel Herreshoff, on the other side of the Atlantic, produced the most beautiful yachts of the Golden Age, from the 1880s up to the First World War.

Jack was said to have designed over three thousand yachts since his practice recommenced in 1945. Nothing like that number had been built, of course, and in 1972, a year after *Gang Warily* was launched, there were 120 yachts recorded in Lloyds that year, the largest being of 46 tons.

Gang Warily was conceived to sail in cold waters, to cruise the Norwegian coast and to cross the Arctic Circle. She needed to be a *home at sea*, seaworthy and fit for cold, wet, miserable weather. This required a charthouse, where a full-scale chart could be laid out, where the sea and scenery could be viewed through thick plate glass windows, the eye travelling from the view to the chart and back to the view again. Parallel rulers and dividers needed to be close at hand, as well as any electronics that were available in 1971, and they were few.

Below, the yacht could sleep five. The heads were located at the forward end with a basin, sail stowage, work bench and long hanging lockers. The saloon had a pilot berth on the port side with an L-shaped settee below that could turn into a double berth. On the starboard side there was a long galley top. The table could be removed and folded against the forward bulkhead. The panelling came from Brunel's SS *Great Britain*. Toward the end of that ship's sea-going life she was working the guano trade off the west coast of South America. The ex passenger vessel's hull was clad with pitch-pine planking to protect her iron sides against the constant bashing and grinding of barges that transported the bird manure to the ship. Some of

Brunel's SS *Great Britain*, sketched by Lear's pupil, Captain Owen Stanley.
Lord Stanley of Alderley

the planking remained with her until she returned to her original building berth in the floating harbour in Bristol in 1970, where it was removed and would have had to have been destroyed. As a member of the ship's restoration committee, I contributed to the funds and bought a couple of planks, which were sawn up by Camper & Nicholson in Southampton. The firm was brave, for the nails that held the copper sheathing and the iron bolts that secured the timber to the ship were still there, hidden, waiting to wreck the saw blade.

I remember taking the harvest of thin planks to Woodbridge by train. The porter – there were porters in those days – said, 'What have you got there mate, a bit of an old chicken house?' He wasn't to see the artistry of Claude Whisstock and his men, who glued the planks on to plywood and polished them with wax and love.

The charthouse contained two bunks and was airy, giving out to the cockpit, with the engine, water and fuel tanks below. The mast, in theory, could be lowered from the mast pulpit and the rig was designed to help, as well as providing a profile of a staysail cutter with a jib-headed main and standing backstays.

In profile, *Gang Warily* had a clipper bow with a figurehead and trail boards. The bowsprit was secured to a little deck of its own so she had the profile of a clipper ship. The stern had a curved, sloping transom with a very small counter. The dinghy, originally wooden but now an inflatable, was carried on davits over the stern, like a Danish trading ketch A large ensign staff with a gold truck, at the same angle as the transom, completed a very satisfactory picture.

Jack Jones asked if I was going to enter for the Round the Island Race. I said I might, and he carried the conversation further by enquiring whether I expected to win or come anywhere within range of a prize. I said no – and that I would think he had failed if he had sacrificed any part of my *home at sea* to finish any more than halfway up the field. He seemed content with that.

Originally, *Gang Warily* was painted black with a white boot top and red anti-fouling. Her upper work was white and the deck a sand colour. When I was the Chairman of the committee building the Sail Training Association's *Sir Winston Churchill*, the question of the colour of that ship came up. I remember John Nicholson of Camper & Nicholson saying firmly 'black'. I asked him why and he replied, 'Black ships never go to hell'. He went on to explain that if you have a wonderful profile and a good sheer, black is a great colour, even if the hull shows signs of wear and tear. On the other hand, white shows every mark and even a great profile does not disguise lack of care and proper maintenance. So black became the colour for *Sir Winston Churchill* and for *Gang Warily*. We were bound for the Mediterranean and the hot Italian sun. Black did not seem a sensible colour, so again borrowing from one of the clippers, shown in Jack Spurling's picture of the *Loch Etive*, a sort of blue-grey was selected. It did not do the same justice as black to her profile, but it may have saved a few blisters. This is less of a problem today with fibreglass, but in 1971 wood was still seen as the right material for a one-off design. Iroko planking on oak frames was the right answer and brought a smile of pleasure to good old Claude.

She was my second *Gang Warily*. The name came from the Drummond motto, meaning 'go carefully'. This arose from the employment of caltraps, four-cornered spikes, one of which was always upright, which disturbed the English cavalry at the Battle of Bannockburn, 1314, when Robert the Bruce, later Robert I, defeated the English under Edward II, even though the Scots were outnumbered three to one. 'Go carefully', therefore, was the order of the day – and not bad guidance for those at sea.

Gang Warily in Danish waters, before her hull was repainted, flying the Royal Cruising Club burgee

3
Edward Lear – the quest

As the tan sails carried us forward, my thoughts returned to Edward Lear. The chronology (Appendix 1) draws a biographical line. Lear's time line will accompany the account of this cruise in search of him. By this method, we may surprise the artist by discovering his ways and his work, along with similar insights into his contemporaries by way of comparison. Usually, biographies follow their subject from birth to death, relying on the author following the trail of the debris of the subject's life, gathered from many places, filing it in date order so that a logical story can be told. This, though, is a voyage of exploration with Edward Lear as the quest.

The imperative of a *voyage of discovery* is that the subject, in this case Edward Lear, is examined as *Gang Warily* slowly passes by or anchors to discover more. Such a voyage is akin to fishing, for the net is cast where there is evidence that Lear has some connection and the haul is then closely examined and recorded.

Edward Lear's meeting with Queen Victoria in 1846 gave a starting place for the voyage 150 years later. However, Lear's time line started on his birthday,

There was an Old Man with a nose, who said, " If you choose to suppose
That my nose is too long, you are certainly wrong ! "
That remarkable man with a nose.

Bowmans Lodge, Upper Holloway.
ESTABLISHMENT FOR YOUNG LADIES'

Bowman's Lodge, Holloway.
Islington Local History Centre

A plaque near the site of Lear's childhood home

12 May 1812, and this should now be celebrated, or should it be postponed until the 13th, for that is what is written on his birth certificate.

Writing to the Reverend E Carus Selwyn on 28 December 1883, Lear states, 'As for memory, I remember lots of things before I was born and quite distinctly being born at Highgate 12 May 1812.' However, the process of registration was peculiar in that Edward's parents registered the births of all twelve of the surviving twenty-one children born to them on the same day (see Appendix 2).[7]

Edward was the twentieth of twenty-one children of the family of Jeremiah and Ann Lear, then living at Bowman's Lodge, Holloway, Highgate, at the corner of Holloway and Seven Sisters Roads. The name of the house descended from the archery field which was part of the same site. The villa was undistinguished, of two storeys with an attic. It was pulled down while Edward was still alive. The stables are still upright but much modified.

The year of Edward's birth saw the world in a disturbed state. Napoleon led 600,000 troops into Russia and some of them out again in the retreat from Moscow. Boney was not exiled to Elba until May 1814, returning to France in February 1815 to begin the Hundred Days. Waterloo ended all that on 18 June 1815. The American War of 1812 was another unsettling event. The backwash of all this, even the victory at Waterloo, was to send shivers around the Stock Exchange. By 1816, it became a personal crash for Jeremiah Lear. He owed over £2,000 in his exchange dealings. Bowman's Lodge had to be rented out, and Jeremiah had to resort to a friend and his bank to allow him to continue to trade as a broker. He must have regretted leaving the family sugar-refining business, where he had been doing reasonably well. Still, he did not go to prison for debt or fraud as son Edward thought. He remained throughout this period a Liveryman of the Fruiterers' Company. A time behind bars would have forced him to resign. However, this upheaval was all too much for the family. Those who could look after themselves did so, seeking employment. The eldest daughter, Ann, who had received a legacy from her grandmother, looked after Edward from the age of four onward and this care continued, even though Jeremiah and Ann returned to Bowman's Lodge for a while.

Psychologists are usually anxious to dredge the past and they would see the seeming desertion by Edward's mother as a significant event in his development. This was complicated by his devotion to his eldest sister. He wrote in his diary on 17 January 1865, 'Ever all she was to me was good, and what I should have been unless she had been my mother I dare not think.'[8]

As Edward became conscious of his appearance, he was convinced he was ugly. Sister Ann jokingly called him a 'Norfolk Biffin' because as a child he was undoubtedly podgy. As he developed, his nose became an exaggerated feature.

Maurice at the chart table

From portraits of his mother and sister Ann, it appears large noses were a family trait. Large noses became a feature of several of Lear's nonsense poems, such as the *Dong with a Luminous Nose*:

> He gathered the bark of the twangum tree
> On the flowery plain that grows
> And he wove him a wondrous nose,
> A nose as strange as a nose could be.

Gang Warily was now in mid Channel and I could see Maurice bent over the chart table, cricking his neck as he transferred the GPS readings to the paper chart. The tide and a little leeway had taken us a touch to the west and, without turning round, he suggested an alteration to the course. Gilly was stretched out reading on the starboard charthouse bunk, resting after delivering a proper sea-going lunch.

The Channel was as grey as the sky and seemed to meld at the horizon. It was difficult to see where one ended and the other began. Watching Maurice at the updated electronic aids, I could not help thinking how cruising under sail had changed in the last thirty years. Landfalls, with, at the most, compasses, depth finder and direction finder, were a navigational hit-and-miss exercise. Without radar, fog in the Channel, with ships crisscrossing, going where they wished without shipping lanes, was at times heart-stopping. Landfall came as a surprise, followed either by doubt or by the glow of self-congratulation. Then we were more akin to the 'old salts' who picked their teeth with a marlin spike, rather than the 'new salts' of today, who navigate electronically and have never grasped a hemp sheet or had to dry their cotton sails after arriving in harbour.

These thoughts brought me back to Edward Lear's childhood. I believe you are able to think more clearly when doing something, like walking, driving a car, or sailing a boat. Somehow the mind needs the body to be occupied to allow the problem-solving side of the brain to work efficiently. Remember Darwin and his sand walk at Down House in Kent, which helped him, among other things, to unravel the ways of the earthworm. Capability Brown (1715–83), the landscape gardener, also understood this with his clockwise circular path within a 'natural' designed landscape that aided philosophical thought. The change of view added extra spice to conversation. Somewhere I had heard the Prince of Wales hit upon the idea of the highly successful Prince's Trust while on the bridge of HMS *Bronington*. It had come as a shooting star, an image to be built on later, but had not disturbed the task at hand. The sensation of wind on the cheek and the occasional flick of salt spray, with hands firmly on the wheel, provided an ideal environment for unravelling aspects of Lear's early life.

The facts are clear from Edward's diaries, and have been interpreted by his various biographers. Vivien Noakes probably knows him best, and writes in her comprehensive and sensitive biography *The Life of a Wanderer*:

> When he [Lear] was only five or six, had come the first attack of epilepsy – 'The Demon', as he called it. It must have been inherited, for his sister Jane was also an epileptic. 'How I remember my sister Jane's epileptic attacks, now!', he wrote in 1873. 'Child as I was then, and quite unable to understand them.' His own seizures were often violent, and for a child they were terrible and frightening. The illness affected his whole life profoundly. He was fearful that one day an attack might leave him paralysed, or that repeated assault would destroy his mind; though he also hoped, until well into middle age, that the disease might loosen its grip as he grew older. It was a constant threat and sometimes he had several attacks a day.[9]

Jane was thirteen when Edward was born and she died prematurely.

Edward's form of epileptic attacks were proceeded by a warning – 'aura epileptica'. As a consequence, at an early age, he learned to make himself scarce when he felt an attack coming on, so few people outside his family noticed his condition. His fear of discovery added to Lear's lifelong feeling of loneliness.

Bertha C Slade, who edited William B Osgood Field's selection of Lear material entitled *Edward Lear on my Shelves* (New York, 1933) gives a short account of Lear's epilepsy. 'Many were our conjectures when suddenly we read in his own words that from the age of seven until his death he was pursued by the "Terrible Demon".'[10] In fact, in several places in the diaries he uses the word epileptic.[11] In his diary for 1882 we read the following: 'I spose the ever presence of The Demon since I was seven years old would have prevented happiness under any sort of circumstances. It is a most merciful blessing that I have kept up as I have and have not gone utterly to the bad, mad, sad.'[12] (The difference in the age of onset is probably due to different recollections as to when the disease struck. Vivien Noakes is probably right.) Field continues:

> It would possibly be the reason why he never married. It would certainly account for his depression and at times his utter loneliness. The attacks were very frequent and came at regular intervals. Often at the end of the month he recorded the number of seizures he had had. For example, in 1859 his record was kept complete with the omission of December, in the following figures: January the 16th, February the 15th, March the 12th, April the 14th, May the 13th, June, July and August 18 each, September the 15th, October the 16th and November the 10th. The attacks usually came in the early evening or in the early morning and on many occasions he noted that he was quite incapacitated for several hours.[13]

Epilepsy is defined by the Epilepsy Foundation of America as 'a physical condition that occurs when there is a sudden, brief change in how the brain works. When the brain cells are not working properly, a person's consciousness, movement or actions may be altered for a short time. These physical changes are called epileptic seizures.'[14]

Edward was led to believe by sister Ann that he was partially responsible for The Demon, and he seemed to believe that the condition was brought on by masturbation. However, such a habit was unlikely to have been blamed for the fits before puberty. In Lear's day, epilepsy was not a condition that could be easily discussed, as it represented a 'touch of the devil'. In any event, sister Harriet was sent to sleep in Edward's room. Her duty was surely not to police self-abuse, but to help him during his turns. The problem of stigma associated with epilepsy is still with us, though obviously not to the same extent. A few years ago a global campaign to highlight the problems caused by epilepsy was launched and called 'Out of the Shadows'.

Epilepsy sufferers have included Van Gogh, who was treated with digitalis, derived from the foxglove. In his painting *Starry Night*, there is a classic example of the halo seen as a side effect of the drug.[15] Prince George, son of George V and Queen Mary, was an epileptic and he died in childhood during a seizure. The sad story of his young life was told in the BBC series *The Lost Prince*. Few people knew about the boy or his complaint.

It is not widely known that Graham Greene, the novelist, born in 1904, was told soon after he left school to devote his life to writing that he had epilepsy. The diagnosis came after an unexplained loss of consciousness. He was many years older before a specialist said that the opinion was wrong. The world would have been poorer without his novels, such as *The Third Man* (1950) and *The End of the Affair* (1951), had Greene been put off his career by a mistaken diagnosis.[16]

In Lear's day there were no anti-epileptic drugs, but now the condition may be effectively controlled with appropriate medication in seventy per cent of cases, though the services kindly given by Harriet Lear still have their place.

I wondered whether Lear's physically active life in later years, which started with romps on the beach at Margate and roaming the Sussex countryside with

Sarah Street at Batsworth Park, Lyminster, near Arundel, lessened the attacks or their severity. The Fund for Epilepsy said that to date there is no research that can confirm this, and so it was probably Lear's own determination to get on that prevented him from being, in his own words, 'bad, mad, sad'.

On top of all this, there were the 'morbids', which wrapped around Lear like a black cloak, that came and went. It is my belief that humorists and comedians go from an entertaining high to a dismal low, especially if they are much on their own like Lear. It may have been the price he had to pay for his gifts in entertaining others, which gilded his letters, gave sparkle to his limericks and peppered his diaries and books. In a way, he needed the oxygen of others to flourish, but was drowned at times in bouts of loneliness and nostalgia.

● The afternoon was sunny and we picked up the Barfleur Light at 20.30. The visibility was down to about four miles and the wind had died away.
– *Gang Warily*'s log, **Wednesday 19 June 1996**

I thought it would take about another hour to reach the Port de Plaisance of the Ville de Saint-Vaast-la-Hougue. So perhaps there was time to consider another side of Edward Lear, and that was his sexuality.

It is fashionable today to see the aura of sex in everything. Perhaps we can blame Sigmund Freud for this. The game of sexual snakes and ladders is endlessly played out to the fascination of the Western World. In Victorian times, religious belief and middle-class ethics marched in tune and drove such thoughts below the dining table. In those days, the press generally thought it should stay there and, in any event, it was no one's business other than the person concerned. Lewis Carroll took pictures of naked or near-naked young girls and society thought the images innocent. He had proposed to Alice Liddell in 1863, his photographic muse and model for *Alice in Wonderland*. He was thirty-one and she was eleven, which upset Alice's parents.

Lord Westbury, caricatured in *Vanity Fair*.
Cadland Archives

As Edward Lear never married, there is, in our world, a question mark over his sexuality. If he was not AC, then he must have been either DC or AC/DC. His letters, limericks, ditties and books have been scoured to produce evidence of a homosexual, or DC side.

On the DC side, there was a bunch of Lear's friends – Wilhelm Marstrand, Chichester Fortescue, Frank Lushington, John Addington Symonds and Walter Congreve – who have been hinted at. However, there is no clear evidence that Lear was homosexual. On the AC side, there is the Hon. Augusta (Gussie) Bethell, daughter of Lord Westbury, the Lord Chancellor. Lear had known Gussie since her childhood and noted in his diary in November 1862, when he was fifty and she twenty-four: 'Dear little Gussie, who is absolutely good and sweet and delightful', to which he added – 'bother'.[17] By all accounts, Gussie was small of stature but full of character, whose energy made her shine. She captivated Lear, but he could not bring himself to propose to her. Gussie married Henry Charles Adamson Parker when she was thirty-six; he died in 1881, and she then became the wife of Thomas Arthur Nash. She died in 1931, aged ninety-three.[18] Lear may have expressed his feelings in the third verse of his song *The Courtship of the Yonghy-Bonghy-Bo*:

'Lady Jingly! Lady Jingly!
Sitting where the pumpkins blow,
Will you come and be my wife?'
Said the Yonghy-Bonghy-Bo
'I am tired of living singly –
On this coast so wild and shingly, –
I'm a'weary of my life;
If you'll come and be my wife,
Quite serene would be my life!'
Said the Yonghy-Bonghy-Bo,
Said the Yonghy-Bonghy-Bo.

Gussie may well have been Lady Jingly.

I could not help wondering what Lord Westbury thought of Edward Lear. The relationship between the two may give a clue to the strength of the romance between Gussie and Edward. A prospective father-in-law is usually cautious about his daughter's potential husband. The first Lord Westbury was twelve years older than Edward Lear and so nearer to him in age than he was to Gussie. There is a clue about the relationship between the two men in a letter that Edward Lear wrote to Gussie on Lord Westbury's death in 1873:

My recollections of your father go back as far as fifty years ago, when you were at Littlehampton: but I seem to remember him more distinctly at Lauderdale House, Highgate, Hackwood and Hinton St George; at all of such places I used to receive unvarying kindnesses from him and your mother ... I used, when I came to England, most frequently to pass my Sundays at Hackwood (near Basingstoke) and generally accompanied your father, who rode a white pony, in rambles about Hackwood Park and the contiguous; and during these excursions I was always struck by the variety, the liveliness and the instructiveness of his conversation.

...

Lord Westbury after he was Lord Chancellor never became the least changed in manner towards me, but was as glad to see me at his house as when he was simple Richard Bethell, and on my frequent visits to England I had only to propose a visit to Hackwood or Hinton St George, to be received with marked kindness. The books of nonsense I wrote from time to time greatly amused him, and when I made that absurd story for the Slingsby children, who went (or didn't go) round the world it was wonderfully funny to hear the Chancellor read the whole aloud with a solemnity befitting the perusal of grave history.[19]

Of course, Edward Lear was referring to *The Story of the Four Little Children Who Went Round the World*:

Once upon a time, a long while ago, there were four little people whose names were Violet, Slingsby, Guy and Lionel and they all thought they should like to see the world. So they bought a large boat to sail right round the world by sea, and then they were to come back on the other side by land. The boat was painted blue with green spots, and the sail was yellow with red stripes and when they set off, they only took a small cat to steer and look after the boat, besides an elderly quangle-wangle, who also had to cook the dinner and make the tea; for which purposes they took a large kettle.

Lord Westbury probably enjoyed the story, as he was a keen yachtsman himself, a member of the Royal Yacht Squadron and the owner of the 155-ton schooner *Flirt*. Lord Westbury was famous for his sharp tongue. He described Samuel Wilberforce (1805–73) as 'a well lubricated set of words, a sentence so oily and saponaceous that no one can grasp it'. This may have been the reason the Bishop was called 'Soapy Sam'.

It is apparent the Lord Chancellor was fond of Edward Lear. He may not have realised his friend's feelings for his daughter.

Edward Lear was really lonely and yearned for close companionship. He was the sort of man who showed his feelings by touching, and no doubt his short-sighted eyes, buried behind spectacles, glowed with pleasure and friendly affection. But he was not homosexual. Recent discoveries have shown there is a condition of asexuality,[20] a condition brought on by the lack of libido. It may be that this part of him had been driven out of Lear by an experience he refers to in his diary on 19 June 1871:

> It is just fifty years ago since he did me the greatest Evil done to me in life, excepting that done by C. – and which must last now to the end – spite of all reason and effort.

Edward was referring to his cousin Frederick Harding. He had just received news of his death. The identity of 'C' is not known. The two incidents are not described anywhere else. The incident with Harding that he records was on Easter Monday, 8 April 1822.[21] Lear is thought to have suffered at one time from a sexually transmitted disease, but it could not have been too serious. A cure for syphilis did not arrive until 1909, when Paul Ehrlich invented salvarsan.

My reverie was disturbed by Maurice, with a glass of white wine in hand. We had rounded Cape Barfleur with its magnificent lighthouse and were about to enter the yacht harbour at Saint-Vaast. There had been no fuss when we sighted land and then identified the lighthouse. No man at the masthead, one hand just below the truck and the other stretched out with a pointing finger, shouting 'land ho!'

Land Ho!
Royal Cruising Club burgee at the masthead

4
Sea battles and sea painters

I remembered that the battles of Barfleur and La Hougue took place in these waters in May 1692. The conflict was between Louis XIV's fleet under Admiral Tourville, which was being prepared to carry troops to invade England in support of the deposed James II, and the much superior Anglo-Dutch fleet under Admiral Russell, who was determined to thwart the Jacobite cause. Tourville's ship, *Le Soleil Royal*, ran aground and was cut out in Cherbourg Bay by the English Admiral Delavall. In another action, Sir George Rooke went into the shallow part of Hougue Bay in his boats and, under the eyes of James II, fired twelve French ships of the line and some transports. It was a brave action, for they were hauled tight inshore under the guns of the fort. The French cavalry, who were to be part of the invasion force, charged into the water, swords flashing. Some of the troopers were pulled from their chargers by seamen wielding boat hooks.[22] James saw all this and exclaimed, rather tactlessly, to the French officers in his entourage, 'None but my British tars could have done so gallant a deed!'[23]

There was an Old Person of Grange, whose manners were scroobious and strange;
He sailed to St. Blubb, in a Waterproof Tub,
That aquatic Old Person of Grange.

Lord Melfort, a Jacobite Drummond, whispered to Louis that part of the British fleet was disaffected and would desert William and Mary. In particular, he named Rear Admiral Richard Carter of the *Duke*. Carter was fighting gallantly when he was hit by a ball. His last words were, 'Fight the ship as long as she will swim.'[24] An American Royal Academician, Benjamin West (1738–1820), painted two studies of the battle. Surely if there were any spirits or 'mere men' about, they would be seen in these waters.

⬤ St Vaast is a pleasant place. The yacht marina no doubt has done something to lift the town. It was all oysters and fish when I last came here in the first *Gang Warily*. We dried out against the wall. Gilly pointed out that the flats above the shops were occupied, unlike in Britain where in some cases the shopkeeper has pinched the staircase to gain more floor space downstairs.

– ***Gang Warily*'s log, Thursday 20 June 1996**

J M W Turner captured a view of *Fisherfolk at St Vaast, La Hougue*. French fishermen and women are jousting in boats by the fort. The fort was designed by the celebrated military architect Sébastien Le Prestre de Vauban (1633–1707), and was joined to the mainland by a long granite causeway. To the left is the town of Saint-Vaast-La-Hougue. The spire of the Mariners' Chapel can be seen. The view was taken from the beach at Morsalines, just south of the town, looking east.[25]

Edward Lear held Turner in great esteem: 'Copy first the works of God, and then the works of Turner.' Peter Levi quotes this ringing phrase in his biography of Lear, attributing the words to Edward Lear.[26] It might have been an instruction from sister Ann, who had encouraged Lear to draw from his earliest days. She recognised his talent and may have given him a copy of Daniel Defoe's *Robinson Crusoe*, with evocative illustrations by Thomas Stothard (1755–1834). These images brought the story to life and emphasised the power of illustration.

While in Sussex with the Streets, Lear had the good fortune to meet Lord Egremont and saw the Turners at Petworth. He noticed that Turner brought together in his watercolours and other pictures the traditions of classical landscape and the more precise record, a mark of the traditional landscape artist. Turner responded to the classical landscape and admired the idylls of Claude

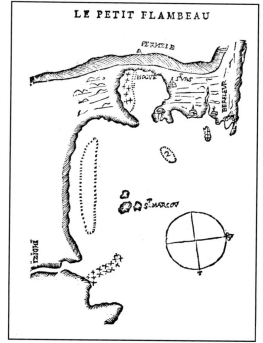

An early woodcut map, showing La Hougue and the Saint-Marcouf islands.
Cadland Archives

Lorrain (1600–82) and Nicolas Poussin (1594–1665).

Again, while with the Streets, Edward Lear, aged eleven, met William Drewitt, an amateur naturalist. Drewitt may have sparked Lear's interest in ornithology and the painting of birds, which he later practised at the London Zoo. Lear became astonishingly good at the painstaking yet lifelike capture of birds and animals on paper, drawn from life.

The appreciation of Turner's abilities came later, when Lear met him at the Marlborough Street premises of the lithographer Charles Hullmandel. Amongst the artists gathered there were Clarkson Stansfield (1793–1867) and James Duffield Harding (1797–1863).[27] Harding was to influence Lear's methods of landscape drawing by emphasising the role of the pencil. Clarkson Stansfield became a longstanding friend of Lear's. He had spent some time at sea, having been pressed into the Navy, and therefore understood the rigging and ways of the ship, never to be one of Lear's strong points. These were 'pressed' into his coastal views, rather than accurately portrayed. Lear may have also met the orientalist David Roberts (1796–1864) at that time.[28]

The Battle of Trafalgar, 1805,
painted by Lear's friend,
Clarkson Stansfield.
Cadland collection

Lear's ability to capture the images of birds from life led him in 1832 to the brave step of publishing on his own account, with Hullmandel's lithographic expertise and the publisher Ackerman's help, his book on parrots, *Illustrations of the Family of Psittacidae.* The venture may not have been a financial success at the time, but it brought the artist to the attention of John Gould, a bird promoter and publisher for whom Lear produced many illustrations, sadly some unaccredited. Another direct result was the introduction to the Stanley family, Earls of Derby, of Knowsley near Liverpool, four generations of whom were to become friends and patrons. The 13th Earl was also President of the Royal Zoological Society, which owned the London Zoo.

As a sailor and navigator, I was interested to discover that Charles Hullmandel introduced lithography to the Admiralty, which made naval charts much clearer.[29] The beauty of the paper chart, now almost lost in the move to the electronic series, is the information it contains on who did the survey and penned the views, together with the dates of the various editions and corrections. Admiralty charts were and are works of art.

Gang Warily slowly made her way in light winds from Saint-Vaast toward Ouistreham, the entrance of the Caen Canal, to join the Royal Yacht Squadron's rally of 1996. I could not resist taking in the Saint-Marcouf islands that lie to the southeast of Saint-Vaast. The islands have always fascinated me. I visited them with David Parkes, the owner of the 40-foot cutter *Joya*, in the late 1960s. David had been determined to spend the night in the moat of the fort on the larger island. *Joya* was not suitable for such an expedition, as she had a draught of over six feet. We were halfway in when we started grinding and bumping on the small rocks. David was not dismayed and laid out an anchor within the moat. With the winch groaning, the engine going and the staysail sheet held right in, which gave us a little list, so reducing the

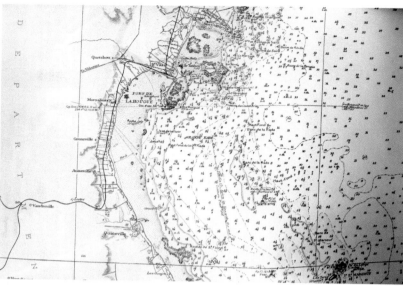

Detail of a late nineteenth-century Admiralty chart showing the approaches to La Hougue.
Cadland Archives

draught, we were successful and spent a quiet night after exploring the ruins of Fort St Marcouf. The fort was recorded by the Norwich painter, John Sell Cotman (1782–1842). He collaborated with Turner in the production of the *Architectural Antiquities of Normandy* in two volumes, published in 1822. This drawing of the fort was the result of working up a sketch made in 1820, as part of his third tour of the region. The fort is now a shadow of its former self, but it was easy to recall this exciting period of the history of the Saint-Marcouf islands.

The two islands, Ile du Large, with the fort and lighthouse, and Ile de Terre, are outcrops of rock commanding the inshore shipping lanes between Cherbourg and Le Havre. In 1796, the French were building large numbers of flat-bottomed barges

Fort Saint Marcouf, near Quinéville, Rade de la Hougue, watercolour by John Sell Cotman.
Fitzwilliam Museum

in the harbours between Antwerp and Cherbourg. These boats were designed to make possible Napoleon's ambition to invade England. The 'landing craft' were the work of an Antwerp naval architect, Muskein, hence their name, *bateaux à la Muskein*.

Captain Sir William Sidney Smith of the *Diamond* captured the islands in July 1795 with five hundred marines. There was no opposition. Napoleon though was outraged and made an attempt at recapture, which was thwarted by a number of British warships in the area. However, the French regrouped in the mouth of the Orne River, more invasion barges were added and a new fleet, together with seven gun-brigs, made for the shores of the larger island. The force was under the command of the Antwerper Lieutenant Muskein. He made the new attempt on 6 May 1798 with fifty-two craft and five to six thousand men. At first light on the 7th, they attacked the British forces under Lieutenant Charles Papps Price. There was no wind, so the British force of four ships in the offing were unable to help. Price only had seventeen guns in the fort, but he managed to sink the first seven barges, so the rest of the French invasion fleet retired. According to a French source, the invaders lost five men, killed or drowned, and fourteen wounded, while the British garrison lost one man killed and four wounded. Price and his colleague Lieutenant Richard Bourne, who was on the other island, were promoted to Commanders.[30]

Thomas Rowlandson (1756–1827), the caricaturist, celebrated the action with a cartoon. In this, the Muskein barges are seen going under, with the soldiers going up in the air. A rather more sober approach was the watercolour worked on grisaille, drawn by I Theobalds, which shows the islands and the disposition of the invading fleet. Wolfe Tone, the Irish Nationalist, noted in his diary: 'What! May

Thomas Rowlandson,
Rehearsal of a French Invasion as Performed Before the Invalids at the Islands of St Marcou on the Morning of Ye 7th of May, 1798.
Cadland collection

the English well say "You are going to conquer England, and you cannot conquer the Iles Marcouf".[31]

Gang Warily was almost as unsuccessful.

● There were three French yachts trying to anchor on the southeast side of the larger Marcouf, close in. They eventually managed to do so. There was not much space for us so we had a look at the northeast side of the Ile de Terre but the smell from the birds, it is a nature reserve, drove us away back to the French. We kept dragging. The bottom seemed to be pure rock. We therefore set sail and headed for Port en Bassin, trailing a mackerel line.

– *Gang Warily*'s log, Thursday 20 June 1996

However, the lock did not open until midnight, so as Ouistreham, a little down the coast, was our actual destination, we headed that way and were through the lock and in the yacht harbour by one in the morning. The Portsmouth ferry *Normandie* seemed to be hesitating in the entrance and came into her berth after us. She was greeted by a cacophony of sound. We later discovered it was the French farmers protesting about the effects of BSE on their livelihoods. I am not sure why this should have been – French BSE was known as JCB (the name of a British-made mechanical digger) as the affected animal was allegedly buried before anyone could have a look at it.

As Commodore (Royal Yacht Squadron) I had to lead the fleet of forty boats in two lines up the canal to Caen, pass and dip to the open Pegasus lifting bridge, the scene of the engagement of the night of 5/6 June 1944 by the 5th Parachute Regiment. Pegasus is the Parachute Regiment's emblem. We moored in the St Pierre basin, surrounded by buildings that rose after the city had been almost destroyed before being taken by the Canadians in June/July 1944.

Gang Warily leading the fleet into the Caen canal.
Royal Yacht Squadron

Apparently, after the war, the Americans suggested bulldozing Caen and creating an American city on a grid system with blocks and broad avenues. The wife of the then mayor, a landscape architect, was appalled by this idea and persuaded the City Council to rebuild on the old medieval street pattern, saving many historic buildings in the process and only replacing those too damaged to repair. This was in contrast to Le Havre, a 1950s city on modern lines with windswept boulevards and grey-brown buildings more in line with an Eastern Block development, drab and undistinguished. These days much has been done to try and alleviate the appearance of Le Havre.

I think the Mayor of Caen thought I could speak French, for my short address had been translated into written French by my sister Annabella, who lives twelve miles south of the city, and spelled phonetically by my wife Gilly, who also suggested a Churchillian beginning to amuse and mask my imperfections. I started: '*Prenez garde, je commence de parler Français!*' I went on in the same Anglicized way. The words went down well.

I had noticed some medieval tiles on the floor of the old Abbey showing two lions (or leopards) *passant gardant*, where our royal coat of arms is emblazoned with three. Hesitantly, for I didn't wish the Mayor to drown me in French words, I asked why he had two lions while we had three. He made a marvellous Gallic reply: 'Why do you find it necessary to have three?'

I discovered afterward that the change came about with King Stephen, who added one to make three. I still could not answer the Mayor's question, 'why?'

PART II

The voyage south

A steamer weathering the *Mascaret* near
Quillebeuf, after an old lithograph

5
Birds or landscapes

At the age of twenty-three in 1835, Edward Lear felt the need for formal instruction, so he enrolled in Sass's School of Art in Charlotte Street, Bloomsbury, where Thomas H Huxley, the great protagonist of Charles Darwin, had also been a pupil. He was consciously, or otherwise, preparing himself for a great artistic change in his life. In Lear's wanderings from the Streets' house in Arundel, he had sketched out of doors as well as capturing the interior of Arundel church. He had also done a landscape or two around the house of his patron, the 13th Earl of Derby (1775–1851) at Knowsley. It was from here that he set off for a sketching tour that was to change his life.

He travelled to the Lake District and stayed at Levens Hall with the Howard family. The root of Levens Hall is a medieval peel tower. Over the ages, the building has expanded, softening the old fortification. Inside, the rooms are symphonies of stone, wood panels and tooled leather wall hangings. Edward showed his enthusiasm for the house and its surroundings in a letter to John Gould (1804–81), the bird book publisher and taxidermist at the Museum of the Royal Zoological Society of London. He wrote:

There was an Old Man who said, "Hush! I perceive a young bird in this bush!"
When they said, "Is it small?" he replied, "Not at all!
It is four times as big as the bush!"

I left Knowsley (only half my work done) on the 12th August for a sketching tour, and really it is impossible to tell you *how* & how *enormously* I have enjoyed the whole autumn. The counties of Cumberland & Westmorland are superb indeed, & tho' the weather has been miserable, yet I have contrived to walk pretty well over the whole ground & to sketch a good deal besides.[1]

This tour was fundamental to Lear's change from a natural-history draughtsman and gifted painter of birds and animals to a landscape painter – a topographical artist. He was conscious of his poor eyesight and how this made some of the fine

work impossible. On 31 October 1836, Lear wrote to John Gould: 'To say truth, I had rather not at all, for my eyes are sadly worse, that no bird under an ostrich shall I soon be able to see to do.' He was putting off doing drawings for a British ornithological book.[2]

Edward wished to use his new-found ability to walk and paint as a profession. His style, in part, was influenced by James Duffield Harding, whom he had met at Charles Hullmandel's studio. It was as though one of his

Edward Lear, *Keswick, 24 September 1836.* Pencil and Watercolour with white. *Reproduced courtesy of Abbot Hall Art Gallery, Kendal, Cumbria, UK*

beautifully executed birds had flapped off, leaving only the landscape behind. Lear's *View of Derwentwater from Keswick* is just such a product of the 'new' Lear.

This change of course is described in a letter to Fanny Coombe, the Drewitt daughter of Peppering House, Burpham, near Arundel, who had married George Coombe:

And now let me inform you of a 'tide of affairs' of your humble servant, first promising, lest your curiosity be overwhelming, that I'm neither going to marry the old Duchess of Gloucester, nor turn cannibal, nor become Bishop of Salisbury, but I am to put into practice a long nursed dream of studying for two years in Rome. My part of undertaking this is a piece or a mass of goodness and friendship scarcely to have been heard of, & for which it is quite out of my power to show sufficient gratitudes. To my exceeding surprise a letter brought me three days ago a sufficient sum to live at Rome for the term I have stated, – and with this an explanation that many friends had been anxious to do me some permanent good ... no less than thirty friends of very different families and connections have arranged in this most delicate & kind manner, – by paying beforehand for commission drawings to be executed in Rome, – to give me this most valuable assistance.[3]

The 'thirty friends' was almost certainly an amusing exaggeration, as the money most probably came from Lord Derby or his nephew, Robert Hornby (1805–57), who had become a friend of Lear.

Edward Lear had previously been to the Continent with John Gould in 1831. He went to look at zoos and to illustrate Gould's *Birds of Europe*. The first edition, printed by Hullmandel, was in five volumes, folio size, with 448 hand-coloured lithographed plates by Elizabeth Gould, worked up from sketches by John Gould. Of the 448, 68 are by Lear. Lear, therefore, was no stranger to travel, and with the advance from Lord Derby he spread his wings again, leaving London for Antwerp with David Fowler on 16 July 1837. Edward had much admired Fowler's drawings of Rome and that must have been part of the motivation. They were accompanied by Fowler's brother-in-law, Edward Gale.

In the early days of the Grand Tour, Antwerp was a favourite port of call. John Evelyn, famous for his book *Sylva: a Discourse on Forest Trees* (1664), visited the city in 1641 and commented, 'There was never a more quiet, clean, elegantly built and civil place than the elegant and famous city of Antwerp.'[4]

In a much later letter to Ann in 1859, Edward described his ideal way of travelling as the 'stopping, prying, lingering mode of travel'. He may well have started this habit on his first visit to Rome. This meander included Brussels, where they met Ann, she staying on for a few months afterward with the community of lay nuns or béguinage, alongside the church of Saint-Jean Baptiste au Béguinage. The companions went on, through Luxembourg to Zell, on the Mosel River, where Fowler became indisposed, eventually returning to England. Lear's picture of the Castle of Eltz, still the home of the Eltz family, in pencil with Chinese white on buff-coloured paper, is evidence of his journey, and of his growing expertise. He continued alone through Germany and was in Frankfurt before crossing (via the St Gotthard Pass) into Italy, where he paused in Florence in early November, finally reaching Rome on 3 December 1837.

The Goodnatured Grey Gull,
who carried the Old Owl, and his Crimson Carpet-bag.
across the river, because he could not swim.

6
The artists' Seine

*G*ang *Warily*'s progress was even slower. At sea and under sail, there is a great temptation to press on, to cover sea miles, particularly when the wind is fair and there is a 'soldiers' wind' anywhere abaft the beam. However, we were entering the estuary of the Seine and with a fair tide made our way to the small port of Honfleur. Le Havre lay in the distance, where cranes and industrial shapes pierced the skyline. The scene was a reminder of Claude Monet's *Impression: Sunrise*, painted at Le Havre in 1872 and credited with providing the Impressionists with their name at their first exhibition in 1874. I cannot banish from my mind the comparison of this picture with A *Town on a River at Sunset*, a watercolour by Turner of 1833. Could Monet (1840–1926) have seen the picture? Could the picture have inspired Monet? Monet had escaped the Franco-Prussian War of 1870 by going to London, where he was much influenced by Turner's pictures.

The port of Honfleur is a delight and a celebration of life by the sea, a bubbling cauldron of sailors, fishermen, unlikely shops and cafés for long lunches, the very place to watch and savour France.

There was an Old Lady of France, who taught little Ducklings to dance;
When she said, "Tick-a-tack!"—they only said, "Quack!"
Which grieved that Old Lady of France.

● The pleasure of the morning was gained through a visit to the Musée Eugène Boudin (1824–98) – dedicated to the great painter, the rooms offered more, much more. They told the story of the artists and schools that flourished here in the middle to late years of the nineteenth century, running into the twentieth. I was particularly taken by an oil painting of an épave, a wreck, in front of the harbour wall at Le Havre by Eugène Isabey (1803–86). He was, therefore, almost a contemporary of Edward Lear. Isabey was one of the first to paint the French coast.

– *Gang Warily's* **log, Saturday 6 July 1996**

Gang Warily had been to Honfleur before, and had sailed up as far as the Abbey of Jumièges. The Benedictine abbey had been rebuilt on the foundations of the seventh-century abbey founded by St Philibert and destroyed by the Vikings. This time, however, we were on more serious business and were to travel through the rivers and waterways of France to the Mediterranean, so, of course, we needed a ladder. The search was not only a good way of practising French but provided an instructive tour of Honfleur. We should have guessed the ladder stockist was on the outskirts of the town. Ladders, like anything else today, were sold by a supermarket with a large car park so pedestrians are not important. So it came to pass, in the Biblical sense, that Charles Nicholson, who was crewing on Hugh and Liz Amherst's *Hal*, and I seemed joined together by a smart wooden ladder wandering back to the harbour. The economic advantages of carrying a ladder are that it is almost impossible to go shopping for anything else. A stage donkey would perhaps bring the same benefit.

It should be explained that ladders are useful, if not essential, on a sailing boat as the canals are shallow along the bank. Deep-keeled yachts cannot put their crew ashore without a fairly long gangplank, and this is what the ladder provides. Further, strapped to the rigging, the ladder helps the crew ashore in locks and alongside wharves.

J M W Turner had his own impediment, a writer called Leitch Ritchie, when he undertook his *Wanderings by the Seine*, the second and third parts of his work entitled *Turner's Annual Tour* (the first was *Wanderings on the Loire*). The three volumes were published by Charles Heath in combination with Turner in the years 1833, 1834 and 1835. There had been great public enthusiasm in the 1820s for illustrated travel books. The volumes describing the Seine included many views we were to glimpse on our way up that river. One of the most attractive is the bird's-eye view of Honfleur. As mentioned, Turner was accompanied by a hack writer, as Leitch Ritchie was unkindly described in the 1895 combined edition of the Seine and Loire.[5] Turner's plan was to walk both sides of the Seine from the ferry port of Le Havre to Rouen and then back along the southern bank to Honfleur, crossing to Le Havre by boat and then returning to England.

Edward Lear may well have seen these volumes. He would have been twenty-two at the time of their publication and already greatly admired Turner. The illustrations could have been part of the reason for his wish to become a landscape painter. The print of Honfleur shows the sixteenth-century Lieutenance or governor's house by the lock entrance to the Vieux Bassin. Turner's vantage point would have been on the high ground to the southeast of the town. Beyond the Lieutenance is another existing building, round-roofed with a belfry. This church is built entirely of wood as a thanksgiving by the town's shipwrights, called axemen, to thank God for the departure of the English after the end of the Hundred Years' War.

Engraving of Honfleur after J M W Turner.
Cadland Archives

Gang Warily left Honfleur and escaped from the lock into the swirling flood of the Seine. The Honfleur tower disappeared in minutes as we were moving at twelve knots over the ground, mostly because of the tide. In the narrowing distance was the magnificent Pont de Normandie, which had opened in 1995. The sun shimmered on the tracery of wires as we flashed underneath. The towers of the bridge are like narrow wishbones that come together in a spire at the top. The wires radiate from each tower supporting the bridge deck. The spider's web caught the sun and radiated a deep gold in contrast to the white of the towers. Sir Philip Dawson, then President of the Royal Academy, described this suspension bridge as one of the great creations of the twentieth century. The sight of it from the river sent a tingle down the spine.

Even with the tide we would not make Rouen in daylight, and regulations forbid navigation at night. There are mooring buoys marked on the *Navicarte – Guide de Navigation Fluviale* for the Seine from Le Havre to Paris, which persuaded us to stop at Caudebec-en-Caux. Just before Caudebec is Villequier, where Victor Hugo's daughter, Léopoldine, and his son-in-law, Charles Vacquerie, drowned six months after their marriage. They lie buried in the same coffin, victims of *le Mascaret*.

The *Mascaret*, or the Seine bore, used to be a spectacular sight at Caudebec. In the flood on the spring tides, the sea water funnelled into the bay of the Seine, particularly in easterlies, and thence into the estuary, where it met the normal river flow going in the opposite direction. Both flows were sandwiched between the river embankments, and a bore, an eight-foot wall of water, travelled upstream, concave in shape with the wave breaking on each shore. The initial wave could be followed by three or four more and then the dangerous *éteules*, silent waves up to sixteen feet in height but subsiding heavily as soon as formed.[6]

Engineering works completed in 1960, together with the deepening of the channel to allow large ships to reach Rouen, have tamed the *Mascaret*. Although still apparent, it has none of the destructive power of the past.

The little town of Caudebec has risen again after a disastrous fire in June of 1940. The Church of Notre Dame, covered with carved stone figures, was untouched – which is providential as Henri IV of France (1553–1610) described the building as 'the most beautiful chapel in the kingdom'. Prosperity from the making of hats and gloves helped to pay for the organ, which boasts 3,325 pewter pipes.

The swirling tide, the change of direction and rapid rise from ebb to flood leads to the recommendation that yachts should moor bow and stern so if one warp or chain were to give way the yacht would still be safe. It would be more comfortable, though, to allow the yacht to swing on one mooring. The log bears witness to the rapid rise of the flood tide.

> ● Gilly posted her letter, while I, a little anxious, looked for the dinghy. There she was, ten metres from the sea wall bobbing happily at her anchor. There was no time to be lost. I ran down the steps and waded into the water, grabbing the painter. The river was up to my waist and with some difficulty I managed to dislodge the anchor.
>
> – *Gang Warily*'s log, Sunday 7 July 1996

The tide picked us up and we were off, bound for Rouen. The tower of the Abbey of Jumièges could be seen through the trees as we whipped by Pouille, a village much favoured by Monet. Edward Lear did not approve of the monkish way of life, judging from his thoughts on the Greek holy men on Mount Athos. He would probably have used the same words about those who followed the Benedictine rule at Jumièges:

> These muttering, miserable, mutton hating, man avoiding, misogynic, morose & merriment-marring, monotoning, many-mule-making, mocking, mournful, minced-fish & marmalade masticating monx.[7]

The abbey was almost overwhelmed by the wooded heights above. Tantalising glimpses of the Castle of Robert the Devil were interrupted by trees. Robert is a mythical character, a smoky representation based on Robert the Magnificent, who became Duke of Normandy when his elder brother died in suspicious circumstances in 1028. Some time earlier, Robert had spied Arlette, a tanner's daughter, from the window of his castle at Falaise when she was washing her clothes in the river – an encounter which had a profound effect on French and English history. At the birth of their son, William the Bastard (later known as William the Conqueror), the legend holds she cried out:

Robert the Magnificent, alias Robert the Devil

> I dreamt that there grew from my womb a great tree which extended its branches so high and so wide that they shaded on one side Normandy and on the other, the whole Kingdom of England.

These magical views were in contrast to the dismal locks of the Flottant Bassin where *Gang Warily* was to be dismasted by the firm of Lozai. The maximum air draught for the French canals, that is to say the distance between the highest part of the boat and the water, is eleven feet five inches. *Gang Warily*, with her mast laid on the charthouse and supported forward by the pulpit, must have had an air draught of six feet. The heel of the mast reached out just short of the end of the bowsprit, while the masthead, with the electronic wind speed and direction equipment, or 'broccoli', was protected by a red plastic bucket and the dinghy that swung in davits on the stern.

> ● The spire of the twelfth-century cathedral of Notre Dame hangs over the city as if it is suspended from the clouds. Maybe God had something to do with its coming, for the two earlier wood and gilded lead spires had been consumed by fire. The first in 1514, the second in 1822. The use of cast iron was planned as early as 1823, but the masterpiece by Alvoine (on the Butter Tower) did not rise until 1876. The spire is the tallest in France at 151 metres. The top is crowned by a weathercock and a cross of red copper. The supporting four pinnacles at each corner of the stone tower are of bronze. The spire is pierced to allow God, or Aeolus, to pipe strongly without damaging this truly wonderful construction. Flaubert didn't like it, though: 'no good for parrots I suppose'.
> – *Gang Warily*'s log, Monday 12 August 1996

[Gustave Flaubert (1821–80) of Rouen brought a parrot into his celebrated and much criticised novel *Madame Bovary*, 1857.]

As we sat in *Gang Warily*'s cockpit, looking at the spire across from our berth near the centre of Rouen, I glanced down at the flowing tidal water and the little eddies that rolled past the hull. A large leaf went by and I remembered that Joan of Arc's heart had been thrown in the river here by her executioner. He had found it among the ashes in the Place du Vieux Marché, where she had been burnt at the stake on 30 May 1431. The execution was soon thought to have been a mistake, as the English in the town whispered that 'they were lost, as they had burnt a saint'. The Pope took longer to come to the same conclusion, for Joan was not canonised until 1920. She was made the patron saint of France and the twenty-metre cross in the square where she died is a national monument of reparation for the Maid of Orleans.

It seems difficult to imagine another scene that took place in Rouen, which is recorded by the Countess of Blessington (1789–1849), in the account of her travels entitled *The Idler in Italy*. Bernard le Bovier, Sieur de Fontenelle (1657–1757), Permanent Secretary to the French Academy of Sciences, was looking forward to a plate of asparagus dressed with oil when he was surprised by an unexpected visitor, the Abbé Terrasson, who proposed dining with him. Fontenelle told him what he was going to have, but the Abbé insisted he would only eat asparagus dressed with butter. The argument was heated and suddenly the Abbé fell from his chair, struck dead with apoplexy. Instead of rushing to the assistance of his one-time friend, Fontenelle ran to the door of the kitchen shouting 'all the asparagus to be dressed in oil, *all* to be dressed in oil'. The anecdote spread through Rouen and asparagus became fashionable and, of course, more expensive. It was difficult for us to respond appropriately, for asparagus was not in season in mid August.

Gang Warily left Rouen astern. It was as though the yacht was looking forward to passage without the muscular thrust or fight against the tide, for at Ampreville there were the sea locks.

> ● We carried the flood almost there as it started at Rouen at 10.30. The tidal rise appeared to be about sixteen feet, perhaps more. The lock keeper, to whom Gilly talked on the hand-held radio telephone, hurried us along. There was just room astern of the cruise ship *Normandie*. This put us into an indent covered at the top by a curved iron plate. That, and the *Normandie*'s continuing propeller wash, put two stanchions under the plate as the water rose, bending them badly. That, thankfully, was the only damage and we extracted ourselves without difficulty, but looking a bit defenceless on the starboard side.
> – *Gang Warily*'s log, Tuesday 13 August 1996

The locks at Ampreville, together with the Poses Dam, divide the Seine, canalising the river above. Napoleon declared that 'Le Havre, Rouen and Paris are but a single town of which the Seine is the main street'.

The Thames could provide a similar 'street'. Lord Desborough, writing in *The Sphere* magazine on 21 January 1928, argued that 'the removal of the tides from London Reaches is, in my opinion, the greatest single measure that can be taken for the benefit of London as a whole.' This was supported by Sir Alan Herbert, and again comparatively recently by the architect Richard (now Lord) Rogers and Mark Fisher, Member of Parliament and one-time Minister of State for the Arts, in their book *A New London*.[8] Looking from the deck of *Gang Warily* on the tideless scene above Ampreville, we said a hearty 'aye' to this great plan.

Gang Warily cut a line through the calm, still water, creating a sight rather than a disturbance. Coot swam lazily, their powerful green legs and feet cleaving the water slowly. They took no notice of us. Perhaps they thought us a giant member of their own family, or would have done if our hull had been her usual black colour.

Paul Signac (1863–1935), a follower of Georges Seurat (1859–91), was a 'divisionist'. He fooled the eye by producing a colour effect by putting dots of pure colour alongside each other, so the eye saw them as one, rather than taking the trouble to mix on his palette. Signac captured the island of Lucas in this way in 1886, two years before Lear died. I think Lear would have considered this method of painting interesting, but not for him.

The town of Les Andelys is a good place to stop and pay respects to Château Gaillard, one of the most impressive ruined castles perched above the River Seine. A salute could be given to Richard the Lionheart, King of England and Duke of Normandy, who built the place beginning in the year 1196. However, we were in France, so the honours went to Philippe Auguste, who stormed the stronghold in 1203, leaving the way open to reduce Rouen.

A magnificent dappled grey horse walked lazily to the edge of the Seine and looked up at us as we passed. You could almost see the quizzical look in his eye, at least the one aimed at us. What the other one was doing I'm not quite sure. The Percheron horse is said to have carried Crusaders and was employed by the French army in the First World War. Percherons are still occasionally used for anything that requires an animal to act as a tug. The home bases of this, the world's most famous heavy horse, are the Perche, Mayenne and Auge regions within Normandy. The animal had strayed a little from its native grasslands. Percherons are now found all over the world.

Vernon is an attractive place to pause. The Archives Tower commands the town and was the keep of the twelfth-century castle, built by Philippe Auguste. E L Maloy, in his book *Our Autumn Holidays on French Rivers*, published in 1880, records Vernon as a sleepy place: 'What struck us most was its stillness. Even the cock, a young and inexperienced one, crowed once very softly.' Today Vernon is quieter than most towns of its size, perhaps because it has been there such a very long time, having been founded by Rollo (860–933), 1st Duke of Normandy. Just across the river and a little upstream at Giverny is Monet's house and garden. It was here the artist experimented with different conditions of weather and light. In August, the borders in the garden are a brilliance of vivid colours, shapes and forms, tumbling from neat, narrow beds.

The next stop on our tour, recommended by my sister, was the Château de Bizy. In 1721, the Marquisate of Bizy was bought by the Count of Belle Isle, grandson of Fouquet, the disgraced Minister of Finance under Louis XIV and builder of the magnificent Vaux-le-Vicomte. Belle Isle created the Petit Versailles, planting the great avenue from the park down to the Seine in 1723. He rebuilt the chateau, the huge stable block and the fountains, and laid out the park. Bizy then became the property of the Duke of Penthièvre. He was an exceptional philanthropist and a much-loved landowner. Indeed, the town of Vernon defied the revolutionaries by honouring the Duke, his kindness and his works and he was not molested by the Red Caps. On the Duke's death, the property was confiscated, partly demolished and abandoned for twelve years.

My sister Annabella told us that Mantes, where we proposed to stop, was a nest of thieves. We found an ideal place to moor at the Halte de Limay, just short of the ruined bridge that was blown sky-high during the Franco-Prussian War (1870–71). Jean-Baptiste Camille Corot (1796–1875), landscape painter of the Romantic school, captured the bridge in one of his pictures. The building at one end that he recorded in his picture is now an antique shop. Corot is seen as a link between the English landscape tradition and French Impressionism. His *pochades*, little sketches done out of doors, *en plein air*, were plays with light and clouds shading the landscape.

In light of my sister's warning, we had battened down the hatches before going wandering and kept a sharp eye out, but there were no masked figures nipping between the buildings carrying bags with *butin*, or swag, written on them.

On Friday 16 August, *Gang Warily* was slowly passing along the Marny arm of the Seine, trying to identify which of the three bridges Claude Monet painted at Argenteuil. He painted this stretch of river from his studio boat, an idea first favoured by Charles-François Daubigny (1817–78), a landscape painter of the Barbizon landscape school. On arriving at Argenteuil, Monet started to search for a flat-bottomed boat that he could convert into a studio. During this, he met Gustave Caillebotte (1848–94), a keen sailor and yacht designer. Edouard Manet (1832–83) painted the boat with Monet and his wife aboard in 1874. Caillebotte was so taken with the idea that he took up painting himself. I cannot think of

Monet's studio boat

a more peaceful or comfortable way of painting in the open air than on a Monet-type studio boat. I think I might be tempted to equip it with an electric motor, rather than use the sculls shown hanging languidly over the side in Manet's painting.

Gang Warily passed the barge capital of France at Conflans-Sainte-Honorine. The port is dominated by the church of St Maclou and the ruined chateau of Mont Joie, which stand out on the skyline. Barges four or five deep lay against each other in rows. August is not a good time for barges as most of the Seine factories are shut for the holidays.

Like all the great buildings and monuments near the Seine, the Eiffel Tower looked better from the river. The bridges of Paris, too, may be properly observed from below. Our destination was the Arsenal, now a marina, in the very heart of Paris opposite the Botanical Gardens.

● *Gang Warily* steamed past Port Mirabeau and then through the great bridges of Paris, sliding beneath, in company with the *bateaux mouches*, loaded to the gunwales with passengers. Modern and hideous they may be, but they are clearly doing a good trade. We went on, leaving the Isle de la Cité to port, looking up at the facade of Notre Dame, which to my mind is not a patch on Rouen Cathedral, but better set.

We had to wait outside the Arsenal Harbour. The lock allows entry to the canal, of which it is a part, while the main road passes over the top. It is a little eerie. *Gang Warily* followed a sort of water-borne chicken coop. We were second into the lock. A well-appointed French motor yacht followed us in and parked herself efficiently on our starboard side, while the chicken coop wandered all over the place ahead of us. Gilly was on the foredeck handling the bow line when the owner of the motor yacht, who was crewed by a lithesome, auburn-haired girl, gave us glasses of champagne. They had just opened the bottle, he announced. What a marvellous arrival.

*– **Gang Warily**'s log, Friday 16 August 1996*

Lear's friend Chichester Fortescue, caricatured in *Vanity Fair.*
Cadland Archives

At the north end of the Arsenal is the Place de la Bastille, a marvellous creation though representing a particularly horrible historical event during the French Revolution. Canons were manufactured here from 1512 onward and so was gunpowder, until the great explosion of 1563 which was heard, so they say, as far away as Melun in the south. Used to dealing in death, the Arsenal provided a home for the Poisoner's Court in 1680, where Monsieur La Voisin used to manufacture poisons which became known as the 'inheritance powder', as they were particularly effective in dispatching relatives.

Leaving Paris was difficult, especially the beauty of the Arsenal's surroundings. The French have managed to keep most of the glass and steel high-rises out of the centre of Paris, recognising that one of the great attractions of the city is its skyline.

Edward Lear passed through Paris in 1858. In a letter to Chichester Fortescue, he wrote that they had crossed from Folkestone and went on to the French capital – 'We crossed to Paris and remained there the 27th and 28th – what a splendid city that has become! I never saw anything like the Rue de Rivoli.'[9]

Melun is forty-six kilometres from the centre of Paris by road. It is a manufacturing centre for brie cheeses, and among other distinctions possesses a book barge, the Librairie Pollen.

● Gilly crawled aboard, mounting her black sides by standing on the charthouse roof and gripping the steel gunwale with determination, followed by a powerful spring. She made her way forward beneath a large canvas awning and looked down into the hold. Staring up at her, surprised, was the bookseller, 'Greetings, Madame', he said. Gilly replied in French, 'I am enchanted to see you. Tell me, do you speak English?' To which he replied, still looking up the ten feet or so, 'No.' Gilly said it didn't matter and continued to ask in French whether we could tie up alongside his bookshop and come and visit him. He was again delighted.

I should mention there are three types of brie – the creamy Brie de Coulommiers, the Brie de Maux and the very strong Brie de Melun.

*– **Gang Warily**'s log, Saturday 17 August 1996*

I remember those very hot days in the middle of August, the river reflecting the heat, making movement almost painful. In the locks, hell was at the top, heaven at the bottom, a reversal. We pressed on.

7
The Barbizon school – *plein air* and impressionism

Three kilometres upstream of Samois-sur-Seine is a modern marina that boasts facilities and provides a good stop for exploring the Forest of Fontainebleau, the ancient Forest of Bière. This, like the New Forest, was created as a hunting preserve. The place has a long pedigree, for the Romans introduced the pheasant and partridge in these woods. Wild boar and fallow deer abounded and François I established a heronry. They used to eat them in those days.

There was an old man in a garden,
Who always begged every-one's pardon;
When they asked him, " What for ? "—He replied " You're a bore !
And I trust you'll go out of my garden."

● Deep in the Forest is the village of Barbizon, which gave its name to the Barbizon school. Painters of this persuasion were inspired by the need to be near the soil and to paint while living in simple peasant cottages, or the Ganne Inn. The Barbizon school, though, was driven by the concept of painting in the open air, *en plein air*, as they said. Ideally, the work was done outside in the open air rather than in the studio. Barbizon art was a direct study of the landscape and nature.

– Gang Warily's log, Sunday 18 August 1996

Their opponents said they painted in prune juice because of the prevalence of browns and greens, which was a bit rough on people like the romantic artist Théodore Rousseau, the leader of the school, born in 1812, the same year as Edward Lear. He died in 1867, twenty-one years before Lear.

A colony of artists already existed in Barbizon in 1821, five years before Lear started work as a professional artist. André Parinaud, in his book about the Barbizon, said:

Like the poets and writers of the time, the artists wanted to be socially committed. Gustave Courbet, Jean François Millet – who came from peasant stock – were social partners of Lamartine, George Sand and Emile Zola. They were defenders of the human condition and the industrial and rural proletariat whom they captured ploughing, in the rain, in winter, reduced to the state of animals.

Today Charles François Daubigny (another follower) would be a champion of the environment, he would call for the protection of rivers, denounce the building of roads and accuse the railways of turning the countryside into a desert. The high priests of the mystical philosophy of nature which was to nourish the dreams of two generations were named, Théodore Rousseau, Millet, Daubigny, Corot and their 'lay brothers and canons' Troyon, Narcisse Diaz de la Peña and Jules Dupré.[10]

Barbizon is fifty-six kilometres from Paris. From 1849, a railway ran from the capital to Melun, leaving a walk of nine kilometres through the woods to reach Barbizon.

John Ruskin (1819–1900), in his autobiography *Praeterita*, tells of his visit to Fontainebleau in 1842, before the railway. The visit clearly moved him and the idea of drawing from nature had strong appeal. Ruskin was not feeling too well. He rested on a bank by the road to see if he could sleep a little.

But I couldn't, and the branches against the blue sky began to interest me, motionless as the branches of the Tree of Jesse on a painted window. Feeling gradually somewhat livelier, and that I wasn't going to die this time, and be buried in the sand, though I couldn't follow the present walk any farther, I took out my book and began to draw a little aspen tree, on the other side of the cart-road, carefully.

Languidly, but not idly, I began to draw it; and as I drew, the languor passed away; the beautiful lines insisted on being traced, – without weariness. More and more beautiful they became, as each rose out of the rest, and took its place in the air. With wonder increasing

every instant, I saw that they 'composed' themselves by finer laws than any known of man. At last, the tree was there, and everything that I had thought before about trees, nowhere.[11]

Ruskin's *Elements of Drawing* was greatly valued by Claude Monet, according to an article by Lawrence Campbell:

In the March 1911 Contemporary Review on 'What is Impressionism?', Wynford Dewhurst quotes Monet as having told a British journalist in 1900 that ninety per cent of the theory of Impressionist painting is in Ruskin's *Elements of Drawing*. This opinion by one of the greatest masters of direct perceptual painting outdoors is remarkable in view of the fact that it is doubtful if Monet could have read English with any real fluency, and that the *Elements of Drawing* was never translated into French. (It was, however, translated into German and Italian.) And yet he may have struggled through it, just as Marcel Proust, known to have had a poor knowledge of English, nonetheless read deeply in Ruskin and was the translator into French of *The Bible of Amiens* and *Sesame and Lilies*.[12]

Another group came to this corner of the Forest, but they preferred to stay at Chailly. Frédéric Bazille, Pierre-Auguste Renoir, Alfred Sisley and Claude Monet did not integrate with the 'prune juicers' but learnt from them. In this way, the seeds of Impressionism were sown.

The birth of the Impressionist movement was painful, but it was through this pain that changes came. The major difficulty was the Académie des Beaux-Arts, which held a yearly exhibition in the Palais de l'Industrie. The 'Salon', as the exhibition was referred to, had a monopoly, and rejected almost all the Impressionists' pictures. Napoleon III was asked to intervene and in 1863 he ordered that an exhibition of rejected works, the Salon des Refusés, should be set up.

Edouard Manet's picture *Déjeuner sur l'Herbe* was there in all its glory, inspired by two classical works, Raphael's *The Judgement of Paris* and Titian's *Le Concert Champêtre*. Philip Hamerton (1833–94), a critic in the *Fine Arts Quarterly* of 1863, wrote:

> Now some wretched Frenchman has translated this (the Raphael and Titian) into modern, French realism, on a much larger scale, and with the horrible modern French costume instead of the graceful Venetian one. Yes, there they are under the trees, the principal lady entirely undressed ... another female in a chemise coming out of a little stream that runs hard by, and two Frenchmen in wide-awakes sitting on the very green grass with a stupid look of bliss.[13]

The description of the hats was wrong, for wide-awakes have a large brim and these did not. Still, he showed how strong the opposition was in those early days to the Impressionists.

It is easier to trace Edward Lear's artistic development than to gauge the influences on Lear of movements in the art world in the United Kingdom and Europe during the period of his working life.

We have seen how his sister Ann guided him in his early years, and have mentioned the influence of the Derby family, starting with Lord Stanley, later the 13th Earl of Derby, whom he met in February 1831 when he was working on his brave project to publish a book on parrots. The high praise he received for this work included the matchless remark by Prideaux John Selby, the celebrated ornithologist, that 'the plates were beautifully coloured and I think infinitely superior to Audubon's in softness and the drawing as good.'[14] He must have been delighted, for John James Audubon (1785–1851) was, and still is, the market leader in bird prints. If Lear's poor eyesight had not forced him into topographical landscape painting, he would have no doubt dislodged the American.

Lear had enrolled at Sass's Drawing Academy in 1834, so that he could gain entry to the Royal Academy Schools. However, lack of finances delayed his going there until 1849. He was a student at the Royal Academy Schools with William Frith (1819–1909) and met William Holman Hunt (1827–1910), one of the founding members of the Pre-Raphaelite Brotherhood, through the painter Robert Martineau in 1852. Hunt, whom Lear called 'Daddy', helped him with his colours

The 14th Earl of Derby, caricatured in *Vanity Fair* in 1869.
Headland Archives

and figures. Lear considered himself to be a 'second-generation member of the PRB'.

This relationship could provide a link between Lear and the art movements that we have discussed. The Pre-Raphaelites started in 1848 and went on until fading away in 1853. The Impressionists, as we have seen, started with the Salon des Refusés in 1863, some years later, but remember, they were born of the Barbizon School, which created the climate for the birth of Impressionism.

I think Brian Read of the Victoria & Albert Museum in London, in his introduction to the catalogue of the Lear exhibition organised by the Arts Council in 1958, set Lear in his place. He wrote:

> Lear's subjects descended from pre-conceptions fashionable in the period of [John] Martin and Turner, but his technique as a watercolourist went even further back to the 'stained drawings' of eighteenth-century masters like Towne, though his style, unlike theirs, was impulsive. He seldom attempted direct watercolour painting in the manner of Peter de Wint, which was practised everywhere by the time he reached middle age. If he could have escaped a little more from the canons of taste prevailing when he was a boy, he would have been a different person, of course, but he might have made an excellent Pre-Raphaelite ... In his own topographical speciality, his vision and technique were based on the transitional Neo-Classical – romantic conventions applied to 'dramatic' or 'picturesque' landscape.[15]

But really, the wonderful thing about Edward Lear was that he could not easily be boxed and labelled.

Jinglia Tinkettlia.

8
Still waters – between the Seine and the Saône

However, we must press on. We now left the broad Seine and turned right, entering the Canal du Loing through the lock at Moret-sur-Loing. Alfred Sisley (1839–99) lived in Moret in a house a hundred metres from the castle, and many of his pictures show the canal. But for us the world suddenly closed in. The trees embraced the river and we glided quietly through a tunnel of green. The fishermen looked at us with narrowed eyes, until they saw we were making no wash and had altered course a little to avoid their lines.

It might be worth quoting the log to show how the locks in this part of the canal work.

● Gilly and I adopted the technique of taking the bow and stern line to the middle of the boat, which I had positioned by the ladder on the lock side. Gilly passed her bow line through the top rung and either held on while I did the

There was an old person of Dundalk,
Who tried to teach fishes to walk;
When they tumbled down dead, he grew weary, and said,
" I had better go back to Dundalk ! "

same thing with the aft warp, or she made her end fast on the forward samson post and I controlled by pulling in on the after line. Once we were up, or down, Gilly stepped off onto the lock side, or climbed the ladder, and helped the lock keeper open one of the gates while he, or she, did the other. I was ready with the warps and the engine to look after the boat while Gilly practised her French by chatting to the lock keeper.

We always let the lock keepers know in the late afternoon where we were going to stop for the night, or during the morning, if a pause for lunch was in prospect. By this intelligence, they were able to gauge how individual boats were progressing in the system. They were unfailingly polite, amused and helpful. A number were university students on vacation. About a fifth were girls. I was told that some of the older men had served in the French navy and that such later employment was a normal progression, or in other words a naval perk.

– Gang Warily's log, Monday 19 August 1996

With the lock keeper at Montbouy

The Pont-Canal de Briare must provide the high point in any water journey through this part of France. The aqueduct carries the canal and the traffic high above the river Loire. This water bridge was opened in 1896. The span is 662 metres long. It is an impressive display of French cast-iron engineering. The decoration

Gilly celebrating our crossing of the Briare aqueduct

matches the style and together they celebrate the achievement, which is so satisfactory that I imagine it gives a glow of pleasure to all who cross.

The canal follows the river Loire, which races seaward far below. Above, at this point, was the hilltop town of Sancerre and the fourteenth-century chateau, both commanding the vineyards of the wine of that name, a delicious white. We later stopped by a chateau on the lock, hoping to purchase. A man in tweeds came around the corner, wearing a cap of

the same cloth and pattern. 'Don't I know you?' he said with a smile. I made a rather non-committal reply, hoping for clues. I learnt that the vineyard, all fifteen hectares of it, belonged to the Château de Thauvenay. The owner introduced himself as the Comte Georges de Choulot de Chabaud la Tour de Thauvenay. Gilly asked him if he could manage with a shorter name and he replied, amused, 'I've already given up two because they would not fit on the label.' The wine was extraordinarily good, flinty, dry, yet without tongue-twisting sharpness. As we departed, we noticed on the map that Verrerie, the chateau of the Stuarts, was just eighteen kilometres away, a good bicycle ride. But this was not to be, for our travelling was coming to an end in August this year. That was our thought as we left *Gang Warily* at Marseilles-les-Aubigny in the capable hands of Richard and Anita Watson of La Chaume du Poids de Fer. They had bought this canal-side property and created a house out of an old farm building, with a workshop. They had put bollards alongside the canal and a number of boats were preparing to hibernate for the winter. *Gang Warily* would be in good hands.

The Canal du Loing

Gilly and I rejoined *Gang Warily* on 5 July 1997. The British newspapers trumpeted that June had been the wettest since records had begun. They went on, with glee, saying that it was 'the wrong sort of rain' and would not do any good. But it was the right sort of rain for us at Cadland in the southeast corner of the New Forest. What the papers should have said, I thought, was that in June when plants are growing apace, the rain is taken up by the leaves as it falls and does not change the aquifer. In this people-centric world of media, plants do not matter. Anyway, we were off to Nevers, the nearest place to the Watsons at Chaume du Poids de Fer, where hopefully there was no rain, as we had to load ship for the next stage of our voyage.

There is a new quay just beyond Cuffy where we secured and my sister Annabella drove us to La Grenoille for Sunday lunch.

● Our waitress was a pretty, slim blonde, with her skirt brief and the wrong way round, with the zip in the front. However, her dress did not prevent her from securing for us three bottles of their Sunny Sancerre.

– *Gang Warily*'s log, Sunday 6 July 1997

Gilly continues the account, as we were off to one of France's most celebrated modern gardens.

● Well content, we headed down the west bank of the river Allier for the great medieval chateau of Apremont, its five round towers dominating the broad valley as far as the eye could see. Below the fortifications Gilles de Brissac created, in 1971 onwards, a very extensive *parc floral* around two large curving lakes dissected by a brilliant red Chinese bridge and adorned with an octagonal Turkish pavilion on a small island.

– *Gang Warily*'s log, Sunday 6 July 1997

Nevers is remembered principally for the polychrome wine cooler in the Musée Municipal Frédéric-Blandin, housed in an old abbey. The cooler is part of the collection of the Nevers Pottery and stands on giant chicken feet. Nevers is famous for pottery, glass and enamelling. In the 1650s, the pottery industry alone employed eighteen hundred workers.

The Visitandine nuns of Nevers had a celebrated talking parrot, Ver-Vert, whose deeds are recorded in the poetry of Jean-Baptiste Gresset in 1733. The nuns apparently had agreed to lend their bird to their sisters in Nantes. He went down-river in a passenger barge, accompanied by the Loire river crew and some dragoons. They schooled him in words and phrases not usually heard in a nunnery:[16]

> For these Dragoons were a Godless lot,
> Who spoke the tongue of the lowest sot,
> ... soon for curses and oaths he did not want
> And could out-swear a devil in a holy font.

The ladies of Nantes were very upset. He was sent back to Nevers, where he was summoned before the Convent's Council of Order. The sentence was that he had to fast, be kept in solitary confinement and principally be silent. Ver-Vert was a model prisoner and the nuns made up to him with every favour – and as a result he died,

> Stuffed with sugar and mulled with wine,
> Ver-Vert, gorging a pile of sweets,
> Changed his rosy life for a coffin of pine.

On the long voyage through the centre of France, moving at three miles an hour, it is easy to gorge like Ver-Vert. Learning French swearwords on the way would be a little more difficult, due to the politeness of the lock keepers. However, aggravating fishermen and other bank users could remedy that situation. The Canal Latéral à la Loire leads southwest from Nevers, passing through Decize and on to Digoin. A week had been reserved for this stretch. This took into account shopping for croissants in the early morning, long sticks of French bread for lunch, time to tie up and search for a good place for dinner, aiming to arrive at our new berth at about six o'clock in order to secure and beautify both the boat and ourselves.

Pierrefitte-sur-Loire was recommended by lock keepers as a good place to stay the night. The small boat harbour had been created, by order of the Mayor of Pierrefitte, out of an old road depot. Shrubs were planted and a quay wall constructed, sadly with not enough water alongside for us. *Gang Warily*, therefore, angled so that the bowsprit hung over the quay wall with the stern several feet away. We arrived early, so found a taxi to take us to Château Dhoury. We found the Vicomte Jehan de Conny all alone in his courtyard keen to issue tickets and a brochure and to show us around himself. There was a small basket tactfully placed for tips for the guide, in which a few coins glinted.

The Vicomte had a strong face, a good nose and a fine welcoming smile. He and his family have owned the castle since 1751. We wandered around after him, peered at the eleventh-century round tower, the twelfth-century gatehouse and the fourteenth-century keep. The different ages of buildings, the owner with his deep knowledge of the place and his family, together with the fading blue of the evening sky, conspired together to provide a scene that is difficult to forget.

Heading towards Digoin

Digoin is reached from the west by an aqueduct, almost as impressive as the one at Briare, though the decoration is not so flamboyant. Digoin possesses an excellent yacht harbour. It was our intention to leave *Gang Warily* here for a month. Across the water there was a small Dutch sailing barge, mast stowed tidily away in the Dutch manner. *Carpe Diem*, a name borrowed from the Odes of Horace, meaning 'seize the day', or make the most of the present time, was owned by an American couple, Rich and Lori Haslacher, who were enjoying a year's sabbatical. Once a day Rich would take his laptop to the telephone booth and send off his emails and collect new ones. French telephone boxes had sockets for such purposes in 1997.

On our return to Digoin, *Carpe Diem* had disappeared. Mechanical problems always arise when you have been away, leaving everything working perfectly. *Gang Warily*'s log records the incident:

● We had decided we would spend Saturday sorting the boat out, which was just as well as the ship's batteries were almost flat. The port captain found an engineer from a garage. He contorted himself into the engine compartment though rather rotund and powerfully built. The filler top snapped off one of the batteries and disappeared into the bilge but he didn't seem to be concerned.

He went off and came back with his mate, his tools and a starter battery which soon had the engine going. He explained what was wrong with the battery charger, giving Gilly a lesson in mechanics, as she was the only one who could understand what he was talking about.

– *Gang Warily*'s log, **Saturday 16 August 1997**

The Basilica of the Sacred Heart and the Benedictine Abbey of Paray-le-Monial is a large, plain structure. The builders eschewed decorative splendour and large-scale design to the glory of God, in favour of abstract beauty. This is composed of the rhythmic combination of light and shadow, space and simplicity, which is conducive to contemplation.

We were now passing through the old industrial heartlands of Burgundy. The Canal du Centre, on which we had been sailing since Digoin, owed its success to the coal and steel industries of Le Creusot, Blanzy and Montceau-les-Mines. In writing the log, I had done some research:

● Joseph-Eugène Schneider and his brother Adolphe really set things going with the Schneider Works at El Crest. First came the power hammer and then the furnace forge in 1924. Armaments, including ships, were part constructed and shipped to the coast. This explosive success was brought to an end by the European steel crisis and bankruptcy followed in 1984. The works are now part of the conglomerate Snecma. Montceau has changed but it is proud of its past. However, almost all of the dirt associated with the 'brass' has disappeared. Certainly it deserves its nickname, or should I say title, today of Ville Floral, proudly stated in flowers as you enter the town. That would have pleased Schneider of Apremont and his remarkable lady.

– Gang Warily's log, Monday 18 August 1997

As we motored quietly through the countryside, I thought of the great attractions of rural France and its timelessness. Frogs echoed this thought with approval. The chorus was really noticeable. The endless repeat by the frogs and the sun blazing down heralded a swarm of bees that flew purposely across *Gang Warily*'s lowered mast. I wondered if they had swarmed from a bee barge. A hundred years ago these bee barges were not uncommon. Bee skeps were placed on the hold cover and the beekeeper would stop where he thought there was a good supply of pollen, wait a day or two for the bees to do their work, and then move on.

On the mirrored surface of the canal lay a dead carp. Inspired by the frogs, I wrote an ode to him, which I think was completed with a glass of Calvados in the hand – Norman inspiration.

Ode to a dead carp

Oh carp, how many summers have you known
Before you floated flipper up and blown?
In early days, escaping from heron's beak,
You survived till now, your scales to dull and reek.
You will join the ooze of the Canal Latéral à la Loire,
With crows and magpies to mourn in croaking choir.

Lear would have made a better fist of this.

● *Gang Warily* came to rest alongside the bank. Just ahead lay a bridge and a little wood. The countryside was made up of small fields. We were near Remigny. A little inn was nestled in the trees and as we supped a big barge slowly came down the river. It was seven o'clock, only a half hour before the locks closed for the night. Suspecting trouble, I ran down the tow path. All seemed to go well until the barge passed and then ping, the after line went and *Gang Warily* gently settled across the canal. The metal pin had popped out of the dry ground and sunk without trace in the canal. I sorted her out, drove the pins almost out of sight at a better angle and she looked comfortable again for the night.

– Gang Warily's log, Tuesday 19 August 1997

Gilly remembers the wild flowers, the blue purple of lucerne, *Medicago sativa*; the white flowers and green seed heads of wild carrot, *Daucus carota*; bright, clear blue devil's-bit scabious, *Succisa pratensis*; pink greater knapweed, *Centaurea scabiosa*; yellow imperforate St John's-wort, *Hypericum maculatum*, close to the water; vivid blue viper's bugloss, *Echium vulgare*; white campion, *Silene latifolia*; and the pale pink field bindwind, *Convolvulus arvensis*, simple, elegant and a delight to the eye.

The Fizzgiggious Fish, who always walked about upon Stilts, because he had no legs.

9
The great rivers – Saône and Rhône

Chalon-sur-Saône is reported to have been Julius Caesar's supply depot during his Gallic campaign. An animal fur fair was held here in the Middle Ages, attracting buyers from all over Europe for the skins of badgers, foxes, pole cat, otter and mink.

We were leaving behind the narrow canal and the chains of locks.

● *Gang Warily* was dwarfed by the sweating walls of the vast lock that gives entrance to the Saône. The drop is 10.76 metres and the final gate is lifted clear on enormous chains, allowing the boat to go underneath. The bottom is dripping water as you pass below. Perhaps amongst them was a drop of goodwill as a parting present from the Canal du Centre.
– *Gang Warily*'s log, Wednesday 20 August 1997

Gang Warily found a quiet and comfortable berth inside Hospital Island at Chalon. The town has a classical look about it, a confident face, commanding the broad

There was an Old Man in a Barge, whose Nose was exceedingly large;
But in fishing by night, it supported a light,
Which helped that Old Man in a Barge.

waters of the Saône. Strangely, we felt the opposite. The small canals had cocooned us. The scent of flowers, cut crops, dark woods, the sounds of birds close by and the incessant chorus of frogs were now a memory.

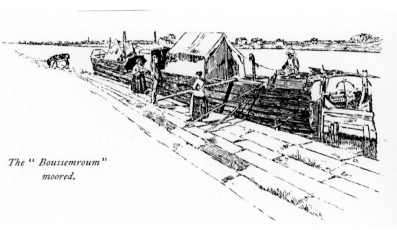

The "Boussemroum" moored.

Philip Gilbert Hamerton came here in the mid 1880s. You will remember his words about Manet and the Salon des Refusés in 1863. Hamerton was the celebrated art critic of the *Saturday Review* and the editor and publisher of *Portfolio*. He was also a small-boat sailor and had developed a catamaran, the *Arar*, in which he explored the Saône. However, we join Hamerton before this, after he has hit on the idea of chartering a *berrichon*, a very narrow eighty-foot canal boat designed for use in the Berri country, which he wished to use to explore the Saône. He was too busy to search for the barge himself, so commissioned a friend. Hamerton was so particular that it must have been a difficult job. He wrote:

A *berrichon*, from Philip Gilbert Hamerton's *The Saône, A Summer Voyage* (1887), illustrated by Joseph Pennell

> My friend has considerable difficulty in finding what I want, as I do not desire to have women and children on board, and almost all these boats are family residences. He tranquilly enquires if I have any objection to a bigamist, as there is a very suitable berrichon with a man and two wives, which I suspect to be an invention of his own; probably the man's wife has her sister with her or some other relation, as I know that whole families live together on the water. My objection to children is, that they would generally be in the way and make noise; as for the sex that we all adore, I would like to know the woman personally before entrusting my peace to her for many weeks. She might possibly be a talker, or even a scold, she might be dirty and slovenly in her habits, all of which would spoil the pleasure of my trip completely, and there would be no remedy against a woman who was established in her own house, under the protection of her own husband.[17]

He might not have wanted women and children, but he had no objection to a donkey. He accepted that every *berrichon* had a donkey on board in its own stable, which was a regular part of the boat, and although at first sight it might have appeared that the donkey would be slow, the fact was that horses only went at a walking pace, and the difference would not have been as great as might appear. Hamerton was happy with the thought that the men could tow the barge when the donkey was tired. His idea was to place a tent just aft of the donkey's stable. The men and pilot, whom he was keen to have, would sleep in the bow, while the *patron* or the owner would have his own quarters aft. In the tent would be billeted Philip Hamerton and his guests, Captain Kornprobst, the artist Joseph Pennell and Hamerton's eldest son.

Zoulou's Farewell.

Another of Joseph Pennell's drawings for Hamerton.

Chalon's favourite son is Nicéphore Niepce, whose statue gazes over the Saône. Chalonians feel a little sore that Daguerre is credited with the invention of photography. Niepce was the actual inventor and Daguerre his commercial partner. Niepce managed to create a permanently fixed image from nature in 1829. Edward Lear was interested in the photographic process from 1863 onward, as he saw it as a substitute for lithography. His initial experiments did not work. A year before he died, he saw a future in the American invention of platinotype. In 1888, the year of Lear's death, another American, George Eastman, brought out the first Kodak roll film camera, which could have solved his problems. The intrepid Julia Margaret Cameron (1815–79), the pioneering portrait photographer whom Lear met with the Tennysons, could have fuelled his interest, but he did not take to her.

Edward Lear's friend Edgar Drummond and his wife Louisa.
Cadland Archives

Gilly and I had time on 20 August to visit the Denon Museum, a classical building mounted on a plinth with only one storey. Etienne Raffort (1802–80), one of Lear's French contemporaries, was on show. Like Edward Lear, Raffort painted Venice. They were both there in 1865 and may have met over an easel.

Lear had mixed feelings about Venice. It may be that he was influenced by his serious-minded companion, Franklin Lushington (1823–1901), who was a lawyer and civil servant as well as Lear's best friend and later his literary executor. Lear's first biographer (1933), Alexander Davidson, certainly thought so, making the point that Venice was not a place to visit with an unsympathetic companion. Lear wrote to his friend and banker, Edgar Drummond (1825–93):

> This city of palaces, pigeons, poodles and pumpkins (I'm sorry to say also of innumerable pimps to keep up the alliteration) is a wonder and a pleasure.[18]

Gang Warily made good speed on the Saône, as there are no speed restrictions and we were able to harness a knot from the stream. At 12.15 on 21 August, the ancient town of Tournus was reached and we found a berth on the quay.

> ● We climbed up the stone steps of the sloping wall above the quay and were soon in the main square and shopping street. This leads to St Philibert's church with its beautiful twelfth-century bell tower, soaring columns and barrel vaulting. One of the vaults was decorated with black and white checker in honour of the Digoin family. The modern glass did not spoil the awe of this dark and soaring space.
>
> – *Gang Warily*'s log, Thursday 21 August 1997

Port de Fleurville, downstream of Tournus, is notable because Philip Hamerton records that he could see Mont Blanc from there with his telescope. Hamerton remembers dining at the inn, which Gilly and I thought we had identified on the bank.

> Our host was not at all aware that Mont Blanc was visible from his window, he'd always taken the mountain for cloud. So we lent him our telescope and made him see the dome and the aiguilles (needle shapes). At first all the snowy parts were warm white, and the aiguille dark by contrast, then the white became rosy at sunset, and after sunset the mountain remained visible for some time as a purple-grey silhouette, both snows and aiguilles dark against the sky.[19]

Mont Blanc is at least a hundred miles from Pont de Fleurville, but it is quite a lump of rock. Even so, we could not spot it.

Edward Lear was keen to paint the Swiss landscape, again influenced by Turner. He travelled to Switzerland in 1854 and did at least three views of Mont Blanc.

In later life, between 1878 and 1883, Lear visited Monte Generosa, near Lake Como. He did not return after his servant Giorgio Kokali of Corfu died there in 1883. Kokali was buried at Mendrisio between lakes Como and Lugano.[20]

Macon is surrounded by vineyards and has an ancient smell about it. Philip Hamerton was here in his catamaran *Arar*. He wrote:

> The most remarkable event in the history of Macon is not of a military nature. It is not the invasion of Attila who pillaged it in the 5th century, nor that of the Saracens in the 8th, or of Lothair in the 9th. There was a great and terrible famine here in the 11th century, but there have been terrible famines elsewhere. There have been fearful religious wars in Macon between the Protestants and the Catholics, but there have been religious massacres in many other cities. Unique distinction of Macon amongst the cities of the world is, that a council of the church was held here in the year 585 during which learned ecclesiastics argued solemnly on the question of whether a woman ought, or ought not, to be considered a human creature.[21]

This remarkable twist was part of a strong desire of the early church to counter the growing influence of a cult that held that Mary Magdalene was closer to Jesus than the apostles. Pope Gregory the Great made her the centrepiece of his sermon from the pulpit at the Basilica San Clemente in Rome in the year 591. After describing her sins, he concluded that it was clear that Magdalene was a prostitute.

But enough about buildings and early churchmen, for Macon is near the centre of Burgundy and the wines from this region are famous all over the world. It is well worth cruising the waters of the Saône between Dijon in the north and Lyon in the south, just for the purpose of eating and drinking the produce of Burgundy. I read that Madame de Pompadour favoured my own preferred red Burgundy, Romanée Conti, while Napoleon went for Chambertin, both in the Côte de Nuits and using the Pinot Noir variety of grape. Meursault heads whites in the Côte de Beaune to my mind. Buxy, to the southwest of Chalon, in the Chalonnaise region, employs the Aligoté grape. The Maconnaise area behind and north of Macon has both Pouilly and Fuissé whites. South of this is the Beaujolais region. Need I say more?

Philip Hamerton spent a night with the Pope. Not the Pope of Rome, but the Pope of the Saône – a fisherman not of souls but of fish. The crew of the *Arar* seem

Mâcon, Towers of St. Vincent and Prefecture.

Macon in 1887 – drawing by Joseph Pennell from Hamerton's book to have just dropped in on the riverbank cottage and asked for a place for the night. Monsieur Batafi had a large black and tan collie which the crew of *Arar* knew from an earlier occasion. When they enquired about the dog, the 'Pope' showed them a *descende de lit*, a rug by the bed, edged in red cloth, clearly his pelt. 'Alas, poor Pataud,' observed Philip Hamerton. 'He loved a comfortable rug and has become the thing he loved.'[22]

On the starboard bank, the distinctive outline of Solutre hill could be seen through the haze of heat. This remarkable jut of limestone was an early hunting ground of the Upper Palaeolithic age. Wild horses and other large animals were chased to the edge of the Rock of Solutre and killed for meat.

Gang Warily slipped through the centre of Lyon, France's second city. We spent the night of 22 August at Neuville-sur-Saône, which Hamerton named the 'Solent of the Saône'.

> ● The quays bordering the Saône are said to be the finest in any city but have been desecrated by hanging car parks outside of them. It is amusing to think that the need for these monstrosities might, with a bit of imagination, be traced back to a flock of crows. Legend has it that two Celtic princes, Momoros and Ante Pomaros, stopped at the coming together of the Saône and the Rhône. They decided to build a town. When they started work a flock of crows settled down around them. The two thought this an excellent omen and called the place 'Crows Hill' or Lugdunum, which in a convoluted way became Lyon.
>
> – *Gang Warily*'s log, Friday 22 August 1997

The Rhône is different to the Saône. Weed, duckweed and *Ranunculus*, or water crowfoot, are the curse of the river in summer. It blocks everything, colonising in great floating rafts, moving to and fro according to the wind. It infests any indents or bays and clogs engine cooling intakes.

The speed of the stream in the Rhône was strong immediately after the locks, and in this dry year about three knots. However, one to two knots seemed about right for the broader and lazier reaches. In 1997, the Rhône provided twenty-three per cent of France's electricity needs. The dark, energetic river moves towards the Mediterranean, interrupted by twelve locks and barrages.

Condrieu and Tournan, where *Gang Warily* rested, were both known for their sailors in the past. The Rhône was then a testing place to navigate, particularly in the winter, and this was further complicated when the Mistral blew. The celebrated writer, François-René, Vicomte de Chateaubriand (1768–1848), called the Rhône a 'great wild river'. Power generation through the barrages and the improvements made by the Compagnie Nationale du Rhône have tamed the river, and the people of Condrieu and Tournan now grow vegetables.

Valence was our next stopping place, a good one for the night or to leave the yacht for a length of time. Napoleon spent some time here, as he was educated at the School of Artillery. Legend has it that he was so keen to learn that he read every

Braving the rain on the Rhône,
Photo: Gilly Drummond

book in the local bookshop. The story does not say whether or not he bought any of them.

The first mulberry was planted on the Valence plain in the seventeenth century. It started the industry based on the silkworms. They seemed to stand up to the Mistral that comes rushing down the mountains from the north. The architecture is adapted to this, for the old houses have no windows on their north sides.

The locks become deeper here. The Écluse du Logis-Neuf has a drop of thirteen metres.

Château de l'Hers

● The locks have become more musical. The floating bollards that descend with you, make mooring a doddle, run on wheels in grooves in the lock wall. Sometimes they seize and complain in notes that would have done justice to a modern symphony, especially as they are against a background of rushing water springing from the walls or gushing from the gates. It would delight a note dabbler, seeming to avoid the semblance of any tune.

– *Gang Warily*'s log, **Monday 25 August 1997**

Montelimar is the centre of the nougat industry, employing local almonds and honey from Provence and the Alpine slopes.

Below Montelimar, the Rhône is squeezed through a short canyon, the Défilé de Donzère. Before improvements were made to tame the river, this was one of the most difficult places to navigate. The deepest lock on the Rhône is the Écluse de Bollène, which has a drop of twenty-six metres. Looking up, the walls seem to close in. The locks gates were raised and *Gang Warily* passed underneath.

At Roquemaure there is a different sensation, for on the opposite bank to the town are the ruins of Château de l'Hers. It stands on a great pimple of rock. The official vintage name of Côte du Rhône originated here over three centuries ago. Pope Clement V (1260–1340), who transferred the Holy See to Avignon, died in the castle. In 1311, Pope Clement ordered the trial of Jacques de Molay, Grand Master of the Templars. He was convicted on trumped-up charges, but before he was burnt at the stake with his knights, he cursed the Pope.

In the biggest lock on the Rhône – the Écluse de Bollène

● About 3, *Gang Warily* was intercepted by Avignon's excellent *Capitaine du Port*, who guided us in from his launch and then hopped ashore to help us secure in the marina. We were under the aura of Pont Saint-Bénézet, the famed Pont d'Avignon. There has been much misinformation about the Pont d'Avignon. The song says '*Sur le pont d'Avignon, L'on y danse tout en rond*', but the dancing took place under the bridge on an island beneath the arches, not on the bridge – *sous* rather than *sur*.

– *Gang Warily*'s log, **Tuesday 26 August 1997**

Avignon's famous bridge

We decided to bicycle and were soon on our way through the crowds that milled about us in the narrow streets. The city had a marvellous feel of the Renaissance, mixed with dollops of the eighteenth century. The eighteenth had, of course, re-discovered the Renaissance and re-interpreted it with proper respect for talent.

The Palais des Papes dominates Avignon, as it was no doubt designed to do. The original concept was a building devoted to prayer which could easily be defended. This great edifice replaced an earlier Palais on the orders of Benedict XII, the third French Pope (1335–42). Seven Frenchmen held office as Pope at Avignon from 1309 to 1377. Political interference was the reason the Holy See moved, with a little encouragement from the French king, Philip the Fair.

The historic reverie was broken by the discovery that I had lost my wallet. Well, I thought I could have left it in the *Capitainerie*. We had paid him a visit and discussed all sorts of things with the ex Navy man before paying for our berth. When we returned to his office, the place was shut and everything would have to wait until the next morning.

The Captain shook his head when we bearded him in his den. Gilly asked him about the police and the telephone number of the Maison du Presse where I had made my last purchase with a card.

The Palais des Papes, Avignon

'You will have to go to the police, not telephone,' he advised. I said to Gilly that I wondered whether it was worth going to the police. She was adamant, 'Yes, let's go.'

● The police station was near the railway just outside the walls. A policeman was at the gate and waved us on to a greyish concrete building, which contrasted badly with most of those inside the walls. Gilly, with her good French, explained. The lady receptionist said she would ring after sending a moustachioed sergeant off to see if anything had been handed in at this station. As she clutched the phone, a smile spread over her face and she pressed the telephone closer to her ear and resisted shaking hands for a few seconds with everyone who entered or passed. 'Yes, yes, it is at the *Police Municipale*, in the Place de Pic.' I could have hugged her but used Gilly instead. The wallet had jumped out of the bicycle basket and had been picked up by the Technical Director of a firm in Perugia, Italy, and she gave me his address. He later refused any reward but said his son of seven years would like a book on dogs. I sent him the biggest, best illustrated book on dogs that it was possible to find. The captain of the port was astonished when we told our story and clearly pleased.

– *Gang Warily's* log, **Tuesday 26 August 1997**

The Rhône is less populated than the Saône. The banks of the river are not fished like the Saône, where there are fishermen dotting each bank. There were no boats drawn up and fewer houses peeping through the trees. The reason is that much of the Rhône is canalised and the stream stronger and less friendly. Beaucaire and Tarascon, opposite one another on the river, are astonishing survivors of France's medieval past. There used to be a famous fair at Beaucaire, but it was destroyed by the railway, which brought a different life. Originally, merchants gathered from all over Europe to do business and enjoy themselves. Cardinal Richelieu (1585–1642) did not upset this when he ordered the castle to be demolished in the seventeenth century, though the soldiers did not do a particularly thorough job as the stone walls still dominate the town.

Tarascon was part of the Holy Roman Empire – the city of Tarasque. The population was said to be terrified by an amphibious monster that every now and then crawled out of the Rhône and ate children and cattle. St Martha is said to have tamed the monster with the sign of the cross and the green Chinese-looking dragon was captured by the people of the town. In celebration of this, each year a huge model dragon is taken through the streets, swinging its great tail, knocking down the unwary.

The castle, in spite of Richelieu, is said to be one of the finest surviving medieval castles in France. In the thirteenth century, the building defended the boundaries of Provence. At that time, Provence was part of the Holy Roman Empire. The Port de Plaisance is nothing like as developed as the one at Avignon. 'There is only about half an amp of electricity,' a bronzed Liverpudlian explained from the deck of *Alan*, his old British-registered Fifie. He went on, 'but then no one comes round for our money'.

Relics of the Roman past of Arles tell of the importance of public entertainment on the fringes of the Empire. There is both an amphitheatre and a theatre. The probable date of the former is the first century AD, while the theatre was built during Augustus's reign, circa 25–5 BC. The remains of these two buildings put a line under the timelessness of Arles.

Sheer joy comes from the newly restored doorway of the Church of St Trophine. The delicacy of the figures and animals raise the spirit, as indeed they were meant to do. On one corner, on the left looking at the doorway, is the representation of St Michael weighing souls by suspending them from their heels.

Gilly and I bought our usual *citron pressé* at La Café de la Nuit, which Van Gogh painted during his time in Arles. He also captured the garden of the hospital in which he was treated for nervous stress. This has been restored to what it looked like in his painting, *The Garden of Arles Hospital*. Vincent Van Gogh was born in 1853, and settled in Arles in 1888, the year Edward Lear died. Van Gogh quarrelled with Gauguin in the same year, and this added to his problems. He committed suicide in July 1890.

Arles is the capital of the Camargue, an alluvial plain produced by the influences of both the Rhône and the Mediterranean. Part is cultivated, part salt-marsh and part delta, pocked by lagoons, dunes and channels to the sea. A system of managing sheep, cattle and horses of the Carmargue has something in common with the New Forest and other areas of Britain where horses and cattle wander freely. The Guardians are like the Commoners of the New Forest. Their herds might include two hundred black bulls and some horses. White horses of the Carmargue are born brown or bay and go white. Horses are the central part of the system and provide the mounts for the Guardians, who look after the animals. They carry a useful three-pronged stick, which acts as a badge of office.

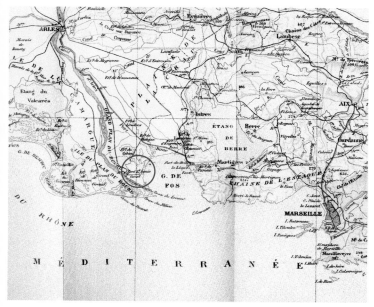

Detail from an old French map showing the Canal St Louis – the short cut from the last stretch of the Rhône to the Gulf of Fos.
Cadland Archives

The last of the great river, as it courses through the ever-changing delta, is not navigable. The lock controlling the canal that leads into the Gulf of Fos, the Écluse de Barcarin, is reserved for commercial vessels. Yachts must use the lock in Port St Louis. There are set opening times, which really apply to the bridge that takes traffic across to the large delta island They de Roustan, cut off by the canal. *Gang Warily* secured, touching the mud, just by the lock at Port St Louis at 12.30. We had to wait two hours for the bridge to open.

The sea canal is extended on the southern side by the Digue St Louis. Once round the end of this, we headed up the channel to the old Port de Carteau, now Port Napoléon, constructed out of a dock built for a dredging company. In 1997, Port Napoléon was only six years old. The marine pontoons were virtually new and the old dredging company buildings had been painted blue and white and acted as covered boat stores, workshops and offices.

Originally, *Gang Warily*'s mast was booked to go in the next day, but the yard team decided to get on with it. The spar was upright within a couple of hours, with the standing rigging in place. This was just as well because the Mistral, the northwesterly wind that rushes down the Rhône valley, started to blow.

We had reached the Mediterranean and salt water. We could dispose of all the old tyres that had protected *Gang Warily*'s topsides through the whole of France. We would soon be turning east and going after you, Mr Lear.

PART III

Cannes, Nice
and the great walk

The Lanterna, Genoa

10
The importance of a clean propeller

D r Samuel Johnson (1709–84) was in no doubt when he wrote 'the grand object of travelling is to see the shores of the Mediterranean'. There is, indeed, a magic about this enclosed sea. The waters seem to register on all senses. The view of the great expanse of azure blue water changes with cloud or wind in a minute to a darker more threatening colour. There is the smell of it. It is not like the tang of the Atlantic, rich in salt and antiseptic. It is softer, much warmer, and it is probably this glow that registers on the nose and gives an attraction not found in other seas. There is finally the sound of it. The sea on the rocky shore registers its own note, which is particularly evident in the time of the Mistral. This wind comes roaring down from the north along the lower Rhône Valley and may last a number of days, reaching 100 kilometres, or 60 miles, per hour. The rush of wind is caused by a high pressure system over the centre of

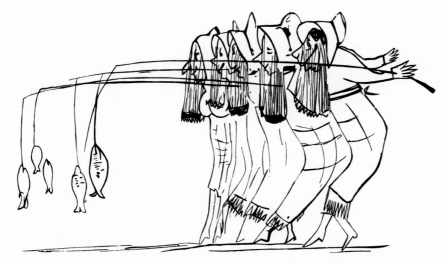

There was an Old Man of Marseilles, whose daughters wore bottle-green veils ;
They caught several fish, which they put in a dish,
And sent to their Pa at Marseilles.

France and low pressure in the northwest Mediterranean and focuses on the Gulf of Lions, which stretches from the Spanish border to Toulon in the east and may have gained its name from the roar of the Mistral. It is important for yachtsmen to watch the barometer and the sky. Sailors often say that the Mediterranean has either too little wind or too much. There is seldom anything in between.

Leaving Port Napoléon to start the voyage eastward was more difficult than I could have imagined and quite outside my experience. The yacht was now well set up, her mast and rigging re-tensioned, sails overhauled and the engine in good order. My nephew, Maurice, and I were anxious to make all speed for San Remo, though there was little wind and the Mediterranean had the appearance of a benign garden pond.

Off the *Côte Bleu*,
approaching Marseille.
Photo: Gilly Drummond

However, try as we might, three knots under power was our best speed. *Gang Warily* has a variable-pitch propeller that had been fitted to provide both extra power at slow speeds when she was being used as a mini oceanographic vessel and as a way to feather out the three-bladed propeller while sailing. A large wheel under the companionway enabled me to alter the angle of the blades from fine, which meant the engine revved to almost a singing tone, to 'paddle wheel', which usually meant the engine stopped dead. This happened when the engine was engaged after sailing, if I was forgetful. What could be wrong? We were not to find out for a day or two.

Slow progress gave time to look around. A few miles to the west, in the Rhône delta, lay that legendary and holy survival Saintes-Maries-de-la-Mer. Each year pilgrims celebrate the arrival on their beach, in AD 40, of a boat without sail or oar that had drifted from the Holy Land. Among others, the three Marys – Mary, mother of James, Mary Magdalene and Mary Salome – were aboard. In complete contrast, the shores of the Bay of Fos reminded me of William Blake's (1757–1827) hymn Jerusalem:

> And was Jerusalem builded here,
> Amongst these dark Satanic mills?

The blue fringe of the Mediterranean to our north erupted into a dark grey-black belching mass. The Port of Fos, together with Marseille, is the largest marine facility in France. The conglomeration includes petrochemical plants, cement, steel and other manufacturing works. The name Fos comes from Fosses Mariennes, the waterway dug by the Romans to provide safe passage from the Rhône. Another reminder of the ancient past is the Graeco-Roman city of Marseille itself, which is reckoned to be the oldest of all the French cities. From two miles off, the morning sun shining on the great pile of buildings – ancient and modern – bristling with tower cranes, the city appears impersonal, without people. Ancient and modern bricks and reinforced concrete are muddled together, masking both the beautiful and the ugly.

France's second city may be taken in at a glance from this distance. The impression of this throbbing, multi-ethnic port is marred by the experience of approaching its centre on land. In a car, it is necessary to fight through the steamy suburbs and characterless streets. There is, therefore, no proper sense of arrival, except by water.

Isolated off shore is the Château d'If. It is Marseille's marine sentinel, a little island in front of the port, made particularly famous by the novel *The Count of Monte Cristo* by Alexandre Dumas (1802–70), where his heroes from the novel were imprisoned. It also played host to the Man in the Iron Mask, along with the Ile Sainte-Marguerite. The mysterious prisoner ended his days in the Bastille, where he died in 1703. There are many conjectures about his identity. One of the most fanciful is that he was the great-grandfather of Napoleon. According to this tale, he had a lover who gave birth to a son who was taken away and given to foster parents in Corsica. As he had no name, he was called Buonapart, taking this from *remis de bonne part*. There is also some confusion over whether the mask was actually of iron or black velvet.

Edward Lear spent a few days in Marseille in December 1866. He stayed at the Grand Hôtel du Louvre before catching the P&O steamer *Pera* for Alexandria to begin his tour of Egypt.

The contrast between the industrial complexes of the Bay of Fos and Marseille, on the one hand, and the dazzling white limestone cliffs of the Calanques, further to the east, is dramatic. This coastal strip is home to the evergreen oak, wild olives, the Aleppo pine, sea lavender and samphire. Rivers have cut through the native chalk to forge deep-sided white fjords. There are nine of these before Cassis is reached in the east. We had hoped to secure a berth in the Calanque de Port-Miou. This small harbour was crammed with boats, as only the French know how. A blue-denimed boatyard worker caught our questioning wave and shouted one word – 'Cassis'. Cassis was the favoured painting ground of Henri Matisse (1869–1954) and Raoul

Dufy (1877–1953). They were part of a movement known as the Fauves. Line and colour were their inspiration. They paid little attention to perspective.

Cap Sicié rises 358 metres out of the sea. Lord Nelson would have known every

Cap Sicié, Near Toulon

inch of this coast and stared endlessly at the great cliff, when blockading the French fleet in Toulon in 1783. 'All we get is honour and salt beef,' Nelson is reported to have said as he tacked backwards and forwards off the Cape.[1]

Gang Warily made about the same progress as Britain's great sailor. The wind was force 5–6 from the east. We thought we would tack round and then bear off for Toulon. On the third tack, the reefed genoa blew out along one of the seams. The engine was not much help in its present state, so the answer was to set the staysail and run for Sanary. The name is a diminutive for Saint Nazaire, who is remembered in the name of the church.

Once secured in the harbour, I went over the side to inspect the propeller. Three blades were thick with barnacles – and I mean really thick. I remembered the shellfish beds around Port Napoléon and the shallow, warm water. The conditions must have been perfect, with the 'lens' of fresh water coming from the river, floating on top of the sea water and further warming the shallows. Without a mask, I could not tell whether these energy-absorbing animals were the common Mediterranean barnacle or the acorn variety, which can grow to three centimetres in height. Monsieur J Juan from Technautic came aboard the next morning and said in a serious tone and matching stern face, 'I always say that in the Mediterranean it is very important to have a clean propeller.' He went on to say, 'Except for your sail, it is what makes the boat go.' He turned his hands in a rotating gesture. Of course, Nelson didn't have propellers, but I could just imagine the engineer's ancestor saying the same about a clean bottom to our naval hero.

Monsieur J Juan looked at the pre-filter in the fuel line. 'It is very dirty,' he said in a matter-of-fact sort of way. 'Shall I tip the residue in the bilge?' I offered him a bucket instead and later, when I was going over the side to have another look at the propeller, this time with a face mask, he observed, 'Don't you think the water is too cold?' I replied that for those who swim in the North Sea or the Channel, the Mediterranean is a like a warm bath. He was not finished with us, and twisted himself into an unnatural position and dipped down into the engine compartment. In a little while, he came out as if he had found one of the yacht's secrets. With the same serious tone, he enquired, 'Do you know she is dripping,' pointing to the freshwater line. 'How do you say circle – he is dead,' stabbing with his finger where a hose clip was hiding. The engineer took the spare I offered him and descended once again to replace the one that had 'died'.

Gang Warily rounded Cap Sicié in no time. We could make 6–7 knots under power, without barnacles – and the headwind had dropped.

Hyères, the pioneer among the Riviera resorts, was soon abeam. Edward Lear referred to Hyères and Saint-Tropez in his letter to Lady Waldegrave of 11 December 1866, written before his departure for Egypt, referring to being delayed in Marseille: 'As it was I went to Hyères and to St Tropez, both of which are bosh.'[2] The word *bosh* came into the English language in 1834 from the Turkish, meaning worthless. It was also the word used for trash and nonsense and, therefore, could almost be a compliment, when employed by the laureate of all nonsense writers.

11
The Book of Nonsense

ang Warily spent a night in the rather soulless harbour of Cavalaire. By lunch the next day, we were off Cannes, now a substantial resort, but only beginning to be developed from a small fishing port in Lear's day. The waters off the town are an appropriate place to consider Edward Lear's great addition to 'bosh'. His contribution to nonsense literature, limericks, rhymes and songs is how he is still best remembered. On 15 February 1886, Lear's popularity as a nonsense writer was confirmed by John Ruskin, writing in the *Pall Mall* magazine in angry response to Sir John Lubbock's 'List of the best 100 books' in an earlier edition. Ruskin's argument was that scholars should not be guided in what they read, and that Sir John should also avoid pointing the new middle-class reading public towards Homer and other 'worthy' texts, which they would surely ignore.

> Surely the most beneficent and innocent of all books yet produced for them is the *Book of Nonsense*, with its corollary carols? – inimitable and refreshing, imperfect rhythm. I really don't know any author to whom I am half so grateful for my idle self, as Edward Lear. I shall put him the first of my hundred authors.

There was an Old Person of Cannes, who purchased three Fowls and a Fan;
Those she placed on a Stool, and to make them feel cool
She constantly fanned them at Cannes.

Ruskin was familiar with Lear, for in his poem *Salsette and Elephanta* he compares the lines jokily to Lear's 'purple mullahs and silvery goreewallahs'. Also, in his ornithological work, *Loves Meine*, he writes of the common dipper, *Cinclus cinclus*. Ruskin takes a dig at Charles Darwin (1809–92), making use of Lear:

> You will please observe that some of the scientific people call it a blackbird – some a thrush – some a starling – and the rest a Cincle, whatever that may be. It remains for them now only to show how the Cincle has been developed out of the winkle, and the winkle out of the Quangle-Wangle – 'Out of the crumpety tree the Quangle Wangle sat'.

Lear's illustrations for Gould would have been well known to Ruskin, for he purchased for his St George's Museum in Sheffield the 'Eyton Collection of Ornithological Plates'.[4] Among the seven thousand hand-coloured illustrations were original watercolour drawings by Lear, later drawn on stone for Gould's works. Ruskin would surely have known also that Lear was responsible for some of the illustrations in Darwin's *The Zoology of the Voyage of HMS Beagle*.

There was a young person of Kew,
Whose virtues and vices were few;
But with blameable haste, she devoured some hot paste,
Which destroyed that young person of Kew.

Lear's first *Book of Nonsense* came out under the pseudonym of 'Derry Down Derry'. The *Oxford English Dictionary* records *derry* in this context as a 'meaningless word in the refrain of popular songs'. The book was published in Lear's year of celebration, 1846. In 1867, Lear settled for three years in Cannes. He found rooms at the Villa Montaret, 6 Rue Saint Honoré, Cannes. Among the Englishmen living in this growing town was John Addington Symonds (1840–93), a native of Bristol and author, among other things, of the six-volume *Renaissance in Italy*. He was also a Fellow of Magdalen College, Oxford, and celebrated as a thinker, which appealed to Lear. Symonds' wife, Katherine, and her sister, Marianne North (1830–90), the flower painter who had wandered the world with her brush, were part of the household. Marianne later gave her collection of flower pictures to the Royal Botanic Gardens at Kew and built a gallery to house them.

The Symondses had a daughter Janet, who was ill and confined to her bed before Christmas in 1867. Lear took his first nonsense song, *The Owl and the Pussy Cat*, to her bed chamber to cheer her up, showing her his drawings, which were quite unlike any of his topographical landscapes. Here was detail to hold the child's attention and to give life to the strange stories.

Ever since Lear's early days at Knowsley when he was first with the Stanley family, Earls of Derby, he could entertain and relate to children. Indeed, children were his route from 'below stairs' to being part of the family in the grand rooms above. Acceptance led to friendships on a much wider scale with some of the most interesting and powerful people of the day. Referring to his first song in a letter to Lady Waldegrave in January, 1868, he wrote, 'I enclose another bit of fun, for some child or other – (I wrote it for Lady Strachey's niece, little Janet Symonds)'.[5] The reference to a 'runcible spoon' in the *Owl and the Pussy Cat* has a strange connection with Admiral Nelson. The runcible spoon is an all-purpose eating implement, basically a spoon with fork tines at the end with a cutting edge on one side. When Nelson lost his arm at Tenerife in 1797

Lear's drawing of the Owl and the Pussy Cat at sea in their pea-green boat

while commanding the *Theseus*, Lady Spencer gave him a fork with a small knife blade attached so that he could cut his food single-handed. To commemorate Nelson's death and celebrate the Battle of Trafalgar in 2005, I had a small number of runcible, or Theseus, spoons made, with Nelson's dates, 1758–1805. The spoons are decorated with the naval foul anchor of the time.

Edward Lear did not invent the limerick verse. The dictionary explains this form of verse came 'from a custom at convivial parties according to which each member sang an extemporised "nonsense verse" which was followed by a chorus containing the words "will you come up to Limerick".' This type of verse may have come to Lear's attention from *Anecdotes and Adventures of Fifteen Gentlemen*, published around 1822, a copy of which may have been in the great library or nursery at Knowsley when Lear was there. The *Sick Man of Tobago* came from this collection:

> There was a sick man of Tobago
> Who liv'd long on rice-gruel and sago;
> But at last, to his bliss,
> The physician said this –
> 'To a roast leg of mutton you may go.'

Lear's typical limerick repeats the first line as the last line with a slight alteration. This provided a sort of chorus for his young listeners. He did not include the Tobago lines in his book, though he illustrated the words, perhaps to show them to children. The original had a night-capped invalid, who may have been rather frightening, so he replaced this with a sailor, pig-tailed, wearing a bum-freezer and slippers.

A typical Edward Lear limerick from the first *Book of Nonsense*, published in 1846, reads:

> There was a Young Lady of Bute,
> Who played on a silver-gilt flute;
> She played several jigs, to her uncle's white pigs,
> That amusing Young Lady of Bute.

Vivien Noakes has made a lifetime study of Edward Lear and has gathered together all his limericks, nonsense songs, stories, alphabets, botany, music and laughable lyrics in her *Complete Verse and Other Nonsense*, with Lear's illustrations. The book provides a complete resource, showing Lear's creative way of entertaining nonsensically.[6]

Gang Warily spent the night in Saint-Jean Cap Ferrat. Eze, the hilltop village, was outlined as the light faded in the west. It is like a gigantic bird's nest atop a rocky hill. Lear painted Nice on 4 December 1864 and then captured Eze from above on 6 December. As we will learn, Lear set out from his house in Nice, 61 Promenade des Anglais, on Tuesday 6 December that year. He climbed the ridge that was to take him up and down all along the Corniche eastward to Genoa. He returned, travelling by diligence and on foot, accompanied by Giorgio, his Suliot servant. In the morning, we could just see traces of the rugged path that commands the Baie des Anges. That fabled shore stretches eastward to San Remo. The port was barely discernible in the morning heat haze. We were soon to return to Nice to follow Lear's footsteps eastward to Genoa and back.

The white-hulled barquentine *Lili Marleen* was anchored off Monte Carlo. I wondered whether the captain had read *Shooting and Yachting in the Mediterranean* by A Bagot, or Bagatelle, as he styled himself. In writing about Monte Carlo, in about the third quarter of the nineteenth century, he recorded that 'sporting facilities are entirely lacking, so it is no use going ashore with your gun.' However, if you did anchor off Monte Carlo, he advised that it was 'unsafe to lie in a sailing vessel. Anchor off gas works and keep steam.' This was before the harbour or the casino were properly in business. John Addington Symonds, Lear's friend, wrote colourfully in his diary for 1886 of the croupiers in the casino. He reported they were either 'fat, sensual cormorants, or sallow, lean cheeked vultures, or suspicious foxes'.

I am not sure that Charles Deville Wells would have agreed. He was the man highlighted in the song *The Man Who Broke the Bank at Monte Carlo*. Wells managed to turn £40 into £40,000. Little good did it do him though in the long term, for he died in prison after being sentenced for fraud.

> ● *Gang Warily* passed Cap Martin before 13.30. Le Corbusier, founder of the movement for high-rise architecture and townscape planning, drowned while swimming off this point in 1965.
> – *Gang Warily*'s log, Saturday 20 December 1997

Le Corbusier, real name Charles Edouard Jeanneret (1887–1965), produced a plan for demolishing the centre of Paris and replacing the old buildings with tower blocks, set in leafy surroundings. He thought the city street had had its day: 'Our streets no longer work. Streets are an obsolete notion. The existing centres must come down.' He went on to declare, 'To save itself, every great city must rebuild its centre.' His ideas were adopted in housing estates that circled Paris, but thankfully the most beautiful and glorious of all city centres was conserved.[7]

San Remo was now on the port bow. The courtesy flag had been changed from the French tricolour to the green, white and red of Italy. Edward Lear had built two houses in San Remo, the first in 1870 and the second in 1880. He also had two cats, Potiphar and the famous Foss. Potiphar soon died, but his twin, the dock-tailed Foss, was to delight Lear until the cat's death in 1887. The second house was designed to mirror the first, so that Foss would know his way around. He bought the land for his house on 25 March 1869 on a plot next door to Walter Congreve's garden in the Corniche. He had liked Cannes because of the Symonds family, but he had left because the only people remaining, as he described them in a letter to Richard Wyatt in 1870, were 'Belgravian idlers, who make calls and go to church daily'.

Gang Warily was to be laid up in San Remo. Dr Giovanni Novi, a great friend, Chairman of the Italian Sail Training Association and past Commodore of the Yacht Club Italiano, had been and was to be tireless in looking after us on the Italian coast north of Rome. He arranged a winter berth at San Remo, under the eye of the harbourmaster, Captain Gavagnin, who had been a driver for the Household Cavalry after Italy withdrew from World War II. Now that *Gang Warily* was safely in his charge, we had time to look at Edward Lear's epic Corniche walk and ride.

Changing the courtesy flag on entering Italian waters.
Photo: Gilly Drummond

Tickia Orologica.

12
Lear's epic walk

Edward Lear had a hectic year throughout 1864. Leaving England on Saturday 2 January, he travelled through France to Marseille and thence by boat to Genoa and then to Ancona on the east coast of Italy. He took a boat from there to Corfu, arriving on Saturday 9 January. After a pause there, he left on Monday 4 April for Athens, arriving on Saturday 9 April. Crete was next and then Greece and then on to Messina and Marseille, returning to London on Saturday 11 June. It was time for a rest, but not for long. On 2 November he left London, arriving in Nice on Saturday the 5th, taking up residence at 61 Promenade des Anglais on Thursday 10 November. There were no lamps or furniture in the house as he had just moved in.

In 1862, Lear had first hit on an idea for mass-producing watercolours and had set himself the task of doing another line of pictures while in his house in Nice in 1864. He called these his 'Tyrants'. He did an outline of the picture, painted it in one colour, leaving that to dry, and then going on to another picture, and so on and so forth. It is easy to imagine a line of pictures on the floor. He slaved away. In his diary for Friday 18 November 1864, Lear notes: 'Seventh day of 240 Tyrants.

There was an Old Person of Nice, whose associates were usually Geese.
They walked out together, in all sorts of weather.
That affable Person of Nice!

Got through 17 of second process – 40 in all.' The process started on 11 November and he recorded in his diary that he 'shut up shop with relief' on Monday 5 December.

Lear's words capture both his exhaustion and his determination. He had been set on the idea of 'walking' from Nice to Genoa and back for some time. I have included the complete account of the walk as far as Genoa, as it captures his everyday thoughts.[8]

Monday, 5th December [1864] – Oh dear me, no rest or peace – and yet this Corniche road must be done. So having risen at 7, I began to pack and didn't breakfast till 10. No letters or papers. After all sorts of trial, I decided on taking a large trunk, and G his box. Did the third process of one small drawing – 22 in all and then shut up shop. At 2, went to Avigdors and got 25 maps, 3 francs, £20 from Drummonds. Found at the diligence office that they could take no luggage after 7 so I took two places for myself and George. 10 fr. the 2 and sent the luggage overnight. Left cards at the Reillys and went home – when I finished all the packing and sent George with the things. At 4 went to Lady Duncan's but clouds and winds arise. Returned to dress and dine at Mr Lyons. Clouds and high winds. Home by 9.30. Finished all packing and went to bed.

The diary entry for Tuesday 6 December is written in a less staccato manner, and it may be this was the start of the proposed 'Corniche book' that was never published.

Winding the hill above Nice in the slow dilly was a bore. However, above Villefranche I got out and walked (it was clear and cold) to the spot I wanted to draw Eze from above, before the diligence came up and its horses returned from Turbie ere I had done. A strangely wild and magnificent coast scene is this, I know no finer. It was bitterly cold and the wind very high – and was glad to have a thick cloak. On to the second point which is equally surprising and this was about 11.30 or 12. Eze is assuredly an astonishing place – and so various. By 2 exactly we got to Turbie, a punctuality highly creditable to my arrangement. Just below the rocky stretch we chose a place for lunch, which being two cold pigeons, sausage, bread and marsala. It was undeniably delightful. We left at 3 and drew once or twice more but not easily in the face of the sun. The rocky scenery is prodigiously fine here about as is the view of Monaco. By 5 we were at Roquebrune, and by 6 at Mentone. A poor fellow of Sardinia – ill from fever, walked with us the last of the way.

Not knowing my particular inn and anxious to escape the town, I stopped at 'The Londres', sending G for the boxes. The first day of travelling on the Corniche was beautiful.

Wednesday, 7th December – Was a grey day in spite of G's optimism. I had to arrange paper – it was 8.30 before I breakfasted. At 9 – went out – near the sea – multitudinous washing women: and sticking to the left entered by a path road through olive groves to the long promontory I wanted to explore. Women gathering olives recall Corfu. No one ever gathered olives as quickly as my mother says George. Olive glades are lovely and the frequent orange gardens, but no sun. Coming out on the sea, a road, pine bordered, runs to the end of the promontory of Cap Martin. Round and over it lovely. Pine trees are everywhere. The view each way very pretty. I drew two times, yea thrice; but lost my knife, which G went to fetch but found not, for through a hole in my pocket it had fallen into my shoe. The fourth time I drew Mentone – but perversely the sun would never shine on it, – and so when about 4, I got by degrees nearer the town I could not see the outline for want of light and much shade. Moreover it was cold. I walked through the town and along the east side where hotels and villas are numberless – and so by sunset (4.15) to Pont St Louis – where I asked about the road from some Frenchmen. We returned reaching our Hotel de Londres at 5.45. There is no small bother as to how to get to San Remo on foot – for diligences only start after 12 and there is the border to contend with which I must be present in body. On whole I fancy the small voiture must be taken to San Remo. Tomorrow I plan to go back to Monaco then back here. Dinner is very good – at 6.15. Since which I have been reading Manel [?] and G has brought my waistcoat, mended. Second day of Corniche travel has been pleasant.

Thursday, 8th December – Did not sleep well. Had a minor epileptic attack but rose at 6.30 nevertheless and having had coffee was off at 7. People here are very industrious and are at work at 6.30.

Morning is fine, greyish but becoming sunnier. Past the heights looking down on the olives and pines of S. Martino and descend below Roquebrune – the road following the sea. Immense gardens of orange and lemon especially the latter. Drew 15 minutes. Long road with no other view but the sea, yet interesting because of the great carobs and olives. Vast rocks tumble down from the upper heights along which you see the Nice road – a threadline. Abundant water, reservoirs account for the vast fertility of this bit of the Riviera, due to its freedom from north and east winds. I am continually reminded of Corfu and the road from Peramo to Benitza. Past several mills and villas, and next, the casino and a great hotel. Here, Monaco, hither hidden becomes visible, but is horribly ugly – like a long box with houses thereon. I voted it undrawable and was surprised to find it so unlike my idea. Going round it, I drew on the west side, but is very little better, and then returning – ascended until I saw the town below me and there drew from 11–12.30. Lunch, by no means good followed and violent sickness. A small steamer came into the port and seeing it move up and down so, helped the sickness. At 1.30 came away – (leaving papers of salt fish surrounded by stones, though G said no one would touch it).

Alas! Monaco is a clumsy place, and 'how unlike those' in Greece and Albania!!! 1.45 talk of the Reids [Sir James and Lady Reid – Governor of Corfu under British rule]. Go up to the town, gardeny walks – walls – three streets (named religiously) clean but narrow. Palace Luogo Morto – (a dead or dull place). Down at 2.20. Priests many, walking 3 abreast, as soldiers. Reeds and figs among olives. 3 p.m. Here and there wondrous bits of grouped carob, olive and rock, but with no composed interest (for drawing): fine studies, but that's all – except for the colour of the rock, hill and sky.

Certainly I had no idea of the richness of this part of Italy: perpetually reminded of Corfu. The profusion of lemons and the sea far below. Before 5 we were at the top and by 5.30 reached the inn. Dinner and bed by 8.30.

Friday, 9th December – Perfectly lovely spring day. Rose at 7, breakfasted at 8. Very good. At 9 went to the east side of Mentone and drew till 12.30. Wonderfully beautiful groves of lemons. What hosts of invalids and invalides! Unwisely I think, but wishing to avoid uncivility, I called on Roberts' [David Roberts, RA] friend Gardiner – Mrs G: six small children. Kindly, vulgar and over hospitable. Pressed me to dine until from weariness I said yes. G who I left as he dawdled, overtook me and staid, when I drew on the east side, and walked back. I growling packed at 5.30 and fled. Dinner as I had anticipated was a bore: but I was amiable as I could be – out of principle and at 9 and Gardiner talking over another, the gossip was odious and I said goodnight.

Ye Gods! What a society! It is as I had known many times – better to be surly and lonely – than social and bored. Mentone is assuredly very beautiful but intolerable and unwholesome because of its crowded Anglicanism.

Saturday, 10th December – Rose at 7.15, fine but grey, a very cold morning. At 7.10 off in a one horse vettura and a funny little dog – luggage behind and before. Soon beyond the Ponte San Luigi, at the Italian Douane, 8 a.m. The officials were utterly courteous and amicable. Above this is some magnificent coast views looking west, perhaps the finest of all: but it is too early to stop here. I thought the same as we reached Ventimiglia at 8.30, from then on we walked sending on the voiture and baggage. The town on the east side is wonderfully picturesque, broken bridge, old houses, etc., etc. Drew though half frozen till I could not hold my pencil – 9.30. Extreme picturesque and varied houses. We went on. There was more traffic and a less interesting road. A good bridge over the River Paglia, inundated low land: a long straight line of road to Bordighera. Ever a cold grey sky. Got to the shore, hoping to find a good view of the place but do not.

Aloes and palms not abundant, but not drawable. Bordighera invisible. Rounded the Cape and finding nothing like I had expected, went on and drew by the roadside, looking back on Bordighera, where the new [railway] tunnel is in the making. No good view: debate whether to return to Bordighera but decide no. Lunch at 1–1.30. Cold fowl and wines. Ever pleasant though it was cold. How many quiet similar hours are to be remembered while memory lasts! 1.45. I move, very cold. Sea even smooth. Railway building in progress. Groups of palms. Village of Ospedaletti, – uninteresting but it is a bay of quiet peace. (Cherry tree leaves still on). 2.45, calm, wide grey wrinkly sea. Ospedaletti, a quiet village by the sea shore, warm and sheltered. Draw 3–3.45. Ascended, the scene ever calm and grey; but there is sadly little to draw and I did not try. Beheld a man climbing telegraph poles with long attachments to his shoes, claws of iron. At the next point many workmen quarrying stone – long low lines of hill to Cape Verde which lies beyond San Remo. By 5.30 got to the large new Hotel de Londres. It was a comfort to wash, and to dine at the 6 o'clock table d'hote. Many English: and two Polish (ladies) who declared themselves hungry at the end of dinner and order a second!

Sunday, 11th December – Grey, but tho' sunless, by no means cold. Breakfast at 8. A mistake in these journeyings, and we do it no more. Out with G, passing the town but finding nothing to draw. The town [San Remo] on a hill slopes back, so you must go a mile or two out to see it, and then it is only a ridge of common buildings. Drew: – but seeing that there is little ahead to draw, go by diligence to Oneglia. Returned, and poled up to convent high above the town, to no purpose, and then descended by very horrid, slippery streets, where but for G, I had fallen several times. To the seaside also, but all to no purpose. San Remo is an absolute failure; came back to the inn and packed. It is now 1 p.m. There don't seem much available in the Corniche. Had some lunch! Good Lord! How horrible to herd with the people I see here – an arrabbiatura in settling accounts. It was the youth who drove me here having taken backsheesh both from the landlord and from me. Finally, I walked to the message office at 3, waited till 3.30, when a diligence arrived with George sat thereon. At 4, no end of a fuss about the place. I didn't care but one lady was furious, she continued to annoy the director for an hour. O, Dio! did she howl. The road seemed to be very uninteresting and dreadfully horrid from long tracks of fallen earth in the last great rains – 40 days of it they say. Obscure torrents and unpleasant villages, roaring sea: no peacock hue bays, nor any other pleasure. At Porto Maurizio where we arrived at 6.15 after starting at 4. Passengers and luggage abounded. The town seems highly picturesque. At 6.45 we got to Oneglia. Sleety rain was falling and after a time I and G got to the Hotel Vittoria where there was a room, – and after a while dinner, not at all bad. The better sort of Italian inn. It is now 9 and bed time.

Monday, 12th December – Rose at 6.30, and was away by 7.15. In the night it had rained and was sunless, grey and cold. A long straight street is the in and out of Oneglia. There follows a suspension bridge over a large torrent. A road – olive edged (all in the world is olives here) brings one and half an hour to near P. Maurizio, where I draw as well as I can – cold and damp included. The people are vastly civil here always. After a time I prowl to the post and go up to the town remembering how well it looked in June last: but now there is no sun – no light and shade – and a deal of gloom and traffic. So, I go back, for there is no more to be done or draw – between rainy droppings – at the bridge and on the shore. Then to the Hotel Vittoria where I get some eggs by way of lunch. At 2 we prowl to the pier and watch the men and women pulling nets, but there is nothing to draw pictorially, so we go up to the opposite hill by the road towards Genoa, and there draw various scenes, but of course, never well, as there is no sun and increasing cloud. I was obliged to sit by the roadside, bothered by mules and cars which is a Corniche drawback. There is also a permanent flea today, abideth by me. I tire sadly of this Corniche – lopsided views and blank grey sea and this everlasting smash of railway cuttings, and blowings up and knockings down. At 4.30, it begins to rain hard and we made a run for the hotel. My, how it did rain! But still they say it is a champ of a moon storm and may be fine tomorrow. A Russian family comes to the room next to mine and makes a horrid row. As for me, I dine at 6, very decently, and the charges are moderate here, and bed (8 p.m.).

Tuesday, 13th December – (Epileptic night) It rained furiously all night and waking at 5 I perceive it was useless to hope to leave this place all day so I, after a while, slept and did not rise until 8. G left at 9. The Russ family next to me – (who had four governesses – English, Italian, German and French) are also weather bound, which is a bore as they make a great row. After breakfast, I began to pen out, and really worked on till 3.30, finishing two drawings and part of a third. It stopped raining about then, so I walked with G, as far as the bridge, the nearly dry torrent of yesterday being now a great river 'rolling rapidly'. Much doubt whether it is best to go back, or on, even if it be fine enough to move tomorrow. Finally, resolved not to engage one of the Nice vittirini now here, but to wait for the chance of fine weather.

Come back at 5 or so, and dined at 6. One feels very well here. Later, tis 8 now, it seems to be clearing and I prepare once more to go onward, the thought of only seeing half of the Corniche being disgusting. Not that I at all report to like it, but I only wish not to leave it 'to see' any longer.

Wednesday, 14th December – At 6 it was quite clear, so at 7, the two items of luggage were taken to the diligence office, marked for Alassio. After cafe, I and G set off, leaving the many governesses and Russians in the act of setting off. It was then quite calm and fine, but grew cloudy before we got up the long coast hill going from Oneglia eastward. At a point where one sees the Val Diano, which is rich and olive covered and runs back from a bay where are Diano and Cervo on the shore. G's hat blew away, but stuck on a stone right over the sea, to which that Suliot, cat like, crawled and regained it. Going downward to Diano, the bay is very pretty, but there was still a prettier view further on, but I did not like to stay, for rain was ahead, so we pressed on and passed the long, long streak of Diano and by a long straight line of road between the olives and Cervo, and round below the town and up the Cape forming the eastern perimeter of the bay. Here the rain came apace, and wind, and it was a bore also to see the horrid land and cliff slips. Beyond in pouring rain, a descent to the flat, over flowing ground where the alarming Andora River even crossed a wooden bridge. Then the village: then a long ascent of Capo Mele, to the lighthouse and down the other side: – here there was a lovely view as far as Noli, and of Laigueglia and Alassio, perhaps the prettiest I've seen – next to Mentone, I have yet seen in these drizzlings. Here, it being noon, we sat on a wall and lunched, but it was awfully cold. Laigueglia is picturesque, and cold as I was, I drew again, when, hurrying on we got to Alassio at 2. But alas! No diligence had come, so we must go to the Belle Italia, and I got housed: vast, airy rooms, – too much show. At 4 the diligence came, and G soon brought the bags and at 5, dinner. Awfully bad. Two English and an American joined in the conversation. It's now 8, and again pouring with rain immensely. A very unprosperous journey!

Thursday, 15th December – It is now 9 a.m. and I rise. A fearful night of pouring rain, high wind, and roaring sea. It is, of course, wholly absurd to think of moving today. What a journey. 10 p.m. All the day from 9 when I rose, to 4, was one great cataract of rain with wind and raging sea – great accompaniments. The two guests are Americans (we breakfast together) and very pleasant. Later I found that she knows Rome well, the Terrys, the Crawfords, the Perkins's, the Storeys and also that he was U.S. consul in Buenos Aires, and knows Farquhar, the Drummonds and others. They kindly asked me to sit with them by their fire, and lent me Dickens' last book, – I, then, lent them Tennyson's and read thereout. So the day wore on, until at 4 rain ceased and Mr. Hudson and I went out 'for a walk' through the one street of the town and up the hill beyond, whence the meritable Riviera point and bay is seen. At 5.30 we dined – very sociably, and later, we had a bottle of marsala: afterwards sitting by the pleasant fire till nearly 10, when I came to bed.

The cookery here is peculiarly vile. Amazing. The diligence has just arrived – from Genoa and I think also from Nice: both, of course, very late.

How am I to get on tomorrow????

Friday, 16th December – Woke at 6, cloudy. Rise at 7. Clearer: and resolved to go on. Pay bill 53 fr. (coffee bad) and having directed the trunks to Finale, leave them with the waiter and set off, 8.30. Very long street of village or city, highly cinquecento [fifteenth-century] and long similar suburb beyond walls. Rise and go by the shore and cliff road. Draw the bay which is only pretty from brightness and 'multitudinous' qualities. About 9.15 descend to Albenga – and came to a marshy plain, olives grown at intervals. Later, the ancient city itself, many towered – the towers I saw in June of this year. It is very Medieval and picturesque, and today being fine and the snow hills clear – a pleasure. While drawing, the two Americans passed and greetings ensued. Walk, by flat road to city, and go round it, also enter it. Very quaint and compact and full of character, and I could willingly stay the night there to see the towers, for which there is not time enough. I recall Amatrice

[Rieti] in the streets and tall houses. Hence the long road between vines and maize fields. I am passing Ponte Lungo – a grand Roman bridge: a broad fine plain and a grand sight for a city. Along the straight long road till I reach Ceriale, at the seaside, about 11.30, or 12. Like all these towns, a street along the shore. Arrive at high rising ground or cape, whence the views are fine both ways. Drew – and at 12.30 lunch on salt fish and bread and marsala. 1.15 off and pass Borghetto Santo Spirito. Old, walled – marshy and flat, semi cultivated with a rapid river. 1.30 hence the road was narrow and between walls to Loano. Very long narrow street, savouring a past grandeur. The river runs close by the east gate of the city (which is a very uninteresting one) and an old man told me all about the accident. The waves were very high, the ford being close by the sea. A cart had just passed and said all was safe. As the diligence entered the water, the stream 'came down' suddenly, three or four feet high – the horses were frightened and the passengers more so, and so 'disgrazia' [trouble]. We cross on a high bridge higher up: the castle of Doria and a convent are picturesque. Low, maize cultivated ground leads on to Pietra – another large plain near which were very large orange and lemon gardens. Beyond, a long straight uphill road. Ever the growing railway aboundeth. Drew a bridge and river scene. Later on reached a village – Borgio. Then on by innumerable rail works towards Capo Di Caprazoppa which we reach about 4. The rolling green sea was magnificent. I turned and draw Finale, very picturesque, till dark. Town by 5. Albergo della China. No luggage came yet. Dined well at 5.30. It is now 7.30 and no dilly. It does not seem the luggage will come, so I must make up my bed. Mean to sleep as best I can: a bore, but one good thing was I was deadly sleepy. At 9, after talking with the intelligent man of Asti, I succumbed to circumstances and came to bed – to sleep in shirt and drawers. It is no use to think of tomorrow – 'sufficient unto etc.'. After a while, I was awakened by the cameriere [waiter] saying that the diligence had come but had brought no luggage.

Saturday, 17th December – Cameriere says the conductor could take no luggage, this diligence going already loaded. What to do? – The same thing may occur again indefinitely and it don't do to go on without luggage. So I decide to send George at once in a one horse trap – (for 12 frs.) to bring back the boxes from Alassio – in case they are not indeed sent on by the next diligence. At 9, went up to the Ponte [bridge] to draw, and George passed me at 9.30. A very grand coast scene: drew until 12. Morning fine, and weather cold, apparently more settled. Back to the Hotel della China and breakfasted. A diligence arriving now has brought no luggage, so I've done rightly to send for it. At 1, set off and walked to Varigotti.

The afternoon cloudier! Not fine. Many pretty bits of scenery along the coast. Returned from the further point I went to at two and drew, and again at the town, until 4.15.

On going back to the hotel, the Suliot came there with the luggage – a comfort. So having nothing more to do at Finale, ordered dinner and the same trap for Savona tomorrow if fine. Dined very well – the cooking here is excellent and the whole hotel recommendable. And so to bed at 9.30.

Sunday, 18th December – Rose at 6. The morning was grey just like yesterday. Paid bill (40.50). A good hotel and got off by 7.30 in the one horse trap. G went into Alassio yesterday. Got to Savona. I knew the road – and shortly beyond, I left the car to go on. Set out to walk. Unluckily it soon began to rain, so I could not draw any part of Capo di Noli, which is certainly immensely grand as a rock and sea scene.

Beyond is doubtless one of the finest views in all the Riviera but all the distance was indistinct.

Stopped – cold and wet, in a lull of rain, to draw Noli and Spotorno. The former (the town of Noli) is very picturesque with towers, fishers abound and I passed outside the town. Along the beach to Spotorno, a place of more pretension with large and painted houses, gardens, oranges, etc. Beyond, the coast is lonely – and by 10.30 – now is rain, now without, we got over the cape opposite the ugly little beastly island of Bergeggi. Further on, the village of Bergeggi is niched into the hill, and then follows a headland with awful landslips and dangerous outcrops of stone, which if it rains much more will diffuse themselves still more to the annoyance of the traveller on the Ligurian Riviera. At the next turn, Vado, was visible, and also Savona. Very plain, but it rained hard, and it was only in a lull at 11.30 that I and G ate luncheon casually standing below a tree – of a cold tunny bottarga – sticking what we could not eat in bits of paper, on thorns: for others benefit. Thence it rained harder and harder and the road was ever between walls – with here and there a few shops, rows of nuts were for sale and some great shut villas: until we reached Savona at 11.15, quite wet – and got to the Hotel Reale, where the luggage had already arrived. It is now 2.45 and being clear, I set out with open (carriage) windows, the rain racing hard into a Corfu like harbour full of boats, recalling other days. *What* a journey! And what to do next?

All the way along the road, the works of the railway tremendous they are – are going on, as if it were not Domenica [Sunday].

Having walked about until 4.45, thereafter came to the table d'hote dinner, and low! no end of a 'mess' dinner – ossifers [officers], and two ladies: two English engineers – youngsters. The dinner became allegro and no end of bottles of champagne were distributed and healths drunk (to all the English and to all the Italians, till we broke up). Then I, sitting with the two engineers, had a bottle of marsala, and very pleasant company till past 8. G came in and I said if it rains, don't call me. Indeed what to do? Cogoleto? or diligence to Genoa?

Monday, 19th December – Pouring rain so I did not rise. Resolved to go to Genoa, believing the road was a decent one, or is it not! G left but I dawdled with Mr Flood, the engineer. Took two places to Voltri. After sharing a table with the intelligent landlord, off at 1. Rain ever pouring, nor did it cease till we passed Albisola. Vehicle odious, jolting, dangerous. Celle, and at 2.40 change horses at Varazze. Very beautiful pine woods and views of the Genoa shore but horribly dangerous turns and landslips. At 3.30, Cogoleto, evening sun red. Falling walls. Leave diligence and walk up mountain – descend to Arenzano at 4. Alarm of falling rox. Arrive at the plain, 4.30. Landslip has covered all the road for a long space, and is still falling. By going onto the railway embankment and walking, we escaped but didn't then get to Voltri before 5.30; just as the rain started. Yet if not for the mistake of a stupid clerk I should have got off after all. We went to the 'Gallo' Locanda [the Cock Inn], a very gallows place; but got not a bad dinner of soup, boiled fowl, fish and wine. The Gallo inn being direful, I go to bed in my clothes, as we must be up at 4. What a day! Precipices, landslips!

Tuesday, 20th December – No sleep. Up at 4. Off at 5. Fine day. Found at Genoa that poor G has forgotten the book! So I sent him back for it: saying next to nothing, as I know his own vexation is quite sufficient punishment. Came to the Grande Bretagne Hotel. By the time I was washed, however, and ready for breakfast, George came back, having found the book just where he left it. The hotel seemed 'neat' and quiet; breakfast good. At 12, went out with G to the Lanterna (lighthouse), and tried to draw two or three times Sampierdarena, but the row and the bother of carriages and having had no sleep, upset me and I could do nothing.

Wonderful to relate it is all cloudy again, and so there seems no hope of settled weather. Return to hotel, and then by the Acquagola [gate], to the view which I want to take looking west, but all was cloudy and I could see nil.

Return sad and disgusted. At 5, dined tete a tete with an intelligent Deputato Garofalo, MP for the County of Terra di Lavoro. At 6 I've come upstairs. What to do next. It is no use to speculate. Have been unwell all day more or less so.

Wednesday, 21st December – Refreshed by long night's sleep. But the morning being heavy and grey, G did not call me till 7.15. As I rose, it grew more hopeful though, the coffee not being available so early, we set off at 7.45 – had coffee in the shop below. Verily magnificent as is Genoa, walking in nailed shoes on its pavements, delights not. At the rail, found there was no train to Voltri until 9.46, so it was cheaper to walk than to wait from 8.15, whereby we walked. The road to the lantern is painful – cars, omnibuses, and slipperyness. Beyond the whole line of hill to Capo Mele, and the one thousand houses in town and villages is a 'marvel' – Sampierdarena is composed of vast warehouses with tramways at one street but two or three parallel streets from the town. To make a shortcut, we went askew, but only came to a vast foundry whence issued one thousand or more men to breakfast: a sight. Next a broad river, but intelligent small boys directed us along it to the high road and a big 'Durazzo' bridge which led to Cornigliano. Here again, a most obliging man went out of his way to show me the station. We were there by 9.30. At 9.50 the train left and we had very comfortable second class seats to Voltri, arriving 10.20. Thence I walked through the town or two towns – and drew quietly: no one bothers: and thus returned repassing the Voltri station at 11.40 and drawing beyond it, near Pra (looking east). All these places are nearly one shore town. The infinite drying of all the linen out of all the windows is a chief characteristic, but the extreme loveliness of the general colour, rising mainly from the beauty of many of the villas, coloured and brilliant, can't be given though it is one of the first characteristics of the Genoa Contorni. At Pra, drew the coast (12.30) now very clear, and then on to Pegli, more of a town than Pra. Draw again near Pegli till 1.30 – and then go on, until we reach the Trattoria della Marina where we have good fish, and a sort of Irish stew, olives and a bottle of really good wine for 4 frs. This half hour, the bright sun and ships beyond, and quiet with G gravely and moderately eating and muttering in Greek, made a pleasant memory. At 2, away: and walked on through Sestri, which contained many beautiful and superb villas, but I drew none – since none would combine with the coast and could only be drawn as elevations. At 3.45, went off to the beach at Cornigliano and drew the outline of Genoa, and then on again, and by 4.30 we were at Sampierdarena, and thus to the Lanterna – after which noise and misery abounded till 6. We reached the Hotel Grande Bretagne. 'Cleaned' and had a most excellent dinner, the Marina Trattoria is by the Francesco Gorgillo. The weather has been lovely.

Thursday, 22nd December – In spite of the last sentence, the morning was quite cloudy, though very cold. Set off, shivering at 7.40 and endeavoured to draw several times, but vainly. Sat trying to go on with the Sampierdarena drawing – the mountains being all more or less clouded – till, my hands could bare it no longer. Whereat, about 11.30, we walked to the Columbus station, and waiting there, I sent G for my thick cloak and gloves – and at 1 we were again at the Lanterna view, which was drawn from a lot of piles of wood by the road side. A luogo comodo universale not far off.

Here we lunched – and well: and I tried to draw vainly again and somewhat less so at the inner barrier – after which I gave it up. And then I walked all through the wonderful streets and palaces to Acquasole [gate], and round the walls till 4, then the hotel 4.30. After 3, the sun had come out, and it was fine, though not for distance drawing. Upon my word this Riviera journey is *a worry*.

Friday, 23rd December – Up at 6. Bright, cold and clear. Coffee at cafe at 7 – and off, 7.15 to the walls, alas! Mountains not clear! Drew till 9.15. Came back – bought photographs, and a box and breakfasted, and it is now noon: and I have written to C.F. [Chichester Fortescue] – F.L. [Franklin Lushington] Eleanor Newsom [Lear's sister] – F. Cooper, the Drummonds and Lady Duncan. Saw a vetturino [cabby] but they ask monstrous prices – 4 frs. to Savona, being Xmas. So I will risk the weather, and send on the luggage to Savona tomorrow, going on foot as far as Cogoleto and to Savona next day. Set out at 1 and drew again at the spot below the Lanterna, a wonderful coast scene – but the hills never became clear. Then I made some useful studies of Genoa ... suffering from the tearing omnibi, raging mules, erroneous asses, and other bores. At 3.15 – we came all athwart the town, and were at sunset on the wall below Cornigliano, but it never became clear. Nevertheless, I think my drawings may be useful. The splendour of Genoa is sunset! And the streets too: also the women and their dresses. Certainly Genoa is a delightful place. Posted six letters. Packed and dined at 6. They at the hotel are profuse in food and moderate in charges – dinner 4 frs. My and G's room – 4 ¹/₂ fr. I was never in so comfortable a hotel as Genoa. A mulatto boy with Buenos Ayres family and French folk at the table d'hote. All things being wound up, I am going to pack and to bed. Hoping for a fine day and a good journey to Nice and home.

There was an old man at a Station,
Who made a promiscuous oration;
But they said, "Take some snuff!—You have talk'd quite enough.
You afflicting old man at a Station!"

13
Gang Warily follows under sail

As Lear begins his long walk back, Gilly and I rejoined *Gang Warily* in San Remo on 6 June 1998. The intention was to sail to Genoa, keeping a close eye on the coast, as we had done from Nice. We hoped to experience, 134 years later, Lear's expedition on foot, carriage and train to Genoa and return in the winter of 1864.

San Remo is a good harbour for yachts with every facility within reach, from ship chandlers and sail makers to engineers and electricians. We returned to the yacht by train – London Waterloo, via the Channel tunnel, to Lille, crossing the platform for the Nice train, taking twelve hours in all. A hire car completed the trip to San Remo.

Gang Warily welcomed us in her gleaming livery of blue-grey paint and light cream upper works. I cannot remember a better finish than that painstakingly

There was a young person whose history,
Was always considered a mystery;
She sate in a ditch, although no one knew which,
And composed a small treatise on history.

achieved by the Roberto brothers. Our part of the final refit took from 6 to 10 June. Before setting sail, we spent some time trying to discover the location of Edward Lear's two houses in the town.

It is clear Lear had a love–hate relationship with the Riviera. He described the rooms in 61 Promenade des Anglais in his diary of Wednesday 9 November 1864: 'They are small but quaint rooms, well arranged – with good back light.' He had lived on the Riviera before, in Cannes, but that was too noisy for him. Noise, as Lear's Corniche diary bears witness, really upset him. His first impression of San Remo was not encouraging, as he wrote in his diary: 'Poled up to convent high above the town, to no purpose, and then descended by very horrid, slippery streets, where but for G, I had fallen several times. To the seaside also, but all to no purpose. San Remo is an absolute failure ...' Lear always judged a place by its paintable views, rather than by whether it was a pleasant area in which to live. This latter dimension gradually became more important

A sketch of San Remo by Lear. Illustration for *The Daisy* by Alfred, Lord Tennyson.
Private collection

to him, however, and by March 1870 he determined to move to San Remo, at the suggestion of a long-time inhabitant and British Consul, Walter Congreve, who was also an estate agent. Lear named his newly built house the 'Villa Emily', after his great niece living in New Zealand.

By the following year, Lear said to Lady Waldegrave, 'I've never met people as accommodating and pleasant as the people of San Remo.'

The joys of gardening were a latent resource that bloomed now that Lear had his own garden. In his diary for 17 February 1871, he records a list of seeds saved for him at Selborne, Hampshire, in the garden created by Gilbert White (1720–93). Gilbert White was a clergyman and naturalist. From 1784 he was curate in his native Selborne and lived at 'The Wakes', observing the comings and goings of the seasons, leading in 1789 to his *Natural History and Antiquities of Selborne*, a classic that has never been out of print. Professor Thomas Bell owned 'The Wakes' between 1844 and 1880. He was a professor of zoology at King's College London, a member of the Royal Society, and chairman of the meeting at which Darwin presented his paper on 'the origin of species'. Bell supplied plants from 'The Wakes', and Lear was a customer. Lear's careful planting in his garden was the inspiration for his nonsense botany and trees.

However, in 1879 his garden in San Remo was blighted by the building of a great white hotel which stole the light of his studio. He had thought he had an agreement with Miss Kay Shuttleworth, the owner of the plot, that nothing would be built there over two storeys in height. He was distraught. Part of the reason for building 'Villa Emily' had been to concentrate on working up his sketches for

Shoebootia Utilis.

Tennyson's poems. By 1880, Lear had calmed down and decided to build another home, using the same floor plan for the sake of Foss, his cat.

The 'Villa Tennyson', this time named after his friend the Poet Laureate, rose on land with only a road and railway between it and the sea. In a letter to Emily Tennyson dated 16 February 1880, Lear's humour shone through: 'My new land has only the road and the railway between it and the sea, so unless the fishes begin to build, or Noah's Ark comes to an anchor below the site, the new Villa Oduardo cannot be spoilt.'[9]

Lear chose the same San Remo builder, Giovenale Gastaldi, who had built the 'Villa Emily'. The new site was on the Corso Imperatrice.

Little is known about the decoration of the new building and we can only assume that Lear hung his own pictures to best advantage in what he described as his 'lower large room or studio'. The pictures would have been on display there for customers. In his bedroom, he placed an engraving of Frederick Edwin Church's (1826–1900) *Heart of the Andes*, painted in 1859. Lear admired Church's other major works, *Aurora Borealis* and *Cotopaxi*, at an exhibition in London. Church was an American landscape painter of the Hudson River School and a friend and follower of Thomas Cole. They worked together in Catskill, New York.

Lear's drawings of the Villa Emily in an undated letter to Lucy Wickham, née Markham. *Hampshire Record Office*

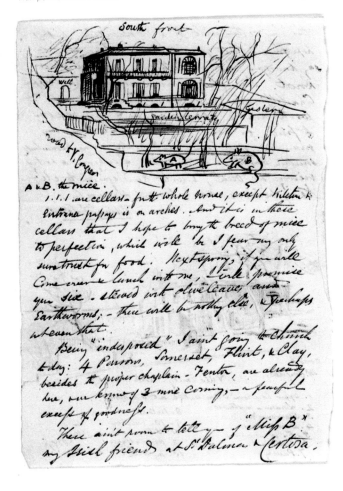

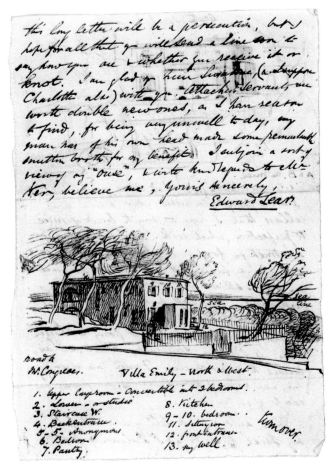

Lear's two villas were damaged in an earthquake in 1887 and repaired. Both were sold by his executors after his death in 1888.[10] Gilly and I could find little trace of Lear's houses. We suspected an old wall might have been part of his garden at 'Villa Tennyson'. However, he is remembered in the La Foce cemetery with Tennyson's lines on his tombstone – 'Died San Remo January 29th, 1888':

> All things fair
> With such a pencil such a pen
> You shadow'd forth to distant men
> I read and felt that I was there.

We stood for a moment in silence under the cypress trees that still live on in many of Lear's drawings of the Riviera. We walked slowly out of the cemetery, in no hurry to leave, though it was time for us to sail again.

● *Gang Warily* left the harbour of San Remo at 15.45, setting the genoa and taking advantage of a soldier's wind. The westerly soon piped up and to my astonishment we nearly reached eight knots, planing down the crested seas. The main was soon stowed and the genoa alone kept her going at almost the same speed. We would be in Alassio by 19.30. Capo Bertha was soon abeam and then came Capo Mele.

– *Gang Warily*'s log, **Wednesday 10 June 1998**

Remember, Lear had said that the view from the lighthouse was 'lovely ... as far as Noli, and of Laigueglia and Alassio, perhaps the prettiest I've seen – next to Mentone.'

Gang Warily at Alassio.
Photo: Gilly Drummond

Out at sea, with white caps topping the racing dark blue waves, it was perhaps even easier to appreciate the run of the land. Lear had always held that the view from the sea was the best, though he did not like the experience. He used to perch on headlands like Capo Mele to capture the scene with his pencil and brush.

As we approached Alassio, we could see that Edward Lear's perch for his drawing of the town was now occupied by a chapel. We were given a welcome by the harbour staff and by Signorina Govanna in the harbour office. She looked at Lear's drawings with interest. She confirmed the chapel and the yacht club were built and established at the same time in 1929.

● Later, I stood where Lear had probably sat, just to the west of the chapel entrance, looking across the town's sweep of beach to Capo Mele in the distance. Just as I was leaving, a man with a plastic bag settled in the same spot and started to extract his drawing block.

– *Gang Warily*'s log, **Thursday 11 June 1998**

Alassio chapel in 1998

Alassio, 16 December 1864.
Watercolour by Edward Lear.
William Osgood Field Collection,
Houghton Library, Harvard University

Edward William Cooke, the marine painter, wrote of Alassio in Christie's catalogue of the sale of ninety of Lear's Mediterranean pictures, 'Alassio – the island of Gallinaria in the distance, famed among the ancients for its breed of fighting cocks.'[11]

● Rain threatened as we entered Loano and the hills behind looked black. Thunder could be heard, with flashes deep in the murk. No one answered our VHF call so we went astern into a gap between two motor yachts. The owner of the one on the inside, dressed in white cotton trousers and a red shirt, said, 'May I help?' with welcome in his eyes. We asked his permission to stay and he said yes, all in English. One of the harbour staff arrived on his Vespa and asked Tony Rillosi if we were friends of his, to which he replied instantly, 'Yes, they are.' He went on to explain to the Assistant Harbour Master that the yacht whose berth we were in had gone to Corsica. Whereupon the port hands set to and tied us up without much help from Gilly or me.

– Gang Warily's **log, Thursday 11 June 1998**

Coffee was Tony's passion and we were soon searching Loano for a café. The old town, with its narrow streets, is compressed around the cathedral whose dome does duty as a sea mark. The old Doria Palace, which is close by, is now connected to the cathedral incongruously by wire that supports a neon star, part of the city's illuminations.

Gilly and I decided to dine at the restaurant alongside the yacht club. We were just about to sit down at the table when the storm struck. The awning shivered, shook and looked as if it was going to take off. *Gang Warily* was surging about and the stern, being only feet off the quay wall, made me anxious that if the bow line parted we would be splintered on the wall. No fender would save her. I jumped aboard and with the engine widened the gap, I took up on the bowline. It was clear we would have to stay aboard. Gilly went back to explain to the madam at the restaurant. She was very understanding. 'I will pack everything up for you and you can eat it on board, even the chocolate cake.' Neatly packed, it arrived complete with grissini torino bread sticks and a bottle of Riviera Ligure di Ponente Pigato 1997 – white. It was now raining hard and Tony's cushions were airborne. I managed to rescue them. The large double one was waterlogged and quite a struggle to recover. It was only afterwards we discovered that this one had flown from another boat to windward.

Later, our dinghy, which I had secured alongside, was flying above the deck, still firmly tethered to the main stays. The apparition surprised Gilly at the washing up as it hovered by the galley porthole.

At times we were heeling at fifteen degrees in a wind that topped 50 knots from the northeast, tearing down the mountains, bent on trouble. Tony would have none of it and before long his lights were out.

⬤ At 11.45 the wind ceased, just like that. There followed an uncanny silence which sleep completed.

– *Gang Warily*'s log, Thursday 11 June 1998

There is a Roman pavement on the second floor of the Doria Palace. The stairs are broad and slope down, making descent easier. This was probably the idea of Giovanni Andrea Doria, the builder and Genoa's great soldier statesmen of the sixteenth century. He swept the seas clean of the Barbary pirates. His family ruled from 1477 to 1737. Convento di Monte Carmelo was reduced to rubble when held by the Austrians against Napoleon at the Battle of Loano on 24 November 1795. Lear noticed the Castle of Doria and the convent and recorded that they were 'picturesque', though he did not think much of the east gate of the city. We left Loano bathed in sunlight, calm and refreshed after the storm.

Finale Ligure, to give the town its full title, nestles under a steep bluff. The distinctive rock from which Lear painted is visible from the offing. The mountain behind the position has been eaten away by a vast quarry.

Gang Warily's bicycles seemed the best way of examining the Lear rock. Wriggling through the traffic, I passed the yellow ochre factory buildings built immediately post-war which belong to Rinaldo Piaggio of Genoa. The rocks are

Finale, 16 December 1864.
Watercolour by Edward Lear.
William Osgood Field Collection,
Houghton Library, Harvard University

The same rocks in 1998.

just to the seaward of the eastern road tunnel entrance and below. We rode out to a gravelled park, reserved for motor caravans, and continued over made-up land to the rocks. These are graced by rough concrete steps to the top and have been transformed from Lear's jagged natural form into a viewing platform. I left the bicycle below and clambered up onto the road over a modern crash barrier. This is where Lear perched before the road was improved. It is on the line of the two-thousand-year-old Via Aurelia that ends in Rome. In Lear's Finale, of 16 December 1864, he could see the cathedral. Although swamped by other buildings, the dome was still visible. Marta Gargiulo, who is in charge of the tourist office, explained that the area was divided into four towns – Finale Ligure – where we were – Finale Marina, Finale Pia and to the north the old medieval town of Finaleborgo. She drove us north to Finaleborgo, which has two castles, one privately owned and modernised. The castles dominate the town. Also nearby was Ligure's oldest theatre, the Teatro Aycardi, built in 1804. The cathedral is medieval but constructed quite magnificently in the Baroque style. It glowed God. Before leaving the port, we had time to visit the old Saracen settlement of Varigotti. Marta explained that the inhabitants were not popular with their neighbours as they wished to secede and form the independent Saracen State of Varigotti.

● We sailed past Capo di Noli and port of Savona, with the light dancing on the waves, making little stars where the sunlight was reflected most strongly.

Our son Aldred was standing on the mole at Varazze. We were soon met by Walter Cingolani. He is a splendid figure of a man with a rubicund face, decorated with a white moustache. Walter was the President of the Lega Navale di Varazze, a most useful national organisation which was started by members of the Yacht Club of Italy and other clubs to gather together all sailors and those working on the shore to help in promoting an interest in things nautical. The Lega Navale is not only a social club but teaches seamanship to adults and children. In some ports, they look after the port and marina facilities. In Varazze, Walter's organisation have formed a sailing school for the blind. He told us at dinner that the Navale has spread round the coast of Italy since it was formed in 1896. Walter had been a boat builder and had specialised in the Gosso Ligure, around five metres in length. The double-enders are seen everywhere pulled up on the beach, or in marinas.

– *Gang Warily*'s log, Saturday 13 June 1998

Captain Gavagnin, Harbourmaster of San Remo, is the 'Master of the Weather' for the Riviera di Ponente, the coast from Ventimiglia to Genoa. His weather

Gang Warily entering Genoa.
Photo: Dr Giovanni Novi

information comes down the wires to the harbour office and to the Lega Navale. We had been warned that the gap in the hills between Arenzano and Voltri is the danger point in the Gulf of Genoa, though only six kilometres of sea. We were told that if the waves were white, looking east from Arenzano, we should put into that port and wait for fairer conditions.

The 'Master of the Weather' forecast a wind strength of 4–5 southeast, so we did not anticipate a night in Arenzano and pushed on for Genoa.

Dr Giovanni Novi and his wife Nucci were in the harbour of the Yacht Club Italiano to meet us, which was a great pleasure. The club is a particularly impressive building on the waterfront with its own mooring facilities. It is the oldest sailing club in the Mediterranean, founded in 1879. The Novis are also impressive. Giovanni then headed his own shipping company and was to become the Chairman of the Genoa Port Authority. He had been President of the Yacht Club of Italy and is now the President of the Italian Sail Training Association. Nucci is very much involved with the International Sailing Federation and was head of the women's section. She later became the Minister of Culture for Liguria.

Arenzano from Voltri.
Watercolour by Edward Lear.
By courtesy of Sotheby's

Their 50-foot sloop *Chaplin*, in which they race and cruise, is looked after in her home port of Rapallo. They kindly asked us to spend a couple of nights with them in their home at Nervi, just east of Genoa. Nucci not only entertained us but loaned us her car to unravel a Lear mystery.

Lear painted a watercolour of the Bay of Arenzano from Voltri. The view looks as far west as the Capo di Noli. In the picture, there is a distinctive fortification jutting out into the sea to the east of Capo di Vardo. In Lear's drawing and at the tip of Punta San Martino there is also a black rock where the Arenzano breakwater now joins the point. Lear's castle appears to lie just to the seaward side of Punta San Martino inside Capo di Vardo. Today, looking west and fixing these points, the castle has disappeared. Could it have been demolished or blown up? This somehow seemed unlikely.

We discovered, by car, that the answer to the puzzle lay in the Port of Savona. The castle has been subsumed in the seaward expansion of the port, now Italy's seventh in trade. A series of black-roofed sheds have been built on land reclaimed from the sea, obscuring the walls of the sixteenth-century Fortezza Priamar, which was prominent in Lear's day. Giuseppe Mazzini, leader of the Young Italy

Sketch by the author
from the same place

movement, was imprisoned there in 1830. In 1864, Lear was witnessing the birth of the Italian nation, for on 17 March 1861, three years before his Corniche walk, the new Kingdom of Italy, under Victor Emmanuel, was proclaimed with Turin as its capital. We were really pleased that we had found Lear's 'lost' castle.

14
Lear walks home from Genoa

I will now 'pencil in' Lear's return to Nice, which, again, gives a clear insight into the way Lear and Giorgio Kokali travelled. Giorgio was Lear's constant companion from 1856 until his death in 1883, having been engaged by him while in Corfu. In a letter to Chichester Fortescue on 11 January 1863, Lear remarked about his way with servants. He admitted that he 'had only had three to date, Hansen, Giorgio and T. Cooper.' He went on, 'The reason of servants being unsatisfactory nine times out of ten is that their hirers consider them as chairs and tables – and take no interest in them as human beings.'[12]

Edward Lear and Giorgio left Genoa on 24 December 1864, retracing the 210 kilometres to Nice. They travelled by train to Voltri, past Arenzano, 'sparklingly pretty'. To their surprise they heard bagpipes. Lear drew Cogoleto, saw the 'house of Columbus, ordinary but repainted' and spent the night in the Locanda d'Italia (inn). He found this to be better than the Gallo, the Cock Inn, where they spent the night on their way to Genoa. Lear mused, 'I wish now, that I knew of the life of C.

There was an Old Man at a Junction, whose feelings were wrung with compunction,
When they said, "The Train's gone!" He exclaimed, "How forlorn!"
But remained on the rails of the Junction.

Columbus well! Cold awful but I tried to draw twice more, while G saved his life by sitting in holes and under walls – smoking. The Suliot, who dines with me is always well bred, quiet and temperate.'

On Christmas Day, a Sunday, Lear and Giorgio went on to Varazze. 'Large town, many ships are building – copper plated.' Celle, a couple of kilometres on, was described as 'interesting, not so much the town, as its accompaniments – a chapel, and an old castle and vast rocks by the wayside.'

'Down the hill of meagre olives, to the town Albissola; larger than it seems, scattered yet presenting nothing to draw.' On they went, ever hopeful, to Savona to stay the night at the Hotel Reale. They again met up with Mr Flood and had a riotous evening in the Regimental Mess. I couldn't help but wonder which British regiment was stationed in Savona at that time. Lear does not mention the missing castle but says that 'Any near good view of Savona is difficult to find, except by boat.' He didn't have time for that and it was probably against his inclination anyway.

On Monday 26 December, Lear had another attempt at painting Savona, 'So down I go to the seaside and in spite of violent and bitter winds, and sand in clouds, I drew tooth and nail as best as I could.'

On, on they went through Vado, Basteggi, drawing at Capo di Noli and even the Isle of Basteggi. For no reason that I can discover, Lear disliked the island. He may have been put off, as he records 'an ugly drunken man here abouts pestered me, but went on, and collapsed into a hedge.' Our two pushed on to Finale, going to the same hotel as on the outward journey, Hotel della China, occupying the same room.

The following day, 27 December, it was pouring with rain accompanied by a howling gale. They took the bus – a three-horsed vehicle – at 10.15 and went through Loano and Albenga, arriving in Alassio by 4.00, a journey of twenty-six kilometres, taking five and three-quarter hours. They stopped for lunch and the 'call of the brush'. They went to the same hotel, La Bella Italia. 'Dinner is brought by a very effete and unclean handmaiden. Peculiarly nasty soup, uneatable fish, leathery cutlet with eatable potatoes, stringy lamb, with admirable turnips and other things wholly uneatable. The poor women are however obliging and do all they can, with the amount of nastiness in the shape of sweets they have sent up is incredible.' The marsala, though, Lear remarks is 'handsome'.

The weather cleared on 27 December and 'in spite of rising at 5.30 could not get coffee or the bill and couldn't leave till 8.' Lear captured Laigueglia, climbed over Capo della Mele and 'took leave of Genoese views' to the east.

Lear believed the valley of Diano 'the most beautiful and rich of all in this Riviera'. With that thought, he reached Oneglia, where again he stayed at the Vittoria, which he observed was 'an honest inn, little show, much attention, and moderate charge.'

The weather may have improved, but the scenery had been degraded by the construction of the coastal mainline. 'At 9.30, S. Lorenzo. Drew all that village by 10 all of which is ugliness, – a continuance of hidden landslips and railway works. At 11, tired of the long earth banks on one side and the sea on the other. San Stephano was near which I drew until 11.30 then we lunched on shore, as noon was striking.'

The two passed Capo Verde, 'ever railway works, an ugliness – breaking of stones and raking of dirt, certainly nothing could be lost by not seeing this piece of road for the whole is ugly.' As if on cue and to take Lear out of his gloom, he hears sweet notes. '*What* memories of Abruzzi bagpipes recall.'

Lear and Giorgio reached San Remo and the Hotel d'Angleterre at 3.30. 'The sunset – seen from an open window is glorious. At 5 p.m. nothing could be more beautiful.' A reversal at dinner, which 'was good but bottle of marsala – vile and undrinkable.'

On Friday 30 December, Lear left the hotel at 7.40, after observing that it was 'vastly clean and nice, cooking good, and W.C. best in all the Riviera.' He left in a four-horse vittura to obtain a view of Bordighera and to experience one of the finest of all Riviera panoramas. He returned to the Hotel d'Angleterre for breakfast at 11.30. He seemed to have taken to San Remo by this time. 'Looked at rooms. I fancy this could have been the nicest winter palace of all.'

Lear arrived at the border customs post at 4.15, after sketching and awaiting the blasting of rocks. His baggage was searched, much to his annoyance. The officials were suspicious because he had walked and sent it on ahead. Once across the border, Lear cheered himself up by going to the bazaar, buying nine photographs for 45 francs and going to the Hotel Londres for the night. 'Tomorrow,' he records, 'I am to walk to Nice and send luggage on.'

On Saturday 31 December, the last day of 'The Walk', it was cold and bright. Lear left soon after 7.00 and walked, sketching when the scenery captured his demanding requirements, catching views of above Mentone, Roquebrune and La Turbie: 'Cloudy sky, Turbie is immensely fine and grand – vast dim lilac headland beyond huge wrinkled face of rock – down, down to the Gulf of Olives; and with the old Roman division tower above all.' Lear's last sketch of the Corniche was of Eze at 4.00 p.m.

Giorgio was sent on to 61 Promenade des Anglais, 'to open and light the rooms.' Lear himself dined at 5.30 at the Hotel du Nord in Nice. He remembered the hotel contained 'a large lot of people – a bore.' At the end of Lear's account, he summed up his feelings about the Corniche walk: 'Conceding the winter season in which I undertook this Corniche tour; it has been wonderfully prosperous. So ends 1864.'[13]

15
Riviera di Levante

ang Warily was still in Genoa, enjoying the hospitality of the Yacht Club of Italy and the kindness of the Novis. The newspaper *Il Secolo XIX* was anxious to cover our search for Edward Lear, so Patricia Albanese and a photographer came to the dock and interviewed the three of us, asking all sorts of questions. When we saw the article in the paper later, it contained a picture of Lear, a view of Rapallo – which we were to visit – and the three of us. The girls waved us off as we set sail for Portofino.

Colourful houses perch on the rocky headlands of Portofino, one of the most famous of all small fishing and yachting ports, now a magnet to tourists in the Riviera di Ponente.

The little port is dominated by Castello Brown. The proper name is the Castle of St George. Roman fragments found in the walls of the tower suggest a long military history. The Romans called the port Portus Delphinus. The Genoese admiral, Andrea Doria (1466–1560) made an alliance with Spain and the engineers remodelled the defences during his time. In 1814, during the Napoleonic Wars, the British attacked the castle and, after one failure, captured the

There was an Old Person of Sestri, who sate himself down in the vestry;
When they said, " You are wrong !"—he merely said, " Bong !"
That repulsive Old Person of Sestri.

Gang Warily in Portofino, with Aldred Drummond recovering the dinghy

stronghold. The cross of St George once more flew from the tower, the flag of both England and Genoa. The British Consul General in Genoa, Montague Yeats Brown, anchored his Cowes-built three-masted lugger *Princess* under the castle in 1870 and fell in love with the old stone walls. He bought the castle, hence the name Castello Brown. He and his family lived there for nearly eighty years. Castello Brown was purchased by the Italian government in 1961 and returned to its original name.

Lear had tried to reach Portofino during his visit to the Gulf of Spezia on 23 May 1860. In his diary he records, 'The views of Portofino from this side are beautiful, but one must stay at La Ruta to do any good.'[14]

Rapallo, at the head of the Gulf of Tigullio on which Portofino also gazes, was a different place in 1860. In his diary for 22 May 1860, Lear was less than complimentary about the town, though keen on its surroundings – 'Intensely lovely hills of olive wood, with thickly strewn houses.'

Lear and Giorgio reached Rapallo at 3.20 p.m. and he wrote:

Dirty, dull place. Poste hotel – ill tempered hostess: particularly filthy room and nasty house. Ordered dinner and went out with G but it rains. I could hardly do anything. Bay of Rapallo dead and shut up. Women make lace. All in contrast to Spezia province. Dinner not very bad. Insisted and got a better room: came to bed at 8. No sleep, fleas, goats, ants, noisy geese – fidgitty sea, lightning all night: crying child and all sorts of *sturbi*.[15]

Lear's diary continues, and he admits that Rapallo was pretty from the west, from where he captured the town in watercolour.[16] On *Gang Warily*, with the awning shading us from the burning sun, we glided gently towards the town. Because of the slow pace, we were able to drink in the magic of Rapallo nestling under the misty outline of the hills behind. With a colour copy of Lear's watercolour sketch of the town of 22 May 1860, I was able to place the high hill and the distinctive

Rapallo, 22 May 1860.
Watercolour by Edward Lear.
William Osgood Field Collection,
Houghton Library, Harvard University

The same view in 1998.

buildings, as though I was at the artist's side (see annotated photograph, below).

On the skyline was the pimple-topped Monte Della Pozze (A). Working to the east was the pointed tower of the Basilica dei Santi Gervasio e Protasio and its Campanile Pendente (B). The long roofed building (C), seemingly next door to the Oratorio di Santo Stephano, with the municipal tower alongside, disguised by scaffolding (D) stood out. Finally, with its feet in the water, stood the Castello Medioevale (E). Lear's sketch, we discovered, was achieved from the root of the Molo Luigi Amedeo di Savoia-Aosta, Duca degli Abruzzi, to give the pier its full title. It is named after the explorer of that name (1872–1933).

The sketch was a sort of halfway house. It was better worked-up than his basic outlines but not finished, for the buildings appear to have been drawn with a ruler, with regiments of windows, almost certainly the right number. The reflection of the town in the water was included and the colours would have acted as a reminder for the finished watercolour. Lear may not have liked Rapallo much because of his experiences in the hotel, but the sketch captures the very spirit of the place. The buildings and the hills behind are so accurately placed in relation to each other that it was possible to drop from the scene of today into Lear's yesterday. As for fleas, they have long gone.

Gang Warily left Rapallo on 19 June 1998 for Chiavari, bound for yet another Lear experience. The wind was stuck in the east, but it was a brilliant hot day. The harbour, under the direction of Commandante Schaffino, greeted us on the eastern mole by the harbour office. Chiavari is a charming old town, and from the harbour heavily but beautifully arcaded. 'The town of porticos' was another name for it, as in the past fishermen's boats were drawn into a porch for shelter. The principal room was built above the open portico, so they looked like a line of boathouses.[17]

There is nothing like local knowledge. Giovanni Novi had helped with our Lear quest. He had suggested we examine the Santuario della Madonna dell'Olivo, built in 1600 on the site of a medieval church. The excitement mounted as we climbed

Chiavari, 22 May 1860.
Watercolour by Edward Lear.
William Osgood Field Collection,
Houghton Library, Harvard University

the path, which started with a few steps and wound its way past memorials that looked like the end gables of houses in miniature. A figure with a load on his head is seen passing one of these in Lear's sketch of 22 May 1860.

By lining up the island-like peninsula of Punta di Sestri with the more distant but larger Punta Manara, both guarding the little port of Sestri Levante, we discovered the place was exactly right.

The same view in 1998.

Maurice, my nephew, returned to *Gang Warily* with Jessica, his wife, arriving from Milan. I think they wondered what I was doing as they stared at a sweating figure on what looked like a ladder on the stern. I was trying to fix the passerelle to the stern capping rail, but none of the bolts appeared to be in the right place for the right holes. I was tempted to punch them into submission with a two-pound hammer.

Sestri Levante, our next stop, was reached on 20 June 1998. The harbour is one of the few ports on this coast that does not have a marina. It was refreshing to secure in the bay and to be helped with the bow and stern moorings by Alessandro, the boatman of the Yacht Club Sestri Levante. The old port is built on a rocky sand bar on which the Romans used to beach their boats. As one guidebook says, the town 'has had the good fortune not to attract the attention of historians through having

Sestri di Levante, 21 May 1860. Watercolour by Edward Lear.
William Osgood Field Collection, Houghton Library, Harvard University

led a peaceful existence'. That is not to say nothing happened here, for Guglielmo Marconi (1874–1937) experimented for the first time with high-frequency radio waves from the tower in the Parco di Castello.

It is worth spending some time looking at maps and charts to collect words like *Fossa Lupara*. It is a bit of a shock to read that Lupara means a sawn-off shotgun! I would have thought it meant something like the lair of the wolf. As observant as ever, Lear comments in his diary on 21 May 1860:

> Beach very fishy, pretty, not clean: far views beautiful. To the house and gardens of the Marchesa Chiuma of Genoa and the latter really exquisite. I do not remember ever to have seen such a mass of beautiful pines together, except perhaps near Thebes in Greece – and the opposite coast, tho' the lines of the hills are not as beautiful as at Spezia, are lovely from the shore.[18]

The Cinque Terre lies east of Punta Mesco and runs in a southeasterly direction to Portovenere and the islands that enclose the Gulf of Spezia. It is a remarkable part of Italy and has been recognised as such by being included in UNESCO's World Heritage List. The guidebook tries to introduce the essence of the Five Lands by distilling its virtues into a single sentence:

> The best approach to the Cinque Terre is by boat, when the full grandeur of the great cliffs with gigantic rocks strewn about the sea at their base, steep slopes covered with vineyards, the coves and inlets and the extraordinary villages, mostly perched on the cliff side, can be seen to the best advantage.[19]

There are five little ports and villages, from west to east, Monterosso al Mare, Vernazza, Corniglia, Manarola and Riomaggiore. *Gang Warily* sailed, or rather drifted, into Vernazza. The harbour was crowded so we anchored outside, looking up at the stone tower. We were told it was hit by a thunderbolt in 1896 and by the German army in the 1940s, but was restored. Vernazza is the centre for the production of the Cinque Terre white wine. This dry white is one of the cleanest-

Vernazza

tasting there is. It seems to contain dew from of the sea. The sweet dessert wine is made from dried grapes, gathered from vines that cover the roofs of houses. The Cinque Terre is worth the journey from any part of the world, and we felt privileged

The coast of the Cinque Terre

Vernazza

to see it from the sea. Many travel by train from Genoa and walk the steep paths and wonder about the women who did much to carve out the terraces and who carried baskets of grapes on their heads, not faltering as they walked on the edge of the precipice.

Edward Lear had good reason to remember the Cinque Terre when walking west toward Genoa from La Spezia above the villages in 1860. He was above Vernazza when he recalled in his diary of 19 May:

Vernazza looks like a small heap of dominoes against the sea. All the landscape is glowering and unpleasant. It would have been quite impossible to visit all five towns, owing to the time taken up by crossing steep abysses between long, long steep paths succeeded always around hillsides: great views of the Modena mountains. Riomaggiore. At 3.40 we are at a point nominato Bocca di Malpertuso, where lives a merry old woman with goats, a flower behind her ear. The pines of M. del Sorrore [Soviore] are in sight. Fernando Galina sorely tried by heavy baggage. 4.50 hideous marshes [?], gravelly paths and slides on the mountain side, and at one turn slipped and fell but caught a chestnut tree some sixty feet down. Happily no hurt beyond a strain. G.K. and F.G. helped me up. It was a good shock. 5 o'clock resume again: but bad bit up hill. 5.30 reach the pine wood, and are above the fifth town Monterosso. More picturesque than the others – bad road ceases. At 6 reach the sanctuary: SM Maddalena [?]: but decide as there is a good road, to go on to Levanto.

Riomaggiore

In this near-fatal walk, Edward Lear appears to have gone from La Spezia up onto Footpath No. 1, which runs from Portovenere to Levanto, at least as far as the Sanctuary. It seems that he did not descend to Monterosso and go to Levanto along the coast, but kept to the high ground. It is quite a remarkable walk, in what appears to be one day. The three of them – Giorgio, Fernando Galina and Edward Lear – left La Spezia at 4.50 a.m., climbing up to Biassa, until reaching Levanto at 7.50 p.m., taking nearly fifteen hours.

In May 2001, Gilly and I walked into the hills from Vernazza to San Bernardino, which lies on the mountainside halfway between Vernazza and Corniglia. I remember how the climb really became a scramble, at times on all fours. The sea side of the hill plunges straight into the deep. We tacked upward, clambering over rocky steps of stone, following a half-buried water pipe that gurgled beneath us. At times, my leg (which I had broken many years ago in Scotland) protested with the shakes and required extra energy to lift it to a higher step. It was not so much the puffing but the feeling of being footloose. Gilly climbed steadily upward, saying the flat was just ahead, but such belief was, as usual, illusory.

Riomaggiore

Vineyards of the Cinque Terre

Maldwin Drummond, Nucci Novi and Gilly Drummond in the Cinque Terre.
Photo: Dr Giovanni Novi

Lear translated Giorgio's feelings about the Cinque Terre walk into his diary of 19 May 1860:

> I am George Sir, I wish to write a truthful thing – There is no need to go again to such places – because you are already too fat and too old.[20]

Lear was forty-eight.

Gang Warily, tacking to the eastward, entered the Golfo Portovenere on the evening of 21 June 1998. We walked up to the chapel that looks over the narrow entrance to the Gulf. The Gulf of Spezia, or the Gulf of the Poets, is one of the most inviting, sheltered sailing areas in the Mediterranean.

PART IV

The gulf of poets and on to Rome

Shelley's yacht *Ariel*

16
The waters of Byron and Shelley

The ancient Byzantine bulwark of the castle on the point of St Peter at Portovenere guards the western approaches to the Gulf of Spezia. The strait separates the three islands of Palmaria, Tino and Pinetto and continues the protection of the waters of the Gulf from the west. In 1494, the defenders of the castle plastered grease on the rocks to prevent the Aragonese from gaining a toehold. For this ingenious defence, the inhabitants of Portovenere were given greater autonomy and tax rebates by the Genoese.[1]

The tower of the church of San Lorenzo acts as a godly exclamation mark above the town. Lord Byron's grotto, with a marble plaque and steps, commemorates the poet's swim across the gulf from Portovenere to Lerici. Two poets, both the 6th Lord Byron (1788–1824), and Percy Bysshe Shelley (1792–1822) are associated

There was an Old Person of Bree, who frequented the depths of the Sea;
She nurs'd the small fishes, and washed all the dishes,
And swam back again into Bree.

with the Gulf of Spezia and for this reason the waters are nicknamed 'the Gulf of Poets'.

Gang Warily was secured in the harbour stern to the quay.

● A narrow street led from the little square, where the entrance gate is of Roman origin, though the main walls were built in 1160. Shops retreat from ornamental door cases and ordinary windows which serve as displays. There are no multiples inside the walls. Motor scooters are the only vehicles that could navigate such streets, but these may be banned, as there is no sign of them. An electric trolley served the shops.

– *Gang Warily*'s log, Monday 22 June 1998

In a democratic way, we decided to be influenced by history and follow in Byron's wake, sailing from Portovenere across to Lerici. The town is dominated by an imposing castle, the foundations of which were laid by the Pisans early in the thirteenth century, and which was much enlarged by the Genoese in the sixteenth.[2] We moored in the bay under the castle on buoys indicated by the Harbourmaster.

Edward Lear sketched the view from below the castle, perhaps from the Scalinata San Giorgio, looking across the straits between Isola Palmaria and Portovenere, indicating on the right of the watercolour the two mountains – Mussorone, 160 metres, and the larger Castellana, 496 metres.

View of Isola Palmaria and Portovenere from Lerici, 15 May 1860. Watercolour by Edward Lear. William Osgood Field Collection, Houghton Library, Harvard University

Lear and Giorgio began their trip to Spezia by travelling from Rome to Civitavecchia on 8 May 1860. They travelled by boat to Leghorn, where, on entering the port, the ship 'smashed a schooner's bowsprit – great fuss'. The two then took tickets for Genoa aboard the *Il Cansilippe*, again changing ships for a very small, crowded steamer making for Spezia. Lear rose at sunrise on 12 May to see 'the beautiful entrance to the Gulf of Spezia'. The two explored the town and surroundings and on the 15th headed for San Terenzo and Lerici, walking along the eastern shore of the Gulf. Lear wrote:

The view from the Scalinata San Giorgio towards Portovenere in 1998

> On the 15th May every promise of a fine day. The giro (round tour) of the Gulf is pretty as are the views of Spezia. Streams – by and by, the world of bog and slosh. A nice woman, who having passed it cooked her feet and legs, amazing. She recommended a collo (a picka back) and so a lad came, who carried me over picka back, G. afterwards. Route along the shore and by and by leaving it to go through gardens and again bits of sea shore. Thence a long rise through a close olive and fig valley and a steep ascent ending in a lovely view of Lerici. Descend (the courtesy of the people impossible to imagine). And so to the high street of San Terenzo, clean compared with the southern towns in general. On the beach is the house of Byron and Shelley, sad looking – but the views are very glorious. Thence by the rocks, through a superb olive wood to Lerici a large town. G. and I had some wine with our breakfast (we arrived at 9) in the osteria (inn) of a very political female. All we observed of the town was very pleasant and agreeable – such beautiful women and children![3]

Lear and Giorgio walked back to San Terenzo, and we followed suit in *Gang Warily* on 23 June.

● *Gang Warily* slipped her moorings and headed north-northwest for San Terenzo. Percy Bysshe Shelley's house, the Villa Magni, smiled at us, buried as it was amongst the apartment buildings. A protecting breakwater has created a 'harbour' since Shelley's day. What is worse, a road now separates his arcaded, green shuttered, white house from the sea. Originally the beach and sea reached the five arches of the arcade. This is clear from contemporary drawings of the house by P D Cambiaso.

– **Gang Warily's log, Tuesday 23 June 1998**

Shelley's house. Villa Magni, San Terenzo

Shelley set out from the house on his yacht *Ariel* in 1822, leaving his wife Mary (Godwin) behind. He was drowned off Viareggio as he returned. A plaque on the house with an inscription taken from one of Shelley's last letters described his affection for the place:

> I still inhabit this divine bay, reading Spanish dramas, sailing and listening to the most enchanting music. My only regret is that the summer must ever pass.

Edward Lear noted later in his diary that the Villa Magni is now 'annually lived in by Captain Cross who resides at Pisa'.

Gang Warily crossed over to Le Grazie, a sleepy place and now the home of the Italian Navy's diving school. The view that Lear noted as 'Porto della Grazie – Spezia – May 16th/17th, 1860' was very recognisable, looking southwest across the Punta del Varignano to the hills that surround Ameglia, beyond Lerici, on the eastern shore. Lear had also come this way, as he had hailed a boat to cross the Gulf from San Terenzo.

On 16 May, Lear sketched a fort, 'Fezzina', putting a question mark after the name. He included the building in a wide view of Spezia from above and beyond Grazie. There did not seem to be any sign of it, so we edged *Gang Warily* into the yacht harbour of Fezzano and headed for the little stone quay, which had once been the main water access to the town. It was just the sort of place *Gang Warily* was designed to stick her bowsprit into.

Spezia – Fort Fezzina,
16 May 1860.
Watercolour by Edward Lear.
William Osgood Field Collection,
Houghton Library, Harvard University

● Gilly wandered to the church and I to the point, climbing up the road that winds above the bay. A dark red and yellow villa was on the left of the road, cut into the hill, leaving a cliff of rock that required netting to stop stones falling on the road. I tried scaling the netting, but that failed so I retraced my steps and found a way up. The building I had glimpsed from below appeared to be part of a fort with a heavy iron grill on one of the windows. A red tiled roof showed the building had been extensively re-modelled. The path petered out into scrub. Long grass at a chained gate with a sign 'cave canem' and a picture of an Alsatian dog warned intruders. I wondered whether the old fort had been knocked down and a new building put on top of it.

– *Gang Warily*'s log, Tuesday 23 June 1998

Spezia, 1862.
Watercolour by Edward Lear.
Courtesy of Guy Peppiatt Fine Art

On Matteo Vinzoni's map of 1773, the point of Fezzano is topped by a building described as 'Guardia di Gamborella'. A little more research was needed, and I determined to visit the library in La Spezia, which would have to be done by car as *Gang Warily* was to be secured for a short period in Porto Lotti, on the eastern edge of La Spezia. The harbour has the reputation of being one of the best marinas in Italy. *Gang Warily* was due to be in their care from 24 June until 17 July 1998.

Wednesday was another blazing day.

● Our elderly taxi driver responded to our call from the gatehouse and just avoided an accident as we pulled out onto the main road. Our objective was the Lea Museum in La Spezia. Signor Lea gave his collection of antiquities, bronzes, religious artefacts and pictures of the city of La Spezia to the town. We were introduced to Dr Andrea Marmori. He spoke little English but the receptionist acted as an excellent interpreter. He thought the castle or watch tower had been pulled down. He mentioned the Torre di San Girolamo and said there were views of the Gulf by A Fossati. The doctor thought the tower had been the subject of one of them. He, too, mentioned Matteo Vinzoni's map of 1773, which is held in the municipal library. We were later given a photocopy of the map on two sheets glued together. Dr Marmori led us into the inner sanctum to look at another map that was high on the wall. Coming back with a stepladder, Dr Marmori took it down. All this evidence confirmed our view that the fort was, indeed, the Guardia di Gamborella.

– *Gang Warily*'s **log, Wednesday 24 June 1998**

17
The death of Shelley

July was to be one of the hottest months Italy had known in recent times. On shore, people were succumbing to heat stroke. This was a strange experience for one who rejoices in sailing in near-arctic waters, and it prompted Gilly to ask why I had been hiding the Mediterranean from her for so long!

We slowly drifted along the coast, drawn along as though the sun was some sort of magnet. The Alps were slashed with white above Carrara. These scars looked strangely natural, as if it was snow rather than man-made marble quarries reflecting a brilliant white. They do not carve into the valley in a square fashion. It is as though they are bent on creating new valleys. The effect is very dramatic, and shows that not all quarrying is without merit in landscape terms. *Gang Warily* sailed into Carrara and we were greeted by Roberto, the harbourmaster, a bronze figure in shorts with a big smile revealing fine teeth.

The marina piers are built of railway iron covered with tyres. At first sight, it looked a rather uncomfortable place to tie up, but the tyres were very effective.

There was an Old Man of Leghorn, the smallest that ever was born ;
But quickly snapped up he was once by a puppy,
Who devoured that Old Man of Leghorn.

● Roberto took the trouble to show us the showers. The new ones, he explained, were heated by the sun, so please use before the sun goes in. The old ones work in the old way and can be employed at any time. The restaurant is good. After taking our details, he shot off. 'I'm very busy. I built all this and now only I run it. I love the place.'

– *Gang Warily*'s log, Sunday 19 July 1998

Gang Warily approached the entrance to Viareggio on Monday 20 July 1998. Here on 8 July 1822, the poet Shelley, together with a friend, Captain Edward Williams, who shared the Villa Magni with him, and Charles Vivian, a sailor boy, capsized in the *Ariel* and drowned. Shelley was identified after it was discovered that he had a volume of Sophocles in one pocket and a volume of Keats in the other. His body was washed up at Viareggio, while Williams and the boy came ashore three miles further south on Tuscan territory near the Tower of Migliarino at the mouth of the Serchio.

The authorities were terrified of disease so Shelley was temporarily interred on the beach and quicklime put over his body. When it came to disinter Shelley, his friends, Lord Byron and Edward Trelawny (1792–1881), were present. Byron asked the latter to preserve the skull for him. He was reluctant, however, as

Model of Shelley's yacht *Ariel*, decked after her salvage.
Russell Cotes Art Gallery & Museum

he remembered Byron had used one as a drinking cup. When the funeral pyre was well alight, Shelley's heart was laid bare and according to legend Trelawny rescued it and it was placed in spirits of wine. All this was too much for Byron, who swam off to his yacht, the *Bolivar*. Another friend, Leigh Hunt (1784–1859), watched the whole process from a carriage. Byron was severely sunburnt from his long swim and his shoulders badly blistered. Shelley's ashes were buried in the English cemetery at Viareggio.

That could have been the end of the story, but Trelawny attempted to salvage *Ariel* and managed to discover, with the aid of two feluccas, the position of the foundered boat two miles from the beach off Viareggio. Everything was still in her so it was unlikely she capsized but more likely was swamped by a big wave. Trelawny had an interest, as it is said he designed *Ariel*. She had the reputation of being 'tender' and it was therefore not surprising that some thought she had capsized. But Trelawny hung on to the story that the yacht had been run down, as he saw an English oar in one of the fishing boats. He called in evidence also the damage to the bulwarks.[4]

Lord Byron was originally going to share *Ariel* with Shelley, and was insistent the 21-foot schooner yacht should be called *Don Juan*. They had endless arguments, even after the name *Ariel* was painted on the stern. In the end, Shelley assumed responsibility for the yacht and Byron built his own, a miniature frigate which he named *Bolivar*. Both were ordered from Captain Roberts and built in Genoa.

Byron had some problems with the authorities in Leghorn (now Livorno). Writing to Edward Dawkins, the British Chargé d'Affaires, on 26 June 1822, before the disaster, he complained:

> I'm obliged to inform you that they refuse at Leghorn to accord permission to cruize in sight of the port in my little yacht – which arrived from Genoa last week. – They also refused to let me have a boat from the port (off the sea-baths which are in shallow water) to undress in when I go out to swim – which I prefer, of course, in deep water. – My yacht was allowed to cruize at Genoa without molestation and which cost me a considerable sum in building, etc. – Is thus rendered perfectly useless to me – and the expense entirely thrown away. It is a little thing of about 22 tons – but a model to look at – and sails very fast. She has nothing obnoxious about her that I know – unless her name (the *Bolivar*) should be so.

He signed the letter, as was his wont, 'Noel Byron'.[5]

Byron was aware that he was not popular with the authorities because of his support of the Italian revolutionaries.

On 15 July, seven days after the loss of *Ariel* and her crew, Byron wrote again to Dawkins:

> Up to this moment I had clung to a slender hope that Mr Shelley had still survived the late Gale of Wind. – I sent orders yesterday to the *Bolivar* to cruze along the coast in search of intelligence – but it seems all over. – I have not waited on you in person being unshaven – unshorn – and uncloathed at this present writing after bathing.[6]

It was Byron's fate to follow Shelley less than two years later. He died of marsh fever at Missolonghi in April 1824 when pursuing his ambition of securing freedom for Greece from the Turks.

Edward Lear recalled the moment he heard of Byron's death, and the feeling was strong enough for him to note years later in his diary of 18 September 1861:

> Do you remember the small yard and passages at [not named] in 1823 and 1824 – when I used to sit there in the cold looking at the stars, and, when I heard that Lord Byron was dead, stupefied and crying.[7]

Lear visited the place where Shelley was cremated under Byron's eyes. He sketched the scene in 1861, when returning from Florence, where he had completed a commission from Lady Waldegrave, who was anxious to cheer him up after the death of his sister Ann.

Shelley's love of the sea passed to his son, Sir Percy, who was a keen yachtsman. In 1853, he sailed his schooner *Ginevra*, 142 tons, from Poole to Valetta, stopping only at Guernsey and averaging 168 miles a day. Sir Percy owned ten yachts between 1854 and his death in 1889. He was a member of the Royal Yacht Squadron and was involved in a celebrated incident at the Castle during lunch in Cowes Week. There had been an election earlier in the week and a red-bearded gentleman by the name of N Power O'Shee, nicknamed The Pirate, was blackballed. O'Shee owned the armed schooner *Daphne*. He anchored his yacht off the Castle, ran his guns out and sent a boat ashore with a note for Sir Percy Shelley. O'Shee believed that Sir Percy had been responsible for the rebuff. The note spelt out that unless Sir Percy came off and apologised to him on his own quarterdeck he would open fire on the Castle. Sir Percy said to those in the room that he was damned if he would. It was only after that great seaman, Sir Allen Young, who knew O'Shee and his reputation well, reminded Sir Percy of the inconvenience of being bombarded at lunch, that he dispatched a note. On receipt, The Pirate dipped his ensign and sailed off into the blue.[8]

Viareggio has a fine marina and is a good place from which to visit Pisa. An Australian in the Club Nautico Versilia, who was sitting on the marble steps outside, said a bus left for Pisa from the station across the canal just before each hour. 'Blue buses,' he added. The bus was air-conditioned, which was a comfort as I was in a froth as the day was very hot.

> ● Along the road to Pisa, we saw a strange sight. On one stretch, about a mile in length just after the Pisa turning which crosses the railway line, was a platoon of girls sitting, or in more provocative poses, spaced about 50 metres apart looking for customers among the passing motorists. One, more ambitious than most, made a pass at our bus!
>
> Gilly and I alighted outside the great enclave that contains both the cathedral and the leaning tower. The tower is undergoing long-term repairs to halt the lean. Basically, this means clever work to the foundations. The original ones were less than three metres in depth for a tower 56 metres high with eight storeys and an estimated weight of 14,500 tons. Its construction started as early as 1174 to the designs of Bonanno Pisano. Another Pisano was responsible for the most glorious creation, the pulpit in the cathedral, supported by columns, one the statue of Hercules, nude with his club.
>
> – *Gang Warily*'s log, **Monday 20 July 1998**

Places that Byron and Shelley no doubt still haunt were on the river. The Palazzo Lanfranchi is instantly known to taxi drivers, while the place that Shelley rented, the apartment at Tre Palazzi di Chiesa, produces a blank stare. Shelley's words, however, are recorded on the riverside:

> Within the surface of the fleeting river.
> The wrinkled image of the city lay,
> Immovably unquiet, and forever
> It trembles, but it never fades away.

18
Elba, Napoleon and the Tuscan islands

On 21 July we reached Livorno, a commercial port where, as usual, we had a great welcome. Known in Lear's day as Leghorn, the port had a mixed reputation. Augustus Hare, an inveterate traveller who wrote *The Cities of Italy* and many other brown cloth-covered travel volumes, said that the charm of the port was the Ardenza, an enchanting walk with shrubberies close to the sea. However, he added, 'There is nothing whatever worth seeing in Leghorn, no one would think of staying there except for sea bathing, but its shops are sometimes amusing.' He goes on to say that 'The place is full of galley slaves who do all the dirty work of the town in red caps, brown vests and yellow trousers.' Surprisingly, Hare's book was published in 1876.[9]

Across from our berth, the round tower of Fortezza Vecchia stood to attention. Shelley wandered round the fort when he was in Leghorn. He nearly drowned, taking a wooden-framed canvas-clad skiff to Pisa with friends. Among them was Edward Williams, who later perished with Shelley. Perhaps Williams was a Jonah and brought bad luck.

There was an Old Person of Pisa, whose daughters did nothing to please her;
She dressed them in gray, and banged them all day,
Round the walls of the city of Pisa.

● A taxi came to our telephone call and we enjoyed a short tour of the town. We were told the best place to dine and enjoy a typical Livornese food was the Cantina Senese in the Borgo dei Cappucini. The place was crowded and our driver had to persuade the owner to let us have a table. 'I told them,' he said expansively, 'that this is the only place to eat Livornese food, so they had to come here.' With that, the owner capitulated and showed us to our table.

The man at the head, busily at work with his face in mussels and clams, but with his back to Gilly, moved his chair, saying that he could not possibly eat with his back to a lady.

– *Gang Warily*'s log, Tuesday 21 July 1998

Cosimo I de' Medici, Grand Duke of Tuscany, saw the potential of Livorno and built a jetty there in 1571. Two years later, tasting success, he dug a canal to link the port with Pisa. The Porto Mediceo was completed during Cosimo II's time in 1620, so in spite of speedboats' wash, which he could not have foreseen, we felt we could raise a glass of Elba Bianco in the direction of both Cosimos.

The Island of Elba is the largest in the Tuscan Archipelago and lies some eighty kilometres south of Livorno. As far as I can discover, Edward Lear failed to visit any of the Tuscan islands. However, Napoleon famously did. He signed the Act of Abdication at Fontainebleau in April 1814 and, thus deposed, lived above Porto Ferraio from 4 May 1814 to 26 February 1815. His house is in the upper part of the town overlooking the sea and the mainland to the north and east. It used to be called the Mill House and was a fine place for a windmill, if not for a deposed emperor. The restorers have tried to bring back the atmosphere of Napoleon's days, with original decorations and by collecting together appropriate furniture, some of which may have been there in the Emperor's day.

The garden was suffering, as it always must have done, from the drought. The terrace commands magnificent views, a constant invitation to escape, which, of course, Napoleon did in the brig *Inconstant*, 18 guns. The small convoy included the schooner *Etoile*, the felucca *Caroline* and three others, together with a chartered merchant ship registered in Elba for all his belongings.

During Napoleon's time on the island, he was known as the 'King of the Mines' because Porto Ferraio was noted as a source of iron. It is said that in those days the natives flavoured their badly made wine with ginger, making it still more indigestible.[10]

Napoleon died on the Island of St Helena on 5 May 1821 of either liver disease or stomach cancer. The picture of the ex-emperor being rowed ashore to begin his exile by British Marines, painted in watercolour by A E Marty, is particularly evocative.

The harbour of Porto Ferraio was crowded, but the British captain of a large American yacht suggested we secure inside him. The idea was to put out an anchor clear of his and come in stern first, throwing him a line. It worked well, but it was not the place to stay for long and so the next day we sailed round to the eastern coast, where it was much cooler, and we anchored in Porto Azzurro.

The old prison broods over all, the watch tower still guards windowless cells, and barbed wire lies rusting. Porto Azzurro used to be called Porto Longone, but the name was changed as it became synonymous with long-term prisoners in the manner of Alcatraz.

Porto Ala on the mainland was our next stop; it was then the summer base for the Italian America's Cup challenge. The port is a modern invention, built with Italian attention to detail, unlike the gloriously natural island of Giglio, another of the Tuscan islands. Giglio means lilies, and in the spring the island is covered with their blooms. The harbour was full so we moved south to the recommended anchorage of Cala Canelle, south of the Le Scole rocks. Captain H M Denham, RN, wrote a series of pilot's guides, including *The Tyrrhenian Sea* which covers this area and is still a must for information and amusement, though long out of date.[11]

● *Gang Warily* weighed anchor at 11.30 and made for the island of Giannutri. The haze, which was nearly a mist, hung over Giglio and extended seawards. The wind, such as it was, more an air, was dead on the nose, so we proceeded under power.

By ten past twelve, the visibility had improved and I could make out the loom of Giannutri, a grey smudge on the horizon. Most of the island is a nature reserve and this extends into the sea for half a mile. The little harbour of Cala Maestra is outside this exclusion, so we looked in. A large ferry seemed to take up much of the harbour, so we decided to investigate the Golfo degli Spalmatoi, a large bay on the eastern side, which again was crowded. We found a spot to drop the hook, in the shallower water marked on the Italian chart as Cala Volo di Notte, which roughly translates as 'The Bay of the Flight of the Night'.

As I was looking at Captain Denham's book, a slip of green paper fell out onto the cockpit floor on which a Lear-like limerick was written –

> There was a young man of Khartoum,
> Who kept a black sheep in his room.
> It reminds me he said of a friend who is dead,
> But he would never tell us of whom.

What with the unexpected limerick, the name of this bay, a bottle of Elba Bianco 1997 and sitting peacefully watching the lights of the other yachts become bright pinpoints, we felt the 'Island of Lilies' was a magical place.

– *Gang Warily*'s log, Sunday 26 July 1998

The next day was pretty good too:

● The day was born white without a patch of blue and the barometer down to 1012. There was little wind. Over to the east, the haze had a yellow band above the sea, which promised clearance and sun later.

– *Gang Warily*'s log, Monday 27 July 1998

Gang Warily was to winter in Cala Galera. We had a wonderful sail across the sparkling sea to the strange peninsula of Monte Argentario, the home of not only Cala Galera but Porto Ercole and Porto San Stefano. Perhaps more importantly, it is a place where Robin and Katie Coventry have their office and look after yachts both summer and winter.

We will pick up Edward Lear again in Rome. We had in fact left him in Pisa, a city that features in another of his limericks:

> There was an old person of Pisa,
> Whose daughters did nothing to please her;
> She dressed them in grey,
> And banged them all day,
> Round the walls of the city of Pisa.

Robin Coventry sat behind his desk, and Katie was similarly placed at right angles. It was very much a double act. Robin had seen service in the Royal Navy in MTBs. After retiring, they moved in steps to Italy, rescuing the old shipyard in 1960, built it up and sold it in favour of brokering and acting as 'fixers' for yachtsmen.

A little further down our pier lay *Bonnie Doone*, an American yacht belonging to Andrew Dossett. This pretty little Herreshoff-inspired yawl was to be left in the marina until crossing back to the West Indies in November. Andrew was keen to stay for a little time in Madeira. He had already sailed around the world the wrong way, basically never going below 40 degrees south. He went through the Red Sea and passed along on to Japan, just right for Los Angeles. His wife was a 'radio ham' and picked up good advice on weather trends and all sorts of information of interest to the mariner. Andrew observed, running the risk of incurring the wrath of feminists the world over, that women want a home to go back to: 'You can take them off for a year, even two, but they must have a nest.'

We were just about to return to ours, but we would be after Mr Lear again next year.

The Enthusiastic Elephant,
who ferried himself across the water with the
Kitchen Poker and a New pair of Ear-rings.

19
The environs of Rome

Gang Warily spent a comfortable winter in Cala Galera. The yacht harbour is sheltered to the east by a hill, crowned by a fort built by Philip II. The harbour itself has all the conveniences and is full of eye-catching yachts in pristine condition, including *Dorade*, designed by the Stephens brothers. She won the transatlantic and Fastnet races in 1931. In 1933, her laurels continued with two Bermuda races and the San Franciso–Honolulu race. She was rescued by the yacht restorer Frederico Nardi and taken to his yard at Porto San Stefano. Frederico came over to Cala Galera to look at *Gang Warily*. He admired the *anatroccolo simpatico* or 'dear little duck' from the way she sat in the water.

My nephew Maurice and his wife Jessica again joined us, and our adventure started early. Gilly and Jessica were changing in the ladies' loo when an Italian woman grabbed Jessica by the arm and exclaimed that a man had come in. Turning to the intruder, she said 'This is the ladies.' The woman, who had short, grey hair, retorted, 'But I am a lady!', which threw everyone into confusion.

We continued south the next day.

There was an Old Man in a boat, who said, " I'm afloat ! I'm afloat !"
When they said, " No you ain't !" he was ready to faint,
That unhappy Old Man in a boat.

● *Gang Warily* was going well under sail, with 10–12 knots of wind, doing 6 knots on a reach. Our destination was Riva di Traiano, two miles southeast of the port of Civitavecchia, which we passed late in the afternoon. A huge cruise ship, *Splendour of the Seas*, was in the harbour, as was a smaller Cunarder, red funnel resplendent. The sight of sights was the Italian naval training ship, a full-rigged ship with white bands on her black hull. She was built by the Royal Shipyard, Castellammare di Stabia, in 1931. The port was constructed by the Emperor Trajan (AD 53–117), the purpose being to serve as the port of Rome.
– **Gang Warily's log, Tuesday 25 May 1999**

Lear used the port, as recorded by Chichester Fortescue in his diary about his first meeting with Lear in 1845. Lear was then thirty-three and Fortescue twenty-two, having just left Oxford. In a rather staccato way, Fortescue records:

Sunday – Lear breakfasted with us ... – (Cornwall Simeon included). Lear came to say goodbye just before our dinner – he has gone by diligence to Civita Vecchia. I have enjoyed his society immensely and am very sorry he has gone. We seem to suit each other capitally, and became friends in no time. Among other qualifications he is one of those men of real feeling. It is so delightful to meet in this cold-hearted world. Simeon and myself both miss him much.[12]

Chichester Fortescue, Baron Carlingford (1823–98), became the Member of Parliament for Louth in 1847. He worked in Ireland as Chief Secretary and then became President of the Board of Trade and Lord Privy Seal. In 1871 he married Frances, Lady Waldegrave (1821–79), who had been married four times before. Frances admired Lear's pictures, and her niece, Lady Strachey, edited two volumes of Edward Lear's letters, published in 1907 and 1911.

The harbour of Riva di Traiano is a beautiful construction and one of the finest yacht harbours *Gang Warily* visited. We were greeted by two admirals, Admiral Mario Giovanni and Admiral Mario Albanasi, and the Harbour Director, Massimo de Notti. We had never had such a reception. On coming aboard and being offered a glass, Admiral Albanasi replied with a twinkle, 'Anything but water.' The remark set the scene for a happy exchange.

Fort of Michelangelo

Just to the south of the harbour is a defensive tower, the Fort of Michelangelo. Although started by others, it was completed by the Master in 1557 and now stands four-square, somewhat diminished by what look like concrete-framed military buildings. The wreck of the old harbour rises from the sea like blackened molars.

There was considerable excitement at the prospect of crossing the bar of the Tiber the next day and sailing up river. There are two entrances to the Tiber, Fiume Tevere, the Fiumicino Canal, and to the south the Fiumare Grande, our chosen route. We had been invited to lie alongside the conserved tug *Pietro Micca*, ex *Dilwara* (1895).

● At 5.15 p.m., Gilly telephoned Pier Paulo Guia of the Circolo Nautico Tecnomar Fiumicino. He instructed us to proceed eastward, up river, keeping to the left-hand bank until we saw a large old tug. I thought he said of steel, but he later explained he meant steam. We paused by a steel trawler, so he was a little puzzled at our late arrival.

– Gang Warily's log, Wednesday 26 May 1999

The tug *Pietro Micca* was magnificently maintained by the Associazione Amici Delle Navi a Vapore 'G L Spinelli', the owners, and in particular by our host, Pier Paulo Guia of the yard. The tug was built in South Shields but moved to Naples before the First World War. She survived two World Wars and now looked new. Indeed, she was off the next day to do a job off Anzio, so the boilers had been fired up. The engine room was a picture and the painters were busy giving last touches to the skylights.

Carla, Pier Paulo's wife, drove us to Ostia Antica.

Lear sketched and later lithographed the castle at Ostia Antica in his *Views in Rome and Its Environs*, 1841. The building is in splendid condition, better if anything than when Lear sat and immortalised it. Built in the fifteenth century by Cardinal Giuliano della Rovere to protect Rome from attack from the sea, it is now inland. Livy tells us that Ostia was founded by Ancus Marcius (640–616 BC), the fourth king of Rome after Romulus. Ostia was both a naval and a commercial harbour. Scipio set off from Ostia in 210 BC to stop reinforcements reaching Hannibal.

You cannot view the layout of these masterpieces of the ancient world without thinking that over the centuries we have not really made any substantial advances in the layout of towns. Indeed, I think we have slipped backward. Over-population has taken its toll and perhaps we have gradually lost faith, so buildings are not put up to the glory of God – or gods, for the Romans had many. The whole plan of Ostia Antica is gloriously celebratory. A strange thought struck me. Is there not a relationship between the days of Trajan and Hadrian and the Victorian period? God and commerce coming together, in these two ages, to mutual benefit.

The castle at Ostia Antica

I pondered the idea of going to Rome in *Gang Warily's* rubber dinghy. We could have safely left the yacht with Pier Paulo and the Circolo Nautico Tecnomar, Fiumicino. However, the spirit of adventure left me when I thought of parking the dinghy in Rome. I suppose we could have deflated the tubes and tried to persuade an hotel to keep the little boat until we wanted to return. I was not quite sure how navigable the upper reaches of the river were. The River Tiber has been silted up since Roman times. The guide to these waters leaves out any mention of the upper reaches.

We wanted to spend a little time in Rome, for Lear had been there from 1837 to 1848. Then there were the sail-bags of clothes. We decided to return in the Roman spring, 2000.

PART V

The Rome of
Edward Lear

The Spanish Steps, Rome

20
No. 39 Baboon Street

The education of wealthy young Englishmen in the eighteenth century was not complete without a spell in Europe. With the aid of a tutor, they savoured, with their own eyes, the vision first gained at school and university. Classical education gave a knowledge of the languages of Latin and Greek, together with an appreciation of ancient history, literature and architecture. Italy, and Rome in particular, was a natural focus, for though Greece was desirable, that land of the ancients was more difficult to reach. Their accompanying tutor was nicknamed the 'bear leader'.

The French Revolution and the Napoleonic Wars brought the Grand Tour to a virtual halt. As a result, the young started to look at their own country – Scotland, Ireland and the Lake District. There was little need for bear leaders at home.

After the Ogre of Corsica, as some called Napoleon, was rowed ashore by the Royal Marines at St Helena, the stream to Europe resumed and became a flood, and Rome was a particular beneficiary. Travel soon became easier with the building

There was an Old Man of th' Abruzzi, so blind that he couldn't his foot see;
When they said, "That's your toe!" he replied, "Is it so?"
That doubtful Old Man of th' Abruzzi.

of the railways, along with the regular and reliable steamer passages that Edward Lear employed later in his travels. The sea, too, played a part in the resurrection of the 'Grand Tour', with the encouragement of the Sailor King, William IV (1765–1837). Some of the yachts were armed with cannon to ward off pirates and corsairs. Yachtsmen such as the Duke of Buckingham and Chandos, on *Anna Liza*, cruised the Mediterranean. The Duke left his great house Stowe to escape his creditors, who were banging on his door, so he built a yacht. A man of good education, the Duke cruised the Mediterranean, visiting Italy and Sicily. While there, he collected, or perhaps more accurately 'liberated', some souvenirs of the ancients.

J H W Pigott-Smyth-Pigott visited Rome from his cutter *Ganymede*, moored in Civitavecchia, in 1842, when Lear was in the capital. He lived on his yacht the year round at that time. The Earl Grosvenor was there too on *Dolphin* in the early 1840s, calling at Civitavecchia to visit Rome, continuing south to Pozzuoli and Capri.

The Cutter *Ganymede*, owned by J H W Piggott-Smyth-Pigott, which Lear may have seen in Civitavecchia in 1842.
Royal Yacht Squadron

The utility of travel was not only a way of resurrecting the ways and works of the ancients. Travel is seen to have advantages in today's education as part of the 'gap year', and the experience of being responsible for one's own progress in a strange place, maybe for the first time, has undoubted value. Samuel Johnson (1709–84) highlighted this in his definition of 'traveller' in his *Dictionary* with an extra dimension. There is 'a common opinion among the Gentiles, that the gods sometimes assume human shape, and conversed upon earth with strangers and travellers.' He was quoting from Bentley's sermons. There would be nods of agreement among romantics even today.

As we have seen, Edward Lear went to Rome to study and improve his skills as a budding topographical landscape artist. He was helped in this by his patron, Lord Derby, who contributed to his expenses between the years 1837 and 1848. Although it is unlikely a contract existed between the 13th Earl and his friend, Lear felt beholden to him and his successors. He earmarked a number of his pictures for the Earl's family, and this continued some time after his long stay in Rome. One of Lear's earliest oils was of Civitella di Subiaco, painted in 1847 and now owned and beautifully displayed in the Clothworkers' Company. This picture was originally painted for James Hornby and shows how Lear had developed his skills in oils during his time in Rome, where he had arrived at the age of twenty-five. The figures in this landscape are successful and yet, as we have heard, Lear enrolled in the Royal Academy Schools in 1850, purely for the purpose of developing this skill. It was also one of the reasons Lear took instruction from Holman Hunt in 1852. He may well have been assisted in this by one of his best friends in the Rome period, Penry Williams.

In a letter to his sister Ann, dated 14 December 1837, Lear describes his rooms, a study and bedroom, on the second floor of No. 39 Via del Babuino, or Baboon Street.[1] The position was very central, being near to the Piazza di Spagna, the Spanish Steps, and to the Accademia Britannica in the gardens of the Villa Borghese just north of the Palazzo delle Belle Arti. The entrance of No. 39 Baboon Street has been turned into a window for Feltrinelli's bookshop.

In my journal that records life away from the boat, I remembered the 'English Quarter', the streets between the Piazza del Popolo and the Spanish Steps, that was Lear's stamping ground:

● The Piazza del Popolo was an entrance from the Via Flaminia via the Porta del Popolo. Lear may have come this way from the north in 1837 in a vetturino carriage with William Theed, sculptor, and Richard Denew, artist, old residents of Rome, as he describes in his letter to Ann of 14 December 1837. He does not mention this incomparable square, through which General Miollis breached the walls of Rome on 2 February 1809.

– Maldwin Drummond's journal, Tuesday 14 March 2000

Walking down Baboon Street towards the Spanish Steps, the Via dei Condotti joins at right angles from the west. In the street between Lear's house and the Steps is the Caffè Greco, now the Antico Caffè Greco, opened in 1760. The Via dei Condotti

Civitella di Subiaco, 1847.
Oil painting by Edward Lear.
By permission of the
Clothworkers' Company, London

Gilly Drummond at 39 Via del Babuino, or Baboon Street, where Lear had rooms

was named after the conduits that supplied water to Agrippa's baths in 19 BC. The café was a gathering place for musicians, writers and artists. Wagner, Berlioz and Goethe were frequent visitors, along with Tennyson, Thackeray and Edward Lear himself.

9 Via dei Condotti, another of Lear's houses in Rome

When Pope Leo XII barred people from entering cafés on 24 March 1824, the owner served refreshments from a window onto the Via dei Condotti. Such actions were brave, as the penalty for disobeying the Pope was three months in the galleys, a punishment still carried on fifty years later, according to Augustus Hare.

The Boat Fountain at the base of the Spanish Steps is of stone, designed by Bernini's father, Pietro, in 1627–29 for Pope Urban VIII. Bernini is said to have thought of the idea when he saw a boat stranded in the Spanish Square by the flood waters of the Tiber around that time.

Lear's name is recorded in the small museum in the Keats/Shelley Memorial, 26 Piazza di Spagna, on his visiting in 1837. John Ruskin, described as a 'painter and writer', visited in 1841.

Edward Lear's next apartment in Rome was at 107 Via Felice, but we did not find it. Vivien Noakes says the house no longer exists. However, Lear then moved back to the English Quarter, No. 9 Via dei Condotti, a front door giving into a large arched hall.

We were now determined to have a look at some of the places Lear painted in Rome.

● The Temple of Venus and Rome, to give this imposing ruin its full name, was a double temple dedicated to Venus and the Goddess of Rome. The Goddess of Rome faces the Forum, while Venus looks toward the Colosseum. The twin structure was the creation of Hadrian between AD 121 and 136, though it was completed by Antonius Pius, so becoming the largest temple in Rome. The site used to support the Vestibule of Nero's Golden House.

The Temple of Venus and Rome

The Colosseum is a short walk from the Arch of Titus. Our objective was the Temple of Venus, painted by Edward Lear in 1840. Lear's view shows the land in front at eye level, yet the Temple is on a plateau several feet up. It soon became clear Lear had drawn his original sketch from the Colosseum's 'windows'. There was a long queue for admittance to the Colosseum, but after a climb, we were exactly at the right level, though not at Lear's exact angle, as the Gallery was wired off.

– MD's journal, Tuesday 14 March 2000

Our search for Lear's views continued.

● Lear's view of Rome from the Pincian Mount was our quest, so we made eastward, reaching Viale delle Magnolie on to the Piazzole Napoleon I and looked east and southeast to St Peter's and the Vatican. There was a slight haze, blueing the buildings on the skyline. The panorama had, of course, changed, yet the major view of St Peter's remained unobscured. The Piazza del Popolo lay below. We walked along the Viale della Trinità dei Monti, passed the Villa Medici, now the Accademia di Francia, which looked as if it had just been cleaned and renovated.

– MD's journal, Tuesday 14 March 2000

Lear had paused to bring alive the fountain in the Borghese gardens. Known as the Piazzale dei Cavalli, the water feature was commissioned by Marcantonio Borghese when he restored the gardens in 1791. A bowl, supported by four raging horses stampeding through the water, were drenched by fountains. The drawing is in the Tate Gallery but it is not dated. The scene must have caught Lear's eye during his first stay in Rome.

In 1838, Lear also captured the Church of Santi Quattro Coronati, in pencil and watercolour. The building looks very much the same today. You can even see where the large clock, which dominated the tower, had been. It has been removed and the spot plastered over. The comparison of views also shows the unkindness meted out by road signs and other street furniture.

The Fountain of the Four Seahorses at the Villa Borghese. Drawing by Edward Lear. Tate Gallery, London

The Basilica of San Pietro in Vincoli appears to have been swallowed by a large modern block since Lear's day. He painted the church in 1842 (four years before the publication of his first nonsense book). The church was consecrated in the fifth century by Pope Sixtus III (432–40), but probably built on the foundations of an earlier building. The chains of St Peter, which were used to bind him in Jerusalem and Rome, are in the confessional. According to legend, they miraculously joined together in the thirteenth century. I suspect Edward Lear enjoyed myths and legend. He was a Christian in the best sense of love and kindness. He could not bear English Sundays, 'deadly AngloSunday, God hating, idolatrous, puritan, Pharisee silence and sermon reading'. He certainly would have admired Michelangelo's tomb of Julius II, crowned by the sculptor's famous Moses.[2]

There was quite a coterie of British painters in Rome in the eleven years from 1837 to 1848. Penry Williams has already been mentioned. He came under the wing of Sir Joseph Bailey, later Lord Glanusk (1798–1885). Penry Williams was born in Merthyr Tydfil. He was a pupil at the Royal Academy Schools, and spent most of his life in Rome from 1822 to 1869.

George Frederick Watts, RA (1817–1904) was another of Lear's Rome contemporaries. He had the distinction of having briefly been married to the actress Ellen Terry. Perhaps Lear's closest friend was the Dane Wilhelm Marstrand (1810–73), who did a portrait of Edward Lear dated 1840.

Lear travelled from Rome to Naples in 1838 with Thomas Ewings, again a graduate of the Royal Academy Schools, who was elected a Royal Academician. Ewings became best known for his Italian subjects. Edward William Cooke, another Royal Academician, was also in Rome. He was employed by Clarkson Stansfield to draw ship details because of his knowledge of the sea and sailing vessels.

Ford Maddox Brown (1821–93) was an admirer, though not a member, of the

The Palatine Bridge, Rome.
Painting by
Edward William Cooke RA,
(1811–80).
Private collection

Pre-Raphaelite Brotherhood. He later came under the influence of Dante Gabriel Rossetti (1828–82). The latter toured France with Lear's friend and mentor, William Holman Hunt (1827–10), whom Lear nicknamed 'Daddy'.

Edward Lear was close to Thomas Hartley Cromek (1809–73) while the two were in Rome. Cromek spent almost his whole time there between 1831 and 1849. Lear, remember, was in the city between 1837 and 1848. Cromek was a highly skilled draughtsman and an accurate and strong colourist. Lear nursed him through a serious illness.

The British artists usually attended the annual art festival in Rome. Lear wrote to John Gould in 1839:

Santa Maria in Cosmedin, Rome, with Campanile in the distance. Painting by Thomas Hartley Cromek. *Private collection*

> I know all the English artists – who are universally kind to me … and our little supper parties in winter, and our excursions in spring and autumn are very lively and agreeable.[3]

Each artist had his own studio and the new wave of wealthy 'grand tourists' did the rounds, buying reminders of their stay for their own collections or for friends. The small sketches could be the forerunner of the postcard. The artists lived agreeably in Rome and most made money, as well as learning their craft. This was still the principal objective. Penry Williams produced a little broadsheet which, as a joke, he called the Civitella Gazette, in which he included a line drawing showing his friends in 'A View of the Serpentara'.

Civitella di Subiaco is a hill village outside Rome. Not many that gathered there on 1 July 1837 are remembered today. For Lear, the record of the gathering and the memory of those days much later brought a warm feeling associated with past happinesses. The same must be said of the Tivoli, again a step away, with the Villa d'Este that crowns the top of the hill. Writing to Ann from Rome on 3 May 1838, Lear's letter bubbles with enthusiasm:

> must now describe my dear little Tivoli as I promised. First then you leave Rome at the San Lorenzo gate – and drive for some time between high ugly narrow high-walled lanes, until you come to the church of San Lorenzo – a very old one of the time of Constantine; it is very beautiful against the wide sky and mountains. After this about ten miles of up and down all over the campagna, I've often talked of, and which you must cross to get away from Rome. All the while you are getting nearer to the blue mountains, and you see Tivoli perched on a rock a great way up. By degrees, the buildings become more distinct and you see quantities of cypress trees – so black – sprinkled about the town. Nearer still – the campagna is very rugged and dreary, and you cross a queer sulphur stream as white as milk – and out of a hideous smell; but shortly afterward the country becomes cultivated – and you drive through plantations of olives and figs – and all kinds of grain. Then you reach the Anio or

Teverone, – the river that runs through Tivoli, and you cross it on a Roman bridge – with fine tomb; you know the old Romans always built their tombs by the road side.[4]

Edward Lear wrote in the same letter to his sister, 'I must now take you to the Villa d'Este – a scene worth walking to Italy from England – if one could see nothing else.' That is surely an invitation.

● We caught the metro from the Piazza di Spagna to Tiburtina and from there took the train to Tivoli. It was a painless journey except for some confusion with the trains. The station master said the Villa d'Este was five minutes' walk, perhaps to encourage us, though we took fifteen. There were virtually no signs and the rather drab approach was discouraging. However, having wiggled through the market, there was the villa, commanding a steep bluff, decorated with the famous garden.

The villa started off as a convent. Cardinal Ippolito II d'Este was a favourite of François I of France, but fell out with his son, Henry II. He decided to retire discretely to Tivoli and converted the building into a country house. He engaged the Neapolitan architect Pirro Ligorio.

The house is empty, rooms leading on to rooms with no furniture. However, the walls and ceiling are decorated with pictures and trompe l'oeil. The picture of the Roman watering place of Baia caught Gilly's attention. Nero had planned to link Baia to Rome, a hundred and sixty miles distant. Little vignettes of hunting and life in general created a linking, room to room.

A small terrace commanded the garden, which dropped away steeply, the main access path and subsidiaries going up and down the slope with paths at right angles to these, breaking the garden into squares and a series of terraces.

Edward Lear's main picture of the house and garden looks up toward the villa. Fascinated by the place, he also drew another the opposite way round, looking down from about halfway or just above the fish ponds. Samuel Palmer and other artistic friends of Lear painted different views, possibly on the same day. Lear selected two for his *Views in Rome and Its Environs*, 1841.

– **MD's journal, Wednesday 15 March 2000**

Samuel Palmer took a different view when he painted the garden again a year earlier in pencil and watercolour. Lear did the same view as Palmer for his proposed book illustrating Tennyson's poems. He called it *The Cypress in the Palace Walk*.

The main theme of the garden is water. There are fountains everywhere, including the Avenue of a Hundred Fountains, where water spouts from the mouths of animals.

Ippolito d'Este, though, dedicated his gardens to Hercules and Hippolytus – strength and chastity. There used to be many statues of Hercules, including one in the niche behind the Fountain of the Dragons, but with alterations by succeeding owners, the symbolism of the founder has been lost. The dragons and Hercules still celebrate the latter's feat of stealing the golden apples from under the noses of the guarding dragons, the eleventh of his twelve labours in the garden of the Hesperides. Golden apples are now part of the d'Este heraldic achievement.

Just as we left the garden, the rains came and we sought shelter for lunch in a café in the main street of Tivoli, and then made our way to the Villa Gregoriana. Tickets bought, we wandered along the steep path that tacked down the side of the gorge. Lear painted the gorge with the Temple of Sybil clinging to the top of this great cleft.

● Rain brought out the smell of the *Viburnum tinus* 'Lucidum' that crowded in on the path. We spotted the strange gothic 'windows' cut into the cliff walls below the temple. We passed through the ruins of the old villa. Commanding all is the noise and occasional sight of the great waterfall. Apparently it is a shadow of its former self because of a hydro-electric scheme further up the Aniene River. Mist rises from the fall and drifts over both sides of the gorge, muting the light. Lower down, when the sun comes through, rainbows appear. We arrived at the place where Lear would have obtained his view. Trees sprouting from below the temple somewhat alter the scene Lear enjoyed. As I passed the kiosk, I asked daughter Frederica, who speaks fluent Italian, to say that the view would be improved by some judicial tree felling. The keeper replied that he was a professor and did not cut down trees.

– **MD's journal, Wednesday 15 March 2000**

The Villa d'Este at Tivoli

Lear strode and rode out beyond Rome into the Roman campagna, the countryside around Rome, with Charles Knight, a close friend whom he first met in 1838. Their adventures together are shown in Lear's cartoons, collected together by Charles's sister, Margaret, Duchess of Sermoneta. In one, Lear and Knight are shown on bucking horses leaving Frascati on 18 July 1842. The caption reads 'Villa Taverna; Lear declares that he considers his horse far from tame.' The horse he had borrowed was a frisky Arab called Gridiron, which he later swapped for a quiet old nag.

Lear went beyond Rome's region, now called Lazio, which lies between the Tyrrhenian Sea and the Apennines, south to the land around the Bay of Naples, brooded over by Vesuvius. He ventured to the east, part of the Apennines, mountainous and wild, to the region known as the Abruzzi. In Lear's day, this southern part of Italy, south of Rome, was all the Kingdom of Naples.

In the cartoon of the two horsemen, the friends were clearly travelling light, but no doubt Lear had a sketch pad and pencil in his tail pocket, though little else. Gradually Lear's painting tours required more equipment and luggage. This was made easier when Giorgio Kokali, his servant and companion, came on the scene in 1857.

Map of the Three Abruzzi.
British Library

Lear remembered in a letter to Lord Carlingford of 22 August 1881 how he had deserved the title 'The Painter of Poetical Topography' awarded to him by Arthur Penrhyn Stanley, with whom he had toured Ireland.[5] This title had raised in his own mind the status of a topographical painter to a more hallowed calling, rather than a picture-postcard artist recording a scene. To balance this, he delighted in calling himself a 'damned dirty landscape painter', which he had overheard himself being described as in Calabria.

Again, in the letter to Lord Carlingford, he remembered that Lady Carlingford had various qualities. One of these was her 'very extraordinary perception of what was beautiful in landscape'. Lear shared her ideas and went about the choice of scene and where to sit.

He first selected his view. The principal object for his drawing had to have a good foreground and good background. He often described the scene as of 'no interest', merely because one of the elements was missing. He certainly did not create a focus or decorate what he saw. He was a true topographical artist.

Hubert Congreve, writing in the preface to Lady Strachey's *Later Letters of Edward Lear*, published in 1911, wrote:

> For some years prior to 1877, I was frequently with him in his studio and we also went on sketching expeditions together, Lear plodding slowly along, old George following behind, laden with lunch and drawing materials. When we came to a good subject, Lear would sit down, and taking his block from George, would lift his spectacles, and gaze for several minutes at the scene through a monocular glass he always carried; then, laying down the glass, and adjusting his spectacles, he would put on paper the view before us, mountain range, villages and foreground, with a rapidity and an accuracy that inspired me with awe-struck admiration.[6]

The second task, usually done on return to his lodgings, consisted of the watercolour washes, the colour following the notes he had written in his own shorthand (e.g. 'rox' for rocks). Then came the final process, the penning out, which he did in sepia ink over the pencil lines. It should be remembered that manufactured pencil then was only around eighty years old. The Faber company used graphite as a lead.

Watercolour paints were made of a ground colour pigment combined with a binder, usually gum arabic. The mixture was brushed on paper with a sable or squirrel-hair brush. Queen Victoria was the first to use a Kolinsky sable brush in 1866. Moist watercolours were introduced by Henry Newton and William Winsor in 1835. The coming of portable paints in little pans and tubes in 1843 made painting expeditions much easier and Lear's impedimenta lighter. Lear's preparations for his major expeditions are described in his book *Journals of a Landscape Painter in Albania and Illyria*, first published in 1851:

> Previously to starting, a certain supply of cooking utensils, tin plates, knives and forks, a basin, etc., must absolutely be purchased. The stronger and plainer the better; for you go into lands where pots and pans are unknown, and all culinary processes are to be performed in strange localities, innocent of artificial means. A light mattress, some sheets and blankets, and a good supply of capotes (a long coat usually with a hood) and plaids should not be neglected: two or three books: some rice, curry powder, and cayenne; a world of drawing materials – if you be a hard sketcher; as little dress as possible, though you must have two sets of outer clothing – one for visiting consuls, pashas and dignitaries, the other for rough, every day work; some quinine made into pills (rather leave all behind than this); a boyourldi, or general order of introduction to governors or pashas; and your teskere, or provincial passport for yourself and guide. All these are absolutely indispensable, and beyond these, the less you augment your impedimenta by luxuries the better; though a long strap with a pair of ordinary stirrups, to throw over the Turkish saddles, may be recommended to save you the cramp caused by the awkward shovel-stirrups of the country. Arms, and ammunition, fine raiment, presents for the natives are all nonsense; simplicity should be your aim when all these things, so generically termed 'the roba' by Italians, are in order, stow them into two brobdignagian saddle-bags, united by a cord (if not, goats-hair sacks); and by these hanging on each side of the baggage-horses saddle, no trouble will ever be given from seceding bits of luggage escaping at unexpected intervals. Until you adopt this plan, (the simplest of any) you will lose much time daily by the constant necessity of putting the baggage in order.[7]

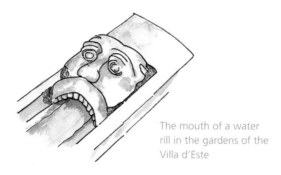

The mouth of a water rill in the gardens of the Villa d'Este

21
Short of tin

I suppose in a strong westerly you would be able to smell the sea in the centre of Rome, twenty-five kilometres away, though the call of salt water is not just the smell. One day there may be a gene that could be introduced during life that both creates a love of the sea and prevents seasickness. Gilly wasn't brought up on the beach and yet she has it, while Edward Lear escaped almost entirely, but he loved the look of it.

Before leaving Rome, there is one more person to meet. Lear met Edgar Drummond (1825–93) in Rome in the winter of 1858–59. He became his friend and banker. Writing from 119 Marina, St Leonards-on-Sea, on 5 August 1859, Lear remembers the Rome days:

> My Dear Drummond, It seems so odd to me not to have seen you – (except once from a cab,) since I came to England, – considering that in one's last Roman days I saw you daily that I must write a line to tell you why I have not tried again to find you, or Mrs Drummond at home.[8]

There was an Old Man of the coast, who placidly sat on a post;
But when it was cold he relinquished his hold,
And called for some hot buttered toast.

He goes on to explain that he was 'preoccupied by the very sudden death of one of my remaining sisters, Harriet [1802–59] who died in Scotland.' He ends in a typically Learish way:

> Do you know this place? [St Leonards-on-Sea] The other end is full of people and swells, but this is remote, and quiet and inhabited by organ grinders and cuttle fish.

In a subsequent letter on 1 October 1859, Lear gives his true feelings about Rome:

> At the end of that month [November] I am going back to that Roman prison but I shall only give [crossed out] this winter. I detested those walls and streets far too much to abide there a week longer than I am compelled to do, believe me.[9]

He was not better pleased by London. Writing to Edgar Drummond on 4 November from 15 Stratford Place, he complained he was 'laid up with flu – cough – asthma and all sorts of beastly superfluous atmospheric disgustables, and fear I must keep close prisoner. On calling at Bryanstone Square [Drummond's London address], I find Mrs Drummond was away: – which, though I did not see her, I was notwithstanding glad of – as London seems to me a frightful horror just now after the long and pleasant seaside summer.'[10]

In another letter to Edgar Drummond dated 21 December 1859, the opening confirmed that they had become sufficiently friendly and close for Lear to address Edgar as 'My Dear Drummond'. He admitted that he was not really at home amongst bankers or those who deal in figures:

> I never ask to see you in the bank – fearing to disturb you: for I know that if anybody spoke to me 'in a sum' I should never get over it.[11]

The letter ended in the same affectionate vein, 'Believe me, yours sincerely', while before he had always signed 'Yours sincerely'.

So who was Edgar Drummond, and what was he like? Edgar Atheling Drummond was the second son of Andrew Robert Drummond by Lady Elizabeth, née Manners, eldest daughter of John Henry, 5th Duke of Rutland. Born in 1825, Edgar entered the Royal Navy on 29 May 1838 as a 'Volunteer 1st Class', at thirteen years of age. He became a Midshipman in 1840 and a Lieutenant in 1845. His first ship was the *Talbot*, Captain Codrington her Commander, on which he was present at the siege of St Jean d'Acre in 1840, where as a Midshipman, he took a boat from one end of the fleet to the other under heavy fire from the Turkish force. He received the British and Turkish medals. He subsequently served on various stations in the *St Vincent, Winchester, Vanguard, Agincourt, Vestel, Dido, Bitterne* and *Daedalus*. On the latter ship, while off the coast of Africa, and Officer of the Watch, he saw a sea serpent, details of which were published in the newspapers on 28 October 1848. Soon after this, he wrote to his father saying that he had a distaste for the career he had chosen and desired to leave the Navy and go into the Army. His father was sympathetic but firm. However, this did not do any good and in October of 1848 the Admiralty granted Edgar's request to go on half pay,

and accepted his resignation in 1854. His elder brother, Andrew John, was none too well, so Edgar entered Drummond's Bank and assisted his father, taking over when the latter died in 1865. He maintained his lands in Hampshire to a high state of perfection, went on long walking tours and, as a member of the Royal Yacht Squadron, cruised in his yawl *Brunette*. Louisa, his wife, died in 1886, two years before his friend Edward Lear. Edgar died in Venice in 1893 from a chill contracted through his habit of taking a walk after dinner.[12]

Edward Lear stayed at Cadland. Both he and Edgar were fond of walking. The latter kept a supply of acorns in his pocket and if he saw a likely place in a hedgerow or open space in the woodland, he would make a hole with his walking stick and pop in one of his hoard.

Edgar Drummond was much involved in a major diplomatic incident in 1870 caused by the kidnapping and eventual murder of his friends and relations in Greece. An expedition to Marathon was organised by Edgar's brother-in-law, Lord Muncaster (1834–1917). They picnicked, and on returning, near the bridge at Pikermi, the party was stopped by a feared band of brigands, headed by Arvanitakis. Many of their escort had fallen behind, too far away to be of much assistance. Two of the gendarmes with the party were wounded defending them, one dying. The women and a little girl were released by the brigands almost immediately. Lord Muncaster was sent off to obtain a ransom of £5,000 for each of the five men. He contacted his brother-in-law, Edgar, and the money was arranged. The brigands also wanted an amnesty and safe passage for themselves. Negotiators were sent out from Athens. The brigands became increasingly nervous and moved their prisoners from place to place, shooting those who did not keep up or tried to escape. In the end, six brigands were shot dead by Greek soldiers and another six taken prisoner. The Dilessi murders, as they came to be know, were a sensation

and all over the British and Greek papers.[13] On 28 April 1870, Edward Lear wrote
to Edgar from Cannes:

> You may imagine how glad I was to see your brother Alfred, who is always anti-melancholic,
> and I had been needing some such remedy. I have a letter from him, date Corfu April 17th
> but he had only then just heard of the capture of Lord Muncaster and the rest of that
> unhappy party. It is this subject that principally urges me to write today – begging you
> will be so kind as to send me a line as soon as you can, for the extracts from the London
> papers in last night's galynarri [?] perplex and distress me extremely. One paper says the
> four captives (i.e. Herbert, Vyner, Boyl (Italian) and Lloyd) were killed. Another report say
> that Lord Muncaster after returning to Athens about the ransom, returned to the brigands.
> All five of the travellers were killed. What is the truth? Poor Mrs Drummond's distress and
> suspense must be dreadful and I truly hope for you may be able to write that her brother is
> saved – wretched as all the rest of the story is.[14]

Those murdered were, as Lear quoted, Edward Herbert, a first cousin of the 4th Earl
of Carnarvon; Edward Lloyd, son of E J Lloyd, QC; Frederick Vyner, a distant cousin
of Lord Muncaster; and Count Alberto de Boyl, Secretary of the Italian Legation in
Athens.

The seven captured brigands were tried and executed, their severed heads
exhibited and photographed on a wall in Athens. Edgar Drummond noted later
that Lord Muncaster was 'probably never able to rid himself of the memory of
it'.[15]

Arthur Penrhyn Stanley, Dean of Westminster, who had accompanied Lear
to Ireland and had been his pupil, together with his brother Owen, preached a
sermon at Westminster Abbey on the Greek massacre the day after the arrival in
England of the remains of both Edward Herbert and Frederick Vyner.

But we must now return to money matters. Lear's accounts held at Drummond's
Bank show how careful he was with money.[16] He tried successfully to keep out of
debt and the management of his financial affairs was a consuming task. The artist
used his charm to strike a good bargain. When staying at the Oatlands Park Hotel
for the winter of 1860–61 and completing his masterwork, *Cedars of Lebanon*,
he was only charged four guineas a week inclusive. The hotel was fashionable
enough to have its arrivals and departures chronicled in the *Morning Post*.[17] He did
find enough resource to respond to charity – the victims of the explosion at Nine
Elms and cholera sufferers in Malta, for example. Financial notes were kept in his
diary and scraps of paper. He was also a great letter writer, and by communicating
with his friends and those who collected his pictures he could persuade even the
most reluctant to buy. He assumed, rightly, that his friends would like to know
how he was doing and what was going on in his studio and gallery. As an example,
he wrote to Edgar Drummond on 22 October (no year given, but must be 1863):

> My dear Edgar Drummond, Thanks for your letter – to which I must send but a brief answer,
> being a proposal I am about to make to you.
> If so be as you have determined to spend ten guineas upon art, there is no help for it:

Lord Muncaster.
Photograph in the Cadland Archives

– only I should prefer your doing so in my own way – thus: – you shall have the Baalbec or any drawing you prefer I should make for you at your own choice for seven pounds seven shillings and no pennies and the book Ionian Views for three pounds three shillings and no pennies which being added together makes ten pounds ten.

Hereby, you will be killing two birds with one stone – in as much as you will have the pleasure of possessing the drawing – and give much pleasure of knowing you have that and the book too: – and as I have known you some years and have passed many pleasant hours with you and Mrs Drummond, I don't think you will refuse my whim upon this subject.

Lear ends with an exhortation about the book:

If you can procure me any subscribers please do: – one hundred copies must be sold to ensure any profit, and as yet I have only got one hundred and twenty-six names.[18]

Judging by the follow-up of 26 October 1863, Edgar Drummond agreed to 'killing two birds with one stone'.[19]

Edgar had a younger brother, Alfred Manners Drummond, often mentioned in Lear's correspondence with Edgar. He, too, was in Lear's sights, as he was both a Lear collector and a determined traveller. Captain Alfred was also a partner in Drummond's Bank.

The Dolomphious Duck,
who caught Spotted Frogs for her dinner
with a Runcible Spoon.

22
The Sea of Circe

Back in the spring of 1999, *Gang Warily* was again in her salt-water element after crossing the bar and leaving the Tiber, the silting river of the ancients (the land expedition to Rome would take place in 2000). The wind was south-southwest force 2–3 and the barometer high at 1023. We set sail and were making nearly five knots – not bad for our old 'duck'.

A skua flapped his lonely way, bright-eyed for gulls from whom he could pinch food. Sweet-hulled fishing boats were nearby and soon dolphins were playing off the starboard bow. A yacht or two with brilliant white sails provided an exclamation mark on the blue of the sea.

● *Gang Warily* was approaching Anzio and by 17.00 Nero's old harbour breakwater had to be avoided. The old stonework was difficult to recognise from the modern sea defence works. Anzio is commanded by a new cathedral that replaced the one demolished by bombs and gun fire during the Allied landings on 22 January 1944. It was difficult to see any old buildings on the skyline. The cathedral tower is square and fluted and now dated.

There was an Old Person of Ischia, whose conduct grew friskier and friskier;
He danced hornpipes and jigs, and ate thousands of figs,
That lively Old Person of Ischia.

Caligula and Nero were born in Anzio, then called Antium. Cicero also had a house there. It seemed appropriate for us to drop the sails and drift off the Villa Borghese and bathe.

Nettuno was next door. The town must have suffered during the Allied landings, yet the old castle with two buttressed towers seems to have survived and modern buildings abut sympathetically. The marina is, of course, a modern, post-war addition. The old town with its winding streets has a charm that is insulated from the modern suburb, designed as a slave to the motor car.

– *Gang Warily*'s log, Thursday 27 May 1999

Nettuno. Lithograph by Edward Lear, from *Illustrated Excursions in Italy*, 1846.
British Library

Edward Lear included a picture of Nettuno in his *Illustrated Excursions in Italy*, published in 1846.

The visibility was not very good when we left Nettuno, but it was clear enough that a grey launch was in pursuit. Once abeam, a smartly dressed policeman ordered us to steer 220 degrees magnetic. Our chosen course for San Felice Circeo was 130 degrees, but the explanation was soon clear. The occasional crump of heavy guns gave us a clue. They were range safety officers. After about two miles on their directed course we started to resume our chosen one, only to find the launch turned towards us again. At noon, Gilly contacted the Coastguard and asked permission to resume our course. He replied, 'yes, anywhere, next stop Casablanca and Tripoli.' This was permission enough. Anyway, it was lunch time so the guns were silent.

During this exchange, Jessica caught sight of what looked like a rocky island soaring into the sky through the mist. 'Wow! What's that?' Then it had disappeared. There were no islands on the chart. It must have been Cape Circeo, which rises vertically from the sea to some 541 metres. Then the vision returned, first as a hazy outline and then, as the mist rolled away, clear as a bell, becoming one of the most dramatic, sudden appearances at sea I can remember. This was perhaps not surprising, as it was here that the goddess Circe had her palace from where, you will remember, she used her undoubted charms upon Odysseus, keeping him under her spell, delaying his voyage for twelve months. I remember reading in Denham's *Tyrrhenian Sea* that Odysseus had taken Hermes' advice. 'When Circe smites you with her wand, draw your sword from your side, and spring at her as if you want to take her life. Now she will fall before you in terror and invite you to her bed – do not hesitate to accept the favours of a goddess.' We were not too wrong in thinking that the headland was an island, for it was virtually so until Mussolini drained the Pontine Marshes which had cut the cape from the surrounding land.

There is a magic about San Felice Circeo. It is difficult to explain. It must be that the goddess is still there, somewhere above the elongated Martello tower.

San Felice Circeo

The five Pontine islands are due south of Cape Circeo. The island of Ponza is the largest. The little town of Ponza was built into and on the rising ground above the harbour. The first colonists were Romans and they carved tunnels into the rock. The dome of the church dominates the waterfront and stares down on the ferry terminal and the fish quay. The Bourbon castle, converted into a house, looks north above the church. It has been much modified. The place is busy with scooters and that 'jack of all works', the Piaggio Ape, or bee, a three-wheeled mini-truck, the workhorse of Italy that supplies all the shops and builders without the need of large lorries blocking the streets.

Of all the small islands, Ventotene wins the prize. We crept into Porto Vecchio at 12.50 on Sunday 30 May, making a hard turn to starboard into the Roman galley port. On the quay was Signor Ciro Alleati, who ran the diving school and was also the Harbourmaster. He offered any help we needed. The Italians have a way of lighting up when pleased – the eyes sparkle, the hands and the whole body moves with internal delight, which is only too visible from the outside.

The town of Ventotene grows out of the harbour of Porto Vecchio. The buildings on the northwest of this little gut are built on the hollowed-out tufa of the galley caves, ancient submarine pens, as it were, of the Roman navy. They extend into the natural rock some fourteen metres, and their mouths have been narrowed from the original 14.5 metres by walls and doors, so that they fit modern purpose – a freezer area for fish, the stores of the Guardia di Finanza, or for diving stores. Diving is a strong industry in these islands and the Guardia are everywhere.

A zigzag road climbs up the hill with steps and provides a shortcut for pedestrians. The square is impressive with its town hall and, opposite, the church. The town hall is an imposing square building, almost a palace, with a museum in the basement. A simple Doric pillar with an inscribed base is the island's war memorial. Somehow these monuments seem sadder in Italy than elsewhere. Perhaps this is an odd statement, but the modern Italian is not a warlike creature. The ordinary people were swept into conflict by Mussolini and they are remembered not as heroes but as the fallen.

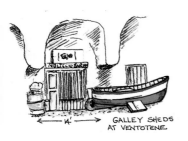

GALLEY SHEDS
AT VENTOTENE.

● There is a plaque on the town hall to Altiero Spinelli, heralded as one of the first during the war to see positive benefit in a united Europe. He was imprisoned on the island by the fascists, along with other visionaries, Eugenio Colomi and Ernesto Rossi.

– *Gang Warily*'s log, Sunday 30 May 1999

It was difficult to shake off the pull of Ventotene and, with regret, we headed across a glass-smooth sea to the island of Ischia, at the northeast entrance to the Bay of Naples. Monte Epomeo, an extinct volcano, rises 788 metres and is easy to see miles away. Pliny the Elder records that an eruption in the seventh century BC drove the Greek settlers away. The Bay of Naples is the place of earthquakes, and I checked with my insurers that they were ready for such an event.

The Greek calls Ischia 'The Land of Monkeys'. We anchored under the point of Lacco Ameno. A swathe of russet foliage climbed the cliff. Gilly was anxious to identify the luxurious growth of plants, so swam ashore. The colour was from the dying leaves of *Euphorbia dendroides*.

The round harbour of Ischia was created from a lake by opening the volcanic crater to the sea, the work of Ferdinand II in 1854. We were secured in the normal Mediterranean fashion, anchoring away from the quay and then securing the stern to the shore, close enough to use the passarelle, or gang plank. A very large Perini Navi ketch entered and we were asked to spring a little sideways when she came astern between us and the smaller ferries. The harbourmaster told me our berth was normally reserved for yachts of over twenty-five metres. I replied that if he allowed us to stay we might grow to that!

Lear also wrote nonsense about Ischia:

There was an old person of Ischia,
Whose conduct grew friskier and friskier,
He danced hornpipes and jigs, and ate thousands of figs,
That lively old person of Ischia.

The heat in this one-time volcano made it difficult to even contemplate dancing. We were pleased to accept the invitation of Dr Giuseppe della Vecchia to visit the Reale Yacht Club Canottieri Savoia in Naples.

Our host had been President of the yacht club for ten years. He said he ran the place like a Swiss German train. Everything is on time, he explained. 'I keep turning the screw a little tighter and things happen.' He added, 'there is a Neapolitan expression that says "my chicken coop is the best in the world". I hold that Naples is the best city in the world.'

Lear did not agree, for he wrote to his sister on 28 May 1838:

Gang Warily in Naples

> If you empty all the streets of all the capitals of Europe into one – then turn in some thousand oxen, sheep, goats, monks – priests – processions – cars – mules – naked children and bare legged mariners – you may form some idea of the Toledo (the main street). Once I walked up it – but would not again for a great deal, as I was nearly deaf and run over (almost) twenty times before I came out of it. It is a dreadful place, – yet at 8 o'clock people lounge and eat ices at every door – although the noise is like all the thunder in the world.[20]

Lear was wandering about Naples and the surrounding area with James Uwins, the painter. He made for Pozzuoli, as did *Gang Warily*. She was going to rest there from 3 June until our return on 20 July 1999. Lear, though, could not leave the place soon enough. In a rather rude letter to John Gould from Rome on 17 October 1839, he wrote:

> I received your nasty, illegible abortion of a note at Naples – whither in company with a friend I had just walked. After that I was taken very ill and owing to the too fine and sulphurous nature of the air, my cough returned and also spitting of blood, and had I not left the neighbourhood of that filthy old mountain Vesuvius I might have died.[21]

Lear was no doubt complaining of Solfatara. This extinct volcano still belches steam and smells of rotten eggs. Sulphurous vapours were valued for medicinal purposes since the Roman times, but clearly did not suit Lear. He did not like Vesuvius either. In the same letter to John Gould he complains:

Roman ship shown on a carved plinth at Naples

> Naples does not please me as a city, altho' no other word but Paradise can be used to express the beauty of its environs, which are unlike any earthly scene beside: – but the town itself is all noise, horror – dirt, heat – and abomination – and I hate it, – nor am I much attached to the seaside residence, not to speak of a beastly volcano whose smoking, groanings, bumpings, thumpings, vomitings, earthquakings and other eccentricities always annoyed me from morn to night. – I was however most fortunate in witnessing one of the finest irruptions known for many years – a midnight scene I can never forget: – I wonder if you will come ever into these places: – but as you would see no kangaroos or marsupial monkeys about the country, I don't believe you would be pleased.

Roly Franks joined us on our return to Pozzuoli. Our first port of call was meant to be the island of Procida to the south, but the weather deteriorated and off Capo Miseno the wind accelerated to 40 knots, which persuaded us to put back into Baia for fuel and a weather forecast. An inky cloud grew rapidly to the northwest and soon the rain came, making the land a hazy blur. However, we managed to shoot into the harbour, noting the barometer had dropped ten points in a very short time. Our initial welcome in Baia was out of the ordinary for Italy. A strong bear of a man advanced down the jetty in the manner of a nightclub bouncer, saying 'You can't stay here!' Gilly managed to calm him down and we were given ten minutes' grace. After hearing the forecast – north-northeast seven, rain, sea very rough – he let us stay until morning.

Baia

Baia was the most fashionable resort in the Bay of Naples from the second century BC to the end of the Roman Empire. Luxurious villas were built for members of the Roman aristocracy. The thermal springs were considered good for health by the Roman doctors and their successors. The baths are dedicated to Venus, Diana and Mercury. A temple of Venus, built of narrow Roman bricks, stands remarkably complete near the harbour. A view of this ruin by William Pars (1742–82) captures the Romantic aura of the building. Thomas Jones (1742–1803) and Francis Towne (1739–1816) also painted the same temple and Turner the city of Naples in 1823.

Gang Warily was allowed a reprieve by our 'nightclub' friend and stayed another night at Baia, but the wind did not retreat much, just enough to let us out, so we again sought the sulphurous peace of Pozzuoli. By the morning of Sunday 25 July, the wind had dropped and was southeast at eight knots. We determined to go to Cornicella on Procida. *Gang Warily* rounded Cape Miseno, creeping under the lighthouse perched on a towering bluff. The great fortified rock of Terra Murata, crowned by the Abbey of San Michele, dominates

Looking over Procida towards Ischia

both the north-coast harbour of Sancio Cattolico and the smaller Marina Corricella. The former was subjected to endless streams of ferries, but mercifully none rounded the corner to Corricella. There, the pink, white and Empress-Maria-Theresa yellow painted houses cling to the rock. The bright colours battle with the darker reds and the natural grey of Roman cement. The sea wall of black basalt prevents the sea from entering the port. A bronzed youth with dreadlocks indicated we could secure alongside a fishing boat lying in the middle of the harbour. Procida is like Ventotene and is another of the 'string of pearls' that stretches from island to island along the Italian coast as you make south. We bathed in the clear water of the harbour, drying ourselves on the rocks – which reminded Roly of the ditty:

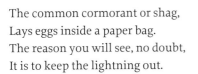

Two views of *Gang Warily* in the harbour at Procida

> The common cormorant or shag,
> Lays eggs inside a paper bag.
> The reason you will see, no doubt,
> It is to keep the lightning out.
>
> But what these unobservant birds,
> Have failed to notice, is that herds,
> Of wandering bears may come with buns
> And steal the bags to hold the crumbs.

This is a modern development of Lear's prime nonsense.

The rain returned, so we uncorked a bottle of Vesuvio, a delicious white wine, before going ashore and dining in a little alcove, sheltered from the weather. There we enjoyed another bottle of white, this time from the island of Ischia.

Heading for Capri with Roly Franks at the helm

We were heading for Capri, and took the precaution of consulting J Luise & Sons Ltd. They were established in 1847 and their card declares they are the Honorary Agent to the Royal Yacht Squadron. We spoke to Paolo Luise, whom we had visited when in Naples. The office was little more than twelve by eight feet, with two desks, faxes and computers and four telephones. Luise's had applied for a larger building first in 1976. There were twenty-four authorities to consult. One planner would say 'we don't like the windows', another 'we don't like the colour', and so on it went. New drawings, new applications, new turning-downs.

'I am working on a berth in Capri. Amalfi is okay', he added. 'Ring me on my mobile.'

Savarona

● The Port of Naples' forecast was 'sea rough, the wind north-northeast force 5, but variable with hazy visibility'. As it turned out, it was too calm. The wind was not strong enough for us to make progress, so we proceeded under power for Capri, arriving just after one o'clock. Anchored off the harbour was the beautiful clipper-bowed, counter-sterned *Savarona*, built in the 1930s and now a cruise ship. The other excitement was *Candida*, the 'J' in splendid condition, her brightwork sparkling and her white hull reflecting the blue of the sea. She was built for Herman Andreae. We had to hang about outside the harbour waiting for permission to enter. After a pause, Gilly telephoned the harbour office and spoke to Captain Amadeo Ferringo, the Harbourmaster. The Luises had taken the precaution of giving us his number. Within five minutes, we were beckoned within and told where to berth – inside the first floating pier, one from the gangway. The harbour was certainly chock-a-block.

– *Gang Warily*'s log, **Monday 26 July 1999**

The island of Capri is an enormous block of limestone. It was colonised by the Greeks. Tamed, the island became the resort of the Roman emperors. Augustus

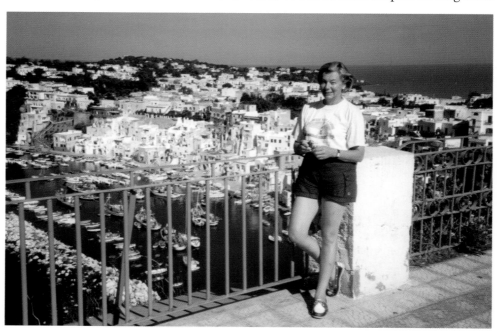

Gilly above the harbour at Capri

lived here and Tiberius built the Villa Jovis on the northeastern tip. In the tenth century, the island was picked at by pirates and the population moved away from the sea to places high above. Ana Capri could only be reached by a flight of 800 steps, called the Phoenician Stairs until a road was built in the nineteenth century. We were drawn upward by the determination to see the villa of Axel Munthe (1857–1949), the Swedish doctor and author of *The Story of San Michele*. He was the personal doctor to the Swedish royal family and, in particular, to their Queen Victoria. Axel Munthe went to Naples in 1884 to lend a hand in treating a cholera epidemic. He had visited Capri aged

Axel Munthe (above) and (left) his house, the Villa San Michele

18 in 1875, and when he had saved enough he returned and built the Villa San Michele, with great care and taste, on the site of a Tiberian villa. We did not take the 800 steps or the road that goes to Ana Capri but were hoisted by funicular. The house is built around the courtyard, called an atrium in Roman times. The garden radiates peace and the cypress avenue, with a water rill down one side, relaxes the garden wanderer, in deference to the head of Hypnos, god of sleep, that decorates one of the rooms.

The taxi driver who took us back said the worst thing about Capri is that everyone knows all about you and you all about them – sometimes before it happens. There was no chance for a second wife! Capri is twenty-nine kilometres from Ischia and twenty-nine kilometres from Naples – a perfect triangle.

● Roly and I sipped the whisky, Famous Grouse, with Gilly drinking the local wine – Tiberio. As darkness fell, some of the edge went off the noise of the town. We listened to Emma Kirkby singing Mozart's *Laudate Dominum*. She praised God for us, for this place.
– *Gang Warily*'s log, **Monday 26 July 1999**

Late July is perhaps not the ideal time of the year to climb the rough road to the Villa Jovis. We tacked upward through the evergreen

The view from the Villa Jovis

scrub oaks and umbrella pines. The villa is just over 350 metres above the sea. The story goes that Tiberius took advantage of this lofty haunt and had people pushed over the edge. Suetonius (c.69–122), the Roman biographer and antiquarian, wrote that:

> On the island of Capri is the place of execution from which Tiberius ordered his victims, after prolonged and skilful torture, to be precipitated into the sea before his very eyes: below a company of sailors beat them with boat hooks until life was crushed from their bodies.

Our progress down was less swift, but a good deal more pleasant. The view from the church, which commands the whole island, and that from the stairway behind Tiberius' leap, which overlooks the cliff of the executions, is one of the world's great panoramas.

The Blue Grotto, Capri.
Oil painting by Edward Lear.
Private collection,
© *Sothebys Picture Library*

Looking south-southwest along the southern coast of Capri is the Marina Piccola, where there is a flat-topped rock, Scoglio delle Sirene, the Sirens' Rock, also known strangely as the Antemoessa, or 'flowery meadow'. Thomas Holroyd painted the view from the Marina Piccola in 1867. This shows the rock with a meadowed top, joined to the shore by a strand, which is no longer there. According to the locals, this is where the Siren sang to lure passing sailors. However, there are rival rocks. Looking eastward from the Villa Jovis are the Galli islands, lying off the Penisola Sorrentina, six kilometres southwest of Positano. Both are identified as the home of the sirens that bewitched sailors. Parthenope was one of them, revered in Naples, where she met her death. We were due to go that way when leaving Capri.

The Blue Grotto in 1999, and one of the boatmen who take visitors inside through the low cave entrance

The Blue Grotto put Capri on the map, as far as tourism is concerned. August Kopisch and Ernst Fries, accompanied by the boatman Angelo Ferraro, described this wonder of the world in 1826. The cave had been used by the Romans as a marine nymphaeum. Boats take visitors from Capri to the small mouth of the cave, two metres wide and a little over one metre high. It is, therefore, necessary to transfer to the bottom of a ten-foot double-ender that takes three plus the oarsman. The boat shoots in and out by pulling on a chain. The blue colour is produced by refraction of light through the water. It is quite eerie. Some of the oarsmen sing well and some badly. The echo improves the voice a little.

I was surprised to discover in a beautifully produced book, *Painters on Capri 1850–1950*, that Lear had done a small oil of the cave.[22] He had adopted his usual way of painting this strange place, positioning

Isole Galli – The Siren Isles, 1844.
Drawing by Edward Lear.
Tate Gallery, London

himself at the far end, looking out toward the entrance. He placed two sirens in a ghostly form in the foreground, but left the boatmen out altogether. When did Lear capture this view? Was it when he visited the Bay of Naples in 1838, some twelve years after the cave was discovered, or was it in June of 1844, when he pictured the Siren Islands off Positano? I believe it was the latter, because both the oil and the drawing contain cartoons, as it were, of the sirens.

We set sail on Wednesday 28 July 1999, heading for Amalfi. The calm of the early morning was broken by strong gusts of wind, reaching 27 knots. The barometer fell five points, almost as we watched. Clouds swirled around the top of Capri. We had almost resolved to remain another day when the weather quietened and the barometer began to step upward.

The Siren Isles in 1999

We were going to pass between the Galli islands and the Sorrentina peninsula. I quickly sketched the islands from the west-northwest at 12.25. Circe's advice was clear:

You will come to the sirens. They will bewitch all men. Whoever sails near them unaware will never again see wife and children once he has heard the siren voices. They enchant him with their clear songs, as they sit in a meadow that is heaped with the bones of dead men, bones on which still hangs their shrivelled skin. Drive your ship past this place and so that your men do not hear their song, soften some bees wax and with it seal their ears. But if you yourself should wish to listen to the sirens, get your crew to bind you hand and foot with ropes against the mast step. In this way you may listen in rapture to the voices of the two sirens, but should you begin to beg your comrades to unloose you, you must make sure they bind you even more tightly.[23]

Odysseus followed this advice, and did eventually make it home. But when the Argonauts passed this way Orpheus sang loudly and sweetly from the *Argo*, and the sirens were dumbfounded and jumped into the sea, where they still are, transformed into rocks. There, they may still claim their victims on a wild night.

Gang Warily passed between the outer mole and the inner pier of Amalfi a little after two o'clock. I had always longed to visit the port, the European home of the compass, and this was redoubled with my interest in Edward Lear and his marvellous rendering of the town in the summer of 1838. Lear remembered Amalfi in a particularly happy way. In his diary of 10 May 1862 he records:

> I do not now suppose that the feeling of happiness can ever come back, but by unexpected and unsought snatches; so I do not strive after it nor mourn that I cannot have it.[24]

Amalfi, 1838. Drawing in black chalk heightened with white on blue paper, by Edward Lear. *Victoria & Albert Museum, London*

Amalfi from the same position in 1999

Gilly and I had a similarly happy experience there, one that will last. That was the joy of discovering where Lear had sat in 1838, in the doorway to the Saracen Tower, to paint his picture, now in the Victoria & Albert Museum.

The Goddess, a tall Greek-looking blonde who had helped us moor up, pointed to the spot where she thought had been the artist's seat. Everyone we spoke to seemed interested in the picture and full of opinions. Before we confirmed ours, we looked at all the buildings that Lear had painted and that were still there.

The white walls of the Hotel Luna, once a convent, rose above us and, though altered, we could pick out the windows and doors which were common to the picture and to reality. The road has been widened and cantilevered out. Two buildings stand out in both Lear's drawing of Amalfi and Turner's sketch (1819) of almost the same view. These are the Torre di Pogerola on high, and on the left edge, the Hotel Cappuccini. The puzzle was the road

Amalfi from the sea

tunnel to Positano. In Lear's drawing the tunnel disappears into the mountain on a level with the Hotel Cappuccini, while the road now cuts through lower down. In due time we found the answer. The dark hole Lear drew by the hotel is now a grotto, as the old road tunnel had collapsed. The modern one is just above the sea. Lear stayed in the Hotel Cappuccini on 5 July 1838 with James Uwins. He signed the visitors' book. The monastery, the original purpose of the building, founded in 1212, was secularised in 1813, and from then on it was a 'locanda', or hostel for travellers.[25]

Amalfi was an important place, Roman to begin with and then the first sea republic of Italy. With the collapse of the Roman Empire, this sea republic was the first to re-establish trade between east and west, carrying and bringing into Italy such exotics as coffee, carpets and paper. Amalfi had its own coinage – the tari – and one of its famous sons was Flavio Gioia, who is said to have invented or perhaps more accurately re-invented the compass, which originally came from China. Amalfi gave the world's navigators the first maritime law – *Tabula de Amalpha* – the book displayed in an imposing case, along with later editions, in the town hall museum.

We were well looked after by the

Gilly checking the email

Gang Warily in the harbour at Amalfi

Heading for Salerno

harbourmaster, Antonio Esposito, and the Greek Goddess, who was his assistant. When we left, Antonio let go our lines and threw a bag of lemons, huge, juicy ones never seen in England, into the cockpit.

Gang Warily entered Salerno on 29 July 1999. We were received with great kindness by Dr Antonio Scocozza, President of the Circolo Canottieri Irno, which

Bath house at Pompeii

was to be not only our base for a few days, but our place for the winter. A secure berth allowed us to explore, and we took advantage by visiting a little village, Corpo di Cava, where Edward Lear stayed in the hills above Salerno and far away from the noise of Naples. He had probably heard that the town below, Cava dei Tirreni, was a recommended stop for those enjoying the Grand Tour. Goethe had been there as early as 1787. Sir Walter Scott and John Ruskin also paused there, enveloping themselves in the great chestnut woods and being entertained by the green and red woodpeckers and treecreepers. Buzzards and kestrels soared above and, on the forest floor, thyme, lavender, borage, violet crocuses and blue anemones formed a carpet.

Gilly, Roly and I went to Pompeii from Salerno. We were enchanted with the House of the Vettii. We found this building an inspiration. The design of the atrium, with an open roof, a window to the sky, with a shallow pool below, provided an ideal living space in this climate. Again, I had the feeling that civilisation is now in retreat. This was reinforced when we visited

Paestum the next day. Edward Lear had the experience too, and writing to his sister Ann on 10 June 1838, he said:

> The next morning at 4, we started in the car for Pesto [Paestum] – the object of our expedition. To get there you cross an immense plain which as you approach the sea grows very desolate and lonely. The peasants have an unhealthy melancholy air – for after June it is so dreadfully unwholesome an atmosphere that strangers cannot stay in it – and the few poor wretches who live in it are always ill. Huge herds of buffaloes you meet continually and one seldom sees a wilder scene. At last you spy the three Temples of Pesto – once a magnificent Greek town and of such antiquity that no one knows anything about them: the Emperor Augustus went to see them as ruins in his time – so judge that they are no chickens – notwithstanding this they are nearly perfect, being of such wonderfully strong architecture although the rest of the city is reduced to nought: vast walls still are to be traced – with an amphitheatre, etc., etc. but only the temples are left whole. One of Neptune has all the outside pillars standing – and everything as it was two thousand years ago: the other two minus their insides, or part of them.

Pompeii – a frieze of chariot-racing *putti*

Well, we know a great deal more about them now. Paestum was founded around 600 BC as Poseidonia, being dedicated to Poseidon, the Roman Neptune, the god of the sea. The afforestation of the hills above the plain and the silting up of the rivers caused the low-lying ground to become waterlogged and marshy and the birthplace of mosquitoes, which carry malaria. The city was not re-discovered until 1752. Lear ended his letter:

A plaster cast of one of the victims of the eruption of AD 79

> To describe these monstrous yet exquisitely beautiful buildings, would be impossible: they are of the simplest, earliest of architecture, and all I can say is that they leave stronger impressions on the mind than anything I ever saw.[26]

Dr Pippo della Vecchia said the buildings' design and build was a greater human achievement than the landing on the moon. Lear added to his next letter to sister

Ann that Paestum, together with Pompeii, was 'alone worth a journey from England'.

It is easy to speculate about Lear's admiration of Paestum. One of his closest friends was Thomas George Baring, 1st Earl of Northbrook (1826–1904). Edward Lear wrote to Chichester Fortescue, who had introduced them, 'He is an extremely luminous and amiable brick and I like him very much.'[27] Thomas Baring became First Lord of the Admiralty in 1880 and before that was Viceroy of India, 1872–76. He lived at Stratton Park, next door to the Grange, near Alresford, Hampshire, which had been bought by Henry Drummond, the brother of Robert Drummond of Cadland. The estate was inherited by his grandson, another Henry, after the early death of his father. At the age of nineteen, he commissioned William Wilkins to build a house of Greek majesty and grandeur in 1804. Young Henry had been taught at Harrow by Dr Drury, the great Greek scholar and family friend, who, as Under Master, had also taught Lord Elgin, imbuing these two young men with a passion for classical Greece. C R Cockerell, who would add to the Grange some years later, wrote 'There is nothing like it on this side of Arcadia.' Paestum inspired Lear, as the Temple of Theseus had inspired Wilkins. Henry sold the Grange in 1817 to the Ashburton Barings.

Paestum – the Temple of Poseidon

One of his drawings of Paestum was selected by Lear to illustrate the poems of Alfred, Lord Tennyson. He started to collect the drawings for the book as early as October 1852, and it groaned on and on after difficulty after difficulty caused by his failing eyesight and technical problems in their reproduction. Lear had hoped that this work would rank with Turner's *Liber Studiorum*.

Northington Grange, Alresford, Hampshire

Also I go on irregularly at the [Alfred Tennyson] illustrations – vainly hitherto seeking a method of doing them by which I can eventually multiply my two hundred designs by photograph or autograph, or sneezigraph or any other graph. In addition to all this, I am at present frequently occupied in cutting, measuring, squaring, and mounting on coloured paper, all the sketches I did this autumn – all very bad though correct and not uninteresting … There, my chicken! don't go for to say I ain't industrious at 72![28]

Lear passed away before his magnum opus was completed. After he died, a selection of his drawings were published in *The Poems of Alfred, Lord Tennyson*, produced by Boussod, Valadon & Co., London, 1889. Only a hundred proof copies were printed, each one signed by Lord Tennyson.

Our seaborne Lear expedition was coming to an end. *Gang Warily* had reached her final objective – the great ruins of Paestum – in 1999. *Gang Warily* had covered some two thousand miles from Queen Victoria's house at Osborne to Salerno by canal, river and sea, with hardly a scratch. The 'paper plan' for 2000 was to sail south to Sicily, perhaps circumnavigating the island. However, in the spring, my nephew Maurice Hochschild, who had been a member of the crew on and off for twenty-five years, indicated that he would like to be the next owner of *Gang Warily*. With a young family, Maurice was keen to have her back in Solent waters, near his cottage at Ashlett Creek, on the Southampton Water.

Gang Warily spent the winter of 1999/2000 in Salerno. Her berth in the marina of the Circolo Canottiere Irno was comfortable and kind and, more importantly, under the eye of Antonio and Raffaela Scocozza. The yard at Cantieri Sorente

Salerno at night

had been responsible for the yacht's refit. They had done a good job and with the assistance of Benjamin, one of the yacht club team on the jetty, she was looking bright and scrubbed. The sun reflected off the water onto the hull, flickering like a broken movie. Someone said that Francesco, the yard manager, was like a *tortolla*, a top you spin. He buzzed and then was off to buzz again, in his shipyard one minute and then off to his van the next.

I have always thought it a wise plan to spend three or four days in port, perhaps living in the town, while the final refit and tidy-up takes place. It wasn't really necessary for that reason at Salerno. However, it was just as well, as when we were unloading our luggage from the local bus in Naples I was pickpocketed and lost a number of credit cards. One of the bustling 'helpers' with our luggage must have been an expert thief, for I felt nothing and my belt loop had not been cut. There was no sign of the chain that I normally attach to my wallet.

An old soldier spotted our distress and said angrily, his medal ribbon dancing on his chest as he gave vent to his feelings, 'such an outrage would not have happened in the time of *Il Duce*.' He gave further emphasis with his stick and led us to the police station, where he gave a similar lecture to the gilded police officer, who stood up and saluted!

I managed to cancel the cards within twenty minutes of the theft, but the thieves had moved smartly and made electronic purchases of up to two thousand pounds before the card was cancelled. The card company accepted the loss.

The misfortune was soon behind us and we could enjoy Salerno. Salernum is said to hark back to 97 BC, if not three hundred years before that. It became one of the most important Roman colonies in southern Italy. Robert Guiscard built churches and restored the fortifications in the eleventh century. He also gave

Salernum the oldest medical institution in western Europe, the Scuola Medica Salernitana, which gained remarkable ascendancy in the twelfth century under, interestingly, 'the strict guidance of the body of Lay Doctors'. Overlooking the town is a large illuminated cross, and just below that, to the south, is the Forte La Carnale, constructed about 1569. This was part of the Spanish Empire in the eighteenth century and no stranger to plague or earthquake. Giuseppe Bonaparte (brother of Napoleon) took the throne in 1806. On 6 September 1860, the town went wild in a great celebration in honour of Giuseppe Garibaldi.

Some remember Salerno as a name for the strategic landing point for the Anglo-American Allied Forces, starting in September 1943. For a year, Salerno was the seat of the Badoglio government. The centre of the city is a maze of small streets, crisscrossed by washing lines, faced with shops, with apartments above. Our stay was made memorable by Antonio and Raffaela Scocozza and Mauro and Theresa Scarlato. Lear remembers 'the bustling and noisy Salerno at night' in 1847. Now it is certainly a lively place and deserves the nickname of the 'City of Socrates'.

23
The call of the Sirens

Our new plan was to leave Salerno and make our way back to Naples, looking at all the places we had missed, and some we had not, the previous year. You could spend a lifetime in the Bay of Naples, around the islands and along the Amalfi coast.

Gang Warily left Salerno on Wednesday 31 May 2000. Capo d'Orso was soon abeam to starboard. We entered Amalfi some two hours after leaving Salerno. Amalfi shone in the afternoon sun, the buildings cascading down the rocks as if piled one upon the other by a child. Signor Esposito, the berthing master, confirmed our place, which we had captured on the mobile telephone. VHF is of doubtful use in these parts, as it is seldom answered. A telephone call could always be a girlfriend. The berthing master, in blue shorts, seemed everywhere, hauling on our bowline so that Gilly could pick it up while I threw him a warp from the stern. We were soon secured and our helper was off to assist another. The

Signor Esposito

There was an Old Man of Vesuvius, who studied the works of Vitruvius;
When the flames burnt his book, to drinking he took,
That Morbid Old Man of Vesuvius.

The author cooling his heels at Amalfi.
Photo: Gilly Drummond

granite wall was decorated with his pots and plants. It was difficult to see when he had time to water them or to grow his glorious lemons. We again wandered into the town, past a beach full of boats, many of wood, being repaired, caulked and painted. Every other place seemed to be a restaurant. Italy seems to run on food and yet the populace is not fat. It must be the olive oil.

Amalfi acted as a magnet to poets. Byron, Shelley and Keats found it a source of inspiration. Longfellow wrote:

> Cross of crimson on the breast?
> Where the pomp of camp and court?
> Where the pilgrims with their prayers?
> Where the merchants with their wares,
> And their gallant brigantines sailing safely into port,
> Chased by corsair Algerines.

Above Amalfi clings the little town of Ravello, which Richard Wagner's wife Cosima described as 'beautiful beyond words'. Wagner used the medieval villa garden of Rufolo as the scenery for the Magic Garden in the second act of *Parsifal*. My nephew Maurice arrived during our wanderings, as if out of the set.

On our return to the yacht, a charter boat had arrived next door and the crew was in party mood. Song continued into the night, until the wind piped and drowned their notes, with some gusts reaching nearly 40 knots. That measure of strength, Signor Esposito explained next morning, matched the number of litres of alcohol taken on board during the day and night. Victims of excess were to be seen crumpled on the quay, in the cockpit akimbo, in the upturned rubber dinghy on the foredeck. The ringleader, a ginger-bearded and moustachioed man in a black T-shirt with a red devil design, came to life and staggered across the plank passerelle, clutching a can of beer, on the dot of eight o'clock, as I was raising the ensign. I would like to think they were celebrating Amalfi's claim to have discovered the compass, or perhaps the Basilica of the Crucifix, founded in the ninth century, but I rather think their boat was a permanent shrine to Bacchus and the god's acolytes her crew.

Towers at Positano

Gang Warily left Amalfi at 16.00, making westward along the magnificent coast of sheer rock that plunges into the foam at its base. We had arranged to pick up a buoy off Positano through contacting the harbourmaster, Signor Lucibello. The telephone was in a box on the beach. For €33 we secured a mooring and the services of a boat and a boatman beyond midnight.

Positano climbs up from the shore and then seems to lose heart, overpowered by the mountains, a mixture of bare rock and greenery. Thirteenth-century round, and seventeenth-century square watch towers guard the shore at each end of the town.

One of the principal purposes of our return was to explore the Galli or 'Rooster' islands that we passed on the way from Capri to Amalfi. Edward Lear sketched these on 12 June 1844. I thought Lear had perched on a headland on the mainland, but as we cruised gingerly through the rock islets, it was clear the artist must have sat on the larger island, Galli Lungo, and that was where he put his cartoon of *A Siren a-Singing to the Argo*. He also sketched *A Blind Doge a-Bathing*. People were doing just that from small boats. We were able to position ourselves exactly on Lear's line and the blue in the distance was the distinctive Faraglioni islands off the southeast point of Capri. These are visible in Lear's drawing.

The 'J' Class *Candida*

Henry Swinburne (1743–1803) had been to the Galli islands, as he records in his *Travels in the Two Sicilies*, published in 1785. He said the islands had been uncultivated and uninhabited since the old hermit San Antonio died.

Another reminder of the past slipped by – *Candida*, altered to rate as a 'J' Class – making east under power. She, too, escaped the call of the Sirens – as did we, passing by under the wheeling herring gulls. The less romantic believe the ancient gull was an inspiration for the Sirens and their voices, they being half woman, half bird.

A little before 14.30, *Gang Warily* rounded Punta Campanella, leaving mainland Italy to starboard. We were heading northeast for Sorrento, where we were to pick up Maurice's wife Jessica. After anchoring for a while outside the harbour, we were invited to secure stern-on to the harbourmaster's finger pier. As we lingered, I minutely examined the cliffs, with hotels above and the port below. I had a picture by the artist E W Cooke (1811–80) labelled 'Amalfi', but it was clearly Sorrento. The main building in the picture is the Casa del Tasso, now the Albergo Tramontano, a smart hotel. Torquato Tasso (1544–95) was a celebrated Italian poet. His house and the hotel were erected on the ruins of the home of Agrippa Postumus, the son of the Emperor Augustus. You could hardly have a more historic foundation than that. A plaque on the museum in the town records the distinguished people who spent time in Positano – Henry Swinburne, 1757; Byron, 1813; Shelley, 1819; J Fenimore Cooper, 1829; Sir Walter Scott, 1831; Charles Dickens, 1845; Harriet Beecher Stowe, 1867–89; Longfellow, 1869; Wagner, 1876; Tolstoy, 1898.

On 4 June we made for Capri again. We entered the harbour just after 5.00. This time the Harbour Director, Signor Amado Ferrino, requested we berth in the private harbour and gave us a prime spot. He came over to shake hands, a seal of welcome.

Staring out through the yachts and over the sea wall, there were crisscrossing ferries, cruise ships, yachts and all sorts of small boats. You could easily believe Capri was the centre of the universe and the spot on earth where everybody wanted to go. Sir Compton Mackenzie and Graham Greene owned the same house after each other. Greene's main haunts were the Gran Caffe in the Piazetta and Gemma's Restaurant on the passage off the Piazetta. You will remember how Graham Greene nearly gave up the idea of being an author because he was wrongly diagnosed with epilepsy. Compton Mackenzie wrote two books here, *Vestal Fire* and *Extraordinary Women*, both tales of wild goings-on on the island, which led to him being banned.

We enjoyed a further two days in Capri and on 6 June left the harbour, making north towards Naples, with all the yachts and ferries seemingly having the same idea. We were on the alert, remembering the little ditty:

Gang Warily in the Bay of Naples.
Painting by Robert King RI RSMI.
Private collection

Here lies the body of Anderson Gray,
Who died protecting his right of way,
He was right, dead right, as he sailed along,
But just as dead as if he were wrong.

Vesuvius commanded the scene as *Gang Warily* sailed north for Naples. The heat haze softened the outline of the volcano. There was no hint of smoke from the top, yet later, in photographs, I thought I could make out a faint shadow.

In the nineteenth and early twentieth centuries, ship painters were encouraged by proud owners to paint their ships and yachts with Vesuvius in the background, for example, the Chevalier Eduardo de Martino, MVO. I was lucky to persuade Robert King, RI, RSMA, to record *Gang Warily* against this famous and traditional backdrop.

With the aid of the mobile telephone, our plan had developed. We booked a berth in the Marina Vigliena, where *Gang Warily* was to be lifted out by the yard – Cantieri Pardopene, under the eye of the yard manager, Signor Giuseppe. The yard had been found with the help of the indefatigable Paulo Luise, the agent. *Gang Warily*'s mast was to be removed and a cradle built so she could be shipped to the UK through the good offices of Dr Captain Nicola De Cesare SA in Salerno. As it turned out, *Gang Warily* was transported to Salerno by road and put on the MV *Gran Bretagna* for Southampton, the voyage taking just over week. The ship sailed between Salerno and Southampton every ten days or so. The plan went like clockwork and *Gang Warily* was soon in the hands of her new owner at Bucklers Hard on the Beaulieu River, without so much as a bruise.

A new chapter in the search for Edward Lear was about to begin.

PART VI

The Kingdom of Naples

Castel del Monte

24
A Sicilian view

With *Gang Warily* dismasted, lifted out, cradled and taken to Salerno to be shipped to Southampton, we had a little time to spare. Gilly and I were determined to make a quick dash to Palermo by fast ferry from Naples to search for the place where Lear had made his sketch for a small oil of the town that my grandfather had purchased. On a faded label on the back of the frame, Lear had penned a legend, 'Palermo, painted by me, Edward Lear, 1872 from drawings made on the spot in 1847, purchased by Edgar A Drummond, Esq, Cadland – Southampton'.

A scribbled postscript to a letter of 26 August 1872, written from Oxford, asks Edgar, 'Has the Palermo come yet?' Lear had been staying at Cadland and the real purpose of the letter was a thank you.

The artist had first visited Sicily with two of his pupils, Leopold Acland, the son of Sir Thomas, and another, the nephew of Stamford Raffles. We know from

There was an Old Person of Gretna, who rushed down the crater of Etna ;
When they said, " Is it hot ?" he replied, " No, it's not !"
That mendacious Old Person of Gretna.

a letter that Lear wrote to the 13th Earl of Derby on 5 June 1842 that he liked Palermo: 'Palermo I think pleased me more than any other city I was ever in.'[1] He could not resist comparing Naples unfavourably with Palermo. With such a recommendation, Gilly and I were determined to visit the place too.

We were told by the ticket office that the Sicilian jet would take six hours. We arrived in the port city at 11.30 in the evening, the Palermo waterside bright with lights. Edward Lear made almost the same trip on his second visit to Sicily, when he caught the steamer from Naples to Palermo early in May 1847. On that occasion, Lear's companion was John Proby (1823–58) a young would-be painter whom he had met in Rome. The two made the best of their stay and were drawn to the Temple of Hera at Segesta and many more at Agrigento. They saw the quarries at Syracuse and, with difficulty, climbed Mount Etna before returning to Palermo. On their return, Lear and Proby decided to celebrate their new-found favourite town with a number of sketches, one of which was turned into Edgar's oil.

Our first task, once we had the keys of our hire car, was to discover Santa Maria di Gesù, the convent from near where we suspected Edward Lear had sketched the picture of Palermo and the brooding Monte Pellegrino.

Gilly and I were advised to take the coast road and then to head south along the Via Diaz. A little map of the one-way square was drawn and absorbed – but we lost our way. Garages and pedestrians were consulted and all gave good-humoured and, no doubt, correct instructions, but we were lost again. However, in the darkest corner, there is always a glimmer of light, and we eventually found the right road and climbed to the convent. We passed through the small settlement of Castello di Maridolce.

Just past the convent, which looked new and perhaps had been rebuilt beyond the old cemetery, the road rose steeply. The surface had been roughly concreted. A cross, recently erected and perhaps the same vintage as the new convent, blocked the road, which up to that point had been lined with old stone walls. To the left was a rubbish dump that we navigated past on foot, down a steep bank. This led to a narrow track between fences. Squeezed in between was a concrete irrigation channel, now almost dry. We walked along it, paddling at times. I was looking at the view and at a photocopy of Lear's picture. This lack of attention allowed me to walk into the frame of a sluice and crash headlong into the channel, damaging one shin and grazing my arm. I was lucky not to break a leg and smash my new camera.

I was trying to close the gap between Monte Pellegrino, 600 metres, and Monte Castellacio, 890 metres. I nearly made it when the channel became a suspended plastic pipe. We continued our scramble past carob, olive, orange trees, loquat, prickly pears and aloe until we reached what we supposed to be Lear's vantage point. A heat haze softened the view of Monte Pellegrino.

There was time to go south to Agrigento on the south coast of Sicily, the one-time Greek city of Akragas. Lear had drawn the Temple of Concord, best preserved

Monte Pellegrino. Oil painting by Edward Lear from sketch of 1847, finished 1872
Private collection

of the Doric temples in Sicily. Lear sketched the temple and did a cartoon of himself and Proby in front of this wonderfully preserved building. The slight angle, showing the columns on the edge of the gorge, made it easy to discover where the two had sat and this was confirmed by the Temple of Juno or Hera Lacinia behind. The building casts a spell over those that have the privilege of seeing it. Fossils of scallop and oyster are to be found in the stone round about.

Lear had a feeling for temples. It was the buildings rather than the ancient religion. His religious views gradually developed, judging from his letters. He wrote to Lady Waldegrave on 15 March 1863, arguing that:

> A broader creed, – a better form of worship – the cessation of nonsense and the curses – and the recognition of a new state of matters brought about by centuries, science, destiny or what not – will assuredly be demanded and come to pass whether bishops and priests welcome the changes or resist them.[2]

Lear's wanderings later in life seem to confirm his disquiet about religion and the quarrels between faiths. Writing to Edgar Drummond from the Hotel Damascus in Jerusalem on 12 April 1867, he said of that city:

> But the city itself is as filthy and as odious as ever, and its different religious sects as opposite as ever to the real spirit of Xtianity. Forms and ceremonies, dogmas and doctrines – all held up to veneration. Charity and tolerance and brotherly love at zero. The longer I live the more I perceived the want of a prayer in our litany, – 'Oh, Lord – remove we pray thee all religion from this world, and give us righteousness and common sense instead thereof.'[3]

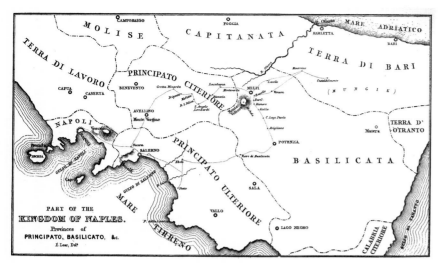

Map by Edward Lear of the provinces of Principato, Basilicato, etc, from *Journals of a Landscape Painter in Southern Calabria, etc*, 1852.
Private collection

The dash to Palermo underlined the importance of following Edward Lear into the southern landscapes of Italy, if our expedition was to be complete. The plan had been to sail south from Salerno in *Gang Warily* to Reggio on the Straits of Messina. We were determined to keep to this logical southern progression, but to add to it Edward Lear's two forays inland, which he describes in his book, *Journals of a Landscape Painter in Southern Calabria, Etc.* The book tells of two expeditions undertaken by Edward Lear and John Proby in 1847. The two journeys were separate, though bound into one volume. Part 1 was the *Journals of a Landscape Painter in Calabri*a; Part 2 was the *Journals of a Landscape Painter in the Kingdom of Naples*.[4]

As we were progressing south, it was logical we should look at the latter journey first, which we did in 2004, and then go on to Calabria in 2005.

In the preface to the joint volumes, Lear differentiates between travel in the northern province and that in the south, in Calabria. He writes:

> The mode of travel which I and my fellow-wanderer adopted while these journals were written was the simplest, as well as the cheapest – we performed the whole tour on foot; except that in Basilicata some of the high roads were well got over in a carriage. In Calabria, a horse to carry our small amount of baggage, and a guide, cost us altogether six carlini daily, no very heavy expenditure; but as there are no inns in that province except on the coach road, which skirts the western coast, the traveller depends entirely on introductions to some family in each town he visits.

Map by Edward Lear of the province of Calabria Ulteriore Prima, from *Journals of a Landscape Painter in Southern Calabria, etc*, 1852.
Private collection

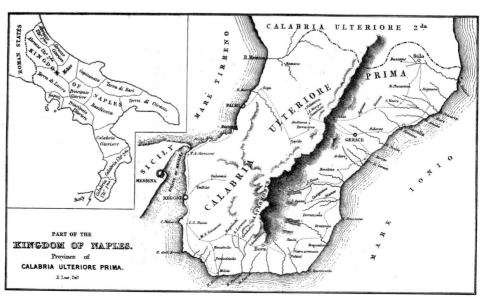

25
Terra incognita

Gilly and I arrived back in Naples on Sunday 26 September 2004. This time, as we were going inland, we travelled by car. Lear is now seen as one of the original green tourists in this part of Italy and so we should have followed his route on foot, perhaps Gilly carrying my paintbrushes, in the manner of Giorgio. We did arrive during the right season of the year, for Lear started this part of his journey on 11 September 1847, having left Reggio in Calabria for Naples on 5 September. Lear and Proby had then travelled by train from Nocera and by carriage to Avellino. We drove from the airport along the motorway to the same place, now Nocera Inferiore, where we turned off, through its twin Nocera Superiore to Montoro, heading in Lear's footsteps to Avellino – or so we thought, but somewhere we took a wrong turning and managed to follow a road up into the hills, ending in a rough, stony track.

Avellino is now a city about the size of Southampton. Our hotel, the Viva, was having a fundamental facelift, as the front of the building had been pulled off, and an enormous hole was being dug in the volcanic grey soil to create a new front – all columns and glass. We headed for Santuario di Montevergine. The monastery

There was an Old Man of Apulia, whose conduct was very peculiar;
He fed twenty sons upon nothing but buns,
That whimsical Man of Apulia.

is high up in the clouds at 1,428 metres. The road corkscrews upward. Lear went up by the old path from the village of Spedaletto, which in turn was a very steep zigzag. The long steps of that path can be seen, as the new road cuts across the old stone paving.

We could now compare Lear's drawing with the sanctuary of today. Edward Lear described the monastery in his journal:

> This celebrated sanctuary, built on the site of a temple of Cybele, as several inscriptions and remains attest, was founded about 1100 AD, and on account of it possessing a particularly miraculous image of the Virgin Mary (not to speak of the bones of Shadrach, Meshach, and Abednego!) its sanctity is great.

As Lear says, great numbers of pilgrims wandered here in his day. We, too, found the place crowded, car-park attendants in blue and red marshalling us for two euro. Many now come by funicular from Mercogliano.

In a note, Lear records:

> It is said that four hundred pilgrims died here in 1611 – some of them having profanely brought up some meat for luncheon. The peasants say that eating meat near the sanctuary will bring on a thunderstorm and hurricane at any time.

Santa Maria di Monte Vergine.
Lithograph by Edward Lear, from
*Journals of a Landscape Painter
in Southern Calabria, etc*, 1852.
Private collection

We passed through stalls selling all sorts of local produce, amongst which I saw locally killed meat. I thought to myself, some people never learn!

Lear thought the monastery had 'Little in itself which could be called interesting except for the great view it enjoys from its isolated and elevated position that constitutes (at least to a landscape painter) its chief charm.' Our two artists remained at Avellino until 15 September, walking and sketching. He thought the town rather busy. 'Here be high roads,' he wrote, 'and rattling carriages, shouting drivers, and crowded markets, and a dining room with a smart waiter.'

Gilly and I followed them on Monday 27 September 2004 to Grottaminarda. We tried to use Lear's route (Route 7), they in a vetturino and we in a Ford Focus.

We were lost again but managed to gaze at the hilltop town of Montefusco, which Lear noticed on 'a high hill beyond' but did not visit. We did, and were enchanted by the place with its commanding views and beautifully restored buildings. A nunnery painted in Maria Theresa yellow with a carved inscription, S. Cat 1818 DA SIEno, over the door caught our attention. The town was quiet but lived-in. The land far below was a mosaic of vineyards, small fields and the occasional olive grove.

The next towns that Lear wandered through, and we shot by, were Pratola Serra and Prata. The former had a main street with one or two fine buildings, but Prata had been swamped in acres of large industrial plants that would have destroyed anything Lear might have seen.

On reaching Grottaminarda, Lear and Proby dismissed their vetturino 'and dined on the universal and useful omelet and macaroni.'

Our hotel in the town, Da Maddalena, was well equipped and spotlessly clean, but the bed was very hard. I had the impression the floor would have had more give. I am told some people like it this way.

We were bound for Frigento, as were our 'leaders'. Lear was not impressed by the paintability of the town:

> Frigento was immediately before our eyes, standing on a very ugly clay hill, and although the grandeur of the shifting clouds, storm, and a rainbow did their best to illumine and set off the aspect of the land, yet we were obliged to confess that our journey lay over a most wearily monotonous country. Nor, on arriving at the foot of the bare hill of Frigento, had we any wish to make acquaintance with Don January Red Flame for the sake of his native place; and it was not until we peeped into a very unsatisfactory osteria at the high-road-side, that we reluctantly resolved to ascend the dismal and ugly cone before us.

The hill must have been bare then, the crops removed and any trees cut at an early age. The rains had probably not set in, so greenery was sparse. Today it was difficult, at this season, to view the town from below because of the flourishing vegetation and youngish trees.

We drove up the bends to the town on its 'clay hill' and we were soon in the square below the municipal buildings. These seemed to have been restored, and while the civic buildings had a 1960s look, all around were pretty town houses with their old marbled door surrounds marked with dates and escutcheons of their owners. The place was a delight.

Armed with Lear's book and the Italian edition,[5] we made for the municipal building. After being passed from one gentleman to another, we ended up with one in a blue suit and a lady who seemed keen to help. Our quest was the well-to-do house where Lear and John Proby had sought shelter for the night of 16 September 1847. Lear had translated the owner's name, Don Gennaro Fiammarossa, as 'Don January Red Flame'. He described his house as 'the only large one in town'. He went on to say:

> Everything in his mansion betokened wealth, and we contemplated with pleasure the comfortable hall with crockery and barrels, and all kinds of neatness and luxury; and until Don Gennaro came, we were pressed to take a glass of wine by the steward and his very nice looking wife.

The kind official looked at his card index for the family and then the census of that time. There were no Fiammarossas and never had been. However, there were, then and now, Flammias and they had their achievement above the door with a representation of a flame and the motto 'Alta Petit Flamma'. The house is in the Via San Giovanni. He gave us a note and asked a young man to show us the way.

'One last thing,' Gilly said in Italian, 'I wonder whether you can say where this place is?' – showing him our yellow folder in which I had placed a photo of a picture I had secured at Christie's. The tinted sepia drawing showed a castle with a high tower above a river. He looked up and met her eyes and without hesitation said, 'Rocca San Felice'. I explained the picture was by Edward Lear. Our young guide soon stood in front of a grand, small house and indicated a doorway with the 'Flame' above.

Sadly, Lear and Proby did not succeed in staying with the Flammias:

> He was expecting an aunt, four cousins (nay, five), three old friends, and four priests who were to pass through Frigento on their way to a neighbouring town; they might come and they might not, but he dared not fill his house.

He suggested a 'capital' inn at Frigento, which turned out to be the very one that Lear had thought 'so palpably disgusting'. The new muleteer found part of the place acceptable and cooked them some poached eggs on a stove in a room, half of which was used as a stable. Finally, they slept well on large heaps of grain.

The year 1847 was an unsettled time in this part of Italy. Lear was worried about the atmosphere of unrest. There had been a number of revolts by the *Carbonari* patriots, who fought the Austrian occupation and were crushed by them. The Young Italy movement had been founded in 1831 by Giuseppe Mazzini. The period was known as the *Risorgimento* and led to the 'First War of Independence' against Austria, led by Charles Albert of Savoy, King of Sardinia. Charles Albert seemed to have been succeeding, but the Austrians counterattacked. In 1849 Charles Albert abdicated in favour of his son Victor Emmanuel II, who appointed Camillo Cavour as his minister. The unrest may have made people less hospitable to those who came with letters of introduction. It was also unsettling to a man like Lear, who wandered about armed only with brushes and needed peace to practise his art.

We followed Lear's footsteps to the next place of his interest, which he called 'Mofette', or 'skunk'. In a hollow basin near Terme di San Teodoro, there was a black pool smelling faintly of sulphur. Lear wrote:

> The water, if water it be, is as black as ink, and in appearance thick, bubbling and boiling up from a hundred springs which wrinkle on its disastrous looking surface.

Most of the pond we spied was covered with reeds and surrounded by willow trees. A faint hum from a pumphouse indicated that water may still be being extracted. We soon arrived at the Terme di San Teodoro, which is now dominated by an enormous pink building for guests to take the waters for the benefit of their health.

Lear and Proby made their way southeast to Sant' Angelo dei Lombardi. They had passed our next quest, Rocca San Felice. Earthquakes and weather have slightly altered the profile, but part of the tower was still sticking up on its mound. Frigento's town clerk was absolutely right. The river is now a trickle, probably because much of it is extracted by quarries, agriculture and the demands of a growing population. Lear admired the place but suffered a disappointment.

Rocca San Felice. Ink and wash sketch by Edward Lear, 1847. *Private collection*

> In an hour or two we reached Rocca San Felice and passed through it. Around this little town, in itself picturesque, there seems to lie the only pretty scenery we had observed since we left Avellino; but a coming storm prevented our lingering to sketch even this single bit of character.

Rocca San Felice in 2004

We now have the evidence that at least Lear's pencil was hard at work. He may have finished the scene, as was his way, later.

Lear considered the hill town of Sant' Angelo dei Lombardi 'one of those places (and in Italy there are but few such) having no goodly aspect or form in themselves, and placed so as to command a wide panorama below, but no foreground, tree, or rock to set off against its abundant extant'. Such were Lear's requirements for a good picture.

In our motor, we made northeast on Lear's road, through Bisaccia to Lacedonia. Lear and Proby had lunched at Bisaccia and changed a donkey for two mules at Lacedonia, reaching Melfi and the Castle of Prince Doria. Gilly and I stayed the night below Lacedonia in the Hotel Val Tuscano, run by a Ukrainian helped by a French chef. The highlands of Bisaccia were being ploughed for wheat, helped by the need for flour for their particular bread. As the ground rose, wind farms appeared, along with new metal silos for the grain. Wind and wheat seemed the new order.

The artists had problems with another sort of power – a horse they had been promised:

> 'Is the horse coming?' said we to the surrounding idlers. 'Yes, it's on the way; it will be here in half a minute.' A quarter of an hour passes – half an hour – three quarters, and still no horse. 'Where is the horse?' – 'Ah, Signori, they are saddling it.'

Edward Lear and John Proby rushed to the stable and found that the fabulous quadruped was calmly lying down. The need was remedied by a man with two mules who was bribed to go to Melfi. They reached the town just before sunset on 17 September 1847.

In 2004, we found our way up to the great castle of Melfi, on a broad road, and parked in the entrance. The main rooms are now without the grand furniture of Lear's day and given over to an archaeological display of singular merit of Bronze Age, Roman and medieval artefacts, some from the Etruscan period. There was a stunning pottery mug in the shape of a horse's head and, perhaps of greater note, bronze helmets with attachments for plumes. Lear remembers:

> There is a draw bridge, and sullen gates, and dismal courtyards, and massive towers, and seneschals with keys and fierce dogs, – all the requisites of a feudal fortress of romance.

A bronze helmet and drinking vessel, in the museum at Melfi.
Photos: Maldwin Drummond

The castle was founded in 1043 by Robert Guiscard, on a precipice at the edge of the city, its site the cradle of an extinct volcano.

Our travellers spent four days at the castle in great comfort. Just as they were leaving on 21 September Lear pondered:

> But what shall we do when we go out once more into the wide world and its dirty osterias? – After these princely subtleties of luxury, this buttered toast and caffé for breakfast, these comfortable rooms and merry society? The ease and grandeur of the Palazzo Doria in Melfi will have spoilt us, methinks, for rough travelling.

Melfi. Lithograph by Edward Lear, from *Journals of a Landscape Painter in Southern Calabria, etc*, 1852. *Private collection*

Gilly and I stayed in the Station Hotel.

The castle's comforts did not last long, for Melfi was shaken by earthquakes. The steward, Signor Vittorio Manassei, wrote to Lear afterwards in a letter dated 27 March 1852 that the Castle of Melfi had been ruined by an earthquake on 14 August 1851, a fifth of it thrown down, including the Great Gallery and the rooms Lear and Proby had occupied. There were further tremors in 1930. The castle was given to the nation by Prince Andrea Doria Pamphilj and restored between 1965 and 1969. Even that was not the end, for an earthquake in 1980 did general damage to the exterior.

On leaving Melfi, Lear and Proby were accompanied by Don Sebastiano, who looked like Dr Samuel Johnson in a tight blue jacket and trousers. Apparently he had been in the service of the king and was very pompous. 'Il Fattore' was horrified when Lear and Proby decided to walk. He accepted the horses were no good, but thought Lear's explanation that Englishmen 'occasionally walk as a matter of choice' was 'poetical'.

We followed the artists through Lavello on minor roads to Minervino Murge. They enjoyed the town because of its noble prospect northward and for the 'bustle and animation – where well paved streets, good houses and strings of laden mules, proclaim an advance in commercial civilization.'

We liked the attractive bungalows with arched doorways before we climbed

A hitching ring at Minervino

into the ancient town. The castle, which, like Melfi, had been turned into an archaeological museum, is looked after by two girls who were interested in our Lear quest and keen to photocopy the Minervino part of Lear's book.

As we walked back from the castle, most of the shops were closed – from 12 until 4 or 5. A man politely invited us into his restaurant. Determined to complete our walk, we climbed the main street, but said we would be back. Edward Lear mentioned that he had

> encountered in the street Don Vincenzino Todeschi, who on reading a letter of introduction, given to us for him by Signor Manassei, seemed to consider our dwelling with him as a matter of course, and shaking hands with us heartily, begged us to go to his house and use it as our own.

Remembering our invitation, we returned to No. 24 Corso de Gasperi, the Ristorante Pizzeria l'Antico Palazzo, and were greeted by Nicola Balducci, who cooked us lunch. Gilly asked if he knew of the Todeschi family. The restaurant owner, now our friend, replied that they lived ten metres away! He would show us after lunch. What a piece of luck.

We went next door, and there on the bell pushes were the names of the very same family. There were five of them, and each had a flat. Nicola Balducci wanted to introduce us to the Todeschis (now spelt Tedeschi), perhaps all five, and pressed a bell or two, but the owners were still at lunch.

On leaving Minervino, John Proby went north to Canosa di Puglia with Don Sebastiano, while Edward Lear made east for Castel del Monte. Lear thought this 'the dullest possible country, – elevated stony plains – weariest of barren

Castel del Monte

undulations stretching in unbroken ugliness towards Altamura and Gravina.' The ploughed earth he remarked on is still there, but the farm house with its fountain has gone. The piped water and irrigation have seen to that.

The castle gradually unfolded itself as we approached. For Lear, on a horse, the time from first sighting until the building in all its octagonal glory was close to the eye would have taken time. In a car, it was a matter of minutes. It was less than thirty kilometres and Lear took five hours. He called it 'a great hunting palace'. The castle enabled the ruler to move from one stronghold to another for sport that could occupy his court and allow the owner time for affairs of state.

This great white stronghold was built in the thirteenth century by Frederick II (1194–1250) as part of a control mechanism, provided by his network of castles. The octagonal outside is repeated in a smaller form within the building, leaving

Castel del Monte. Lithograph by
Edward Lear, from *Journals of a
Landscape Painter in Southern
Calabria, etc*, 1852.
Private collection

an eight-sided court inside, containing all the accommodation between the two walls.

Edward Lear's 'fat guardino' told of the suicide of the architect of this beautiful building. Frederick had dispatched a courtier to report on how the castle was progressing. The representative stopped at Melfi and in the house of a friend met a girl who took his eye off the ball. He never went near Castel del Monte. Eventually, summoned by the king, he denounced the architect as an impostor. The king sent for the architect and he, anticipating the worst, went upstairs and killed his wife, his family and then himself. Frederick, on hearing of this turn of events, went to see the castle for himself, taking with him the original messenger. When he saw the beauty of the place, he was outraged and dragged the messenger to the top of the highest tower and pushed him off.

The puzzle is, why did Lear sketch the side without the entrance? He was almost certainly following his rule about foreground, middle ground and background. The picture shows the foreground with the track and figures pausing, the middle ground, Castel del Monte itself, and the background, the hills beyond the plain. This, therefore, made the best view, between the sixth and seventh tower.

Lear returned to join Proby in Minervino and, after coffee, over a spirit lamp, proceeded to draw the town. They then made westward to Montemilone and on to Venosa, where the two and their companions arrived at 11 p.m. on 24 September. They were closing in on Monte Vulture, a mountain that is always in view in these parts, and held a particular fascination for Lear. Don Nicola Rapolla's rambling mansion in Venosa provided beds for the night, though their hosts were away. The wives of Don Nicola's two brothers, Peppino and Domenico, 'ladies of considerable beauty', welcomed them, followed by their husbands. 'Don Peppino dressed in the extreme of Neopolitan fashion, and Donna Maria in a riding habit and hat appeared to our amazed senses as truly wonderful and unexpected objects in this land of Horace.'

As far as Gilly and I were concerned, it was now Thursday 30 September 2004. We made for the castle, which in Lear's day had been occupied by Don Peppino and his wife.

The castle is now an archaeological museum, which we went round at some speed as we hoped we might catch the light and Lear's view of Venosa. Our first objective in the town had been accomplished earlier, and that was to find the

Venosa. Lithograph by Edward Lear, from Journals of a Landscape Painter in Southern Calabria, etc, 1852. Private collection

office of the publisher of Lear's Italian edition *Viaggio in Basilicata*. We found Edizioni Osanna Venosa in the Via Appia. When we purchased three copies, they presented us with a print of Lear's view of Venosa and told us from where it had been sketched, across the ravine. It was nearly dark as we stumbled across the stubble. We decided it would be better to return in the morning, so we headed for Rionero for the night.

Looking back on the day, I remembered we had left Melfi after breakfast, passed by Lavello, entered Minervino, where we had lunched and explored, through to Castel del Monte, tarried, back via Montemilone to Venosa, where we paused till dark, and then on to Rionero di Vulture, where we dined and slept. Lear took five days to do the same journey by horse, foot and carriage. He held that you see more if you walk, and he was right.

The sun was playing on the walls of Venosa as we looked across the ravine that Lear had pictured. The town has grown, but the castle and churches are exclamation marks in the panorama. I feel sure Lear would recognise the place. Before leaving Venosa, we followed Lear and Proby into the church of La Trinità, which Lear described as 'an extremely ancient low building with pointed arches; two large stone lions guard the door, and near it is a vestibule containing a single column, around which, according to the local popular superstition, if you go hand in hand with any person, the two circumambulants are certain to remain friends for life.' Gilly and I tried it.

Lear thought the church had been spoilt by neglect and additions. The tomb of Robert Guiscard, and Ademberta, his wife, was shamefully out of repair and the church a disgrace to Venosa. La Trinità has now been sympathetically restored. The old floor, the Roman one, can be seen below and the windowed apse is striking. Holiness radiates from the old stone walls.

We skirted the town of Rionero, leaving the town proper to the north. The search for the rich mansion of Don Pasqualuccio Catena in this modern, growing town was in vain. Lear had described how dinner had been accompanied by the presence of a 'great Barbary ape, who made convulsive flings and bounces to his chain's length, shrieking amain'.

Edward Lear and John Proby visited the monastery of San Michele del Vulture on 28 September 1847. We engaged in the same journey on Friday 1 October 2004, one hundred and fifty-seven years later. The description of our approach to the monastery is virtually the same as Lear's. I wrote in my journal:

● The road took us through vast beech woods, cool and brilliant green, where the sun's rays reach the leaves. Monte del Vulture was above, up on our right-hand side though we could not see the mountain as we were travelling below a thick leafy canopy.

The great white building appeared as the lake came into view. What a wonderful prospect. Peaceful too, if you ignored the tourist paraphernalia of restaurants, souvenir shops, cars and buses. Strangely, as we wandered, anti-clockwise round the lake on a mud path, there was an aura of quiet. Two pedalos made no noise. We found Lear's spot on the shore. The blue-green of the lake, the green of the leaves and the brilliant white of the building, provided a sight to etch the memory.

– MD's journal, Friday 1 October 2004

San Michele di Monte Voltore.
Lithograph by Edward Lear, from
*Journals of a Landscape Painter
in Southern Calabria, etc*, 1852.
Private collection

Lear was more poetic. He had a way with words, but the scene was the same.

When we had reached the western side of the hill, we entered most beautiful beech woods, which continued increasing in thickness and size as we advanced. The path through these shady forests turns inward to a deep dell or hollow, formerly the principal crater of the volcano; and soon through the branches of the tall trees we saw the sparkling Lake of Monticchio, and the monastery of San Michele reflected in its waters. A more exquisite specimen of monastic solitude cannot be imagined.

There may not have been the restaurants and souvenir shops, but the day Lear visited, 'great numbers of peasants were arriving and encamping below the tall walnut trees; forming a fair, after the usual mode of Italians at their feste.'

On the drive to Atella, we came across a scene that Lear would have easily recognised. A shepherd, mounted on a mule, herding sheep. He was accompanied by Alsatian dogs and carried a thick stick painted red. Much of the land round about was ploughed. Italy has a great need for *grano duro* wheat for pasta, so it is not only the subsidy that speeds the plough.

Atella is a sprawling, undistinguished town, despite its pretty name. Thirteen kilometres to the southeast, Castel Lagopesole sits full-square on top of its own personal hill. The castle owes its beginnings to Byzantine times. When the Normans conquered Acerenza and expelled the Greeks in 1061, this set in place the steady growth of the defences, including, most probably, Lagopesole. Our pair of artists arranged a visit to the castle, the last of Prince Doria Pamphilj's possessions in this part of Italy. The castle was a favourite of Frederick II and used as a hunting lodge. Lear found that this 'ancient place has no pretensions to beauty though from a draughtsman's point of view it was more picturesque, at a considerable distance than drawn close to.' However, he liked the aspect from the south, 'whence it combines as part of the landscape, within the plain and Monte Voltori beyond'. Signor Manassei, Prince Doria's agent, was staying in the castle, which Lear described as 'modernised and comfortable'. In the evening, Lear admitted, 'There was the inevitable charm which eventide in Italy brings even to the least promising scenery; the

Monte Vulture (Voltore)

deep purple Monte Voltore, its long lines blending with the plain, across which the last crimson lights were flickering; the dark copse-wood around; the smoke rising from the hamlet of Filipopoli; the goats and flocks wandering in the valley-common below, – these, joined to somewhat of the wild-world solitude in the scene, through a sentiment of beauty even over Castel del Lagopesole.' Lear could certainly compose a good picture with words.

We dropped down to Potenza, built again on a hill, which is now largely obscured by the suburbs. From an artist's point of view, Lear found Potenza 'as ugly a town for form, detail and situation, as one might wish to avoid'. He was emphasising his difficulties with a pencil. Potenza today may be even more difficult to draw, particularly from the south, as the roads press upon the town, but the way the buildings climb the hill and cluster at the top is attractive to the eye.

Lear did not stay there anyway, but went on to Vietri di Potenza, which he refers to as Di Basilicata, which 'left a strong impression of beauty on our minds and full of really fine scenery and material for good landscape'. This continued until they reached Eboli, from where the blue Gulf of Salerno was visible. On 4 October 1847 they arrived at Paestum, which we had visited from *Gang Warily* in 2000. From there, John Proby and Edward Lear went to 'bustling and noisy Salerno by night and then on to the beautiful Corpo di Cava, on to Nocera, and then by rail from Pompeii to Parthenope.' Parthenope, the Siren, gave her name to the city of Naples and from 1799 the French ruled. The Parthenopaean Republic was instituted, followed by a kingdom under Joseph (Giuseppe) Bonaparte. All this came to an end in 1860 with the arrival of Garibaldi, who ended the rule of the Bourbons in Sicily and southern Italy.

Edward Lear summed up the second part of his expedition to southern Italy, from 11 September to 4 October 1847, in a letter to Chichester Fortescue on 16 October:

> Avallino is certainly exquisite, and so is Mte. Vergine when not in a fog, – But of Apulia we saw little, only from hills apart, because why? the atmosphere was pisonous in Septbr [*sic*]. Nevertheless Proby went on to Cannae, and I believe found one of Annibals shoes or spurs, – also a pinchbeck snuffbox with a Bramah lock belonging to a Roman genl. – I rather chose to go see Castel del Monte, a strange record of old F Barbarosa and which well paid no end of disgust in getting at it. We saw the tree Horace slept under at Mte. Volture, and were altogether much edified by the classicalities of Basilicata.[6]

They both reached Rome on 14 October 1847 and there parted. John, Lord Proby, eldest son of the Earl of Carysfort, whom Lear labelled 'an excellent companion', died in 1858. The family felt he had overdone himself, having caught the Roman disease while there and straining himself following after Edward Lear.

We were less tested by our travels, and made our way to Brienza, topped by the remarkable castle, and then southwest through Polla and Sant' Arsenio. We were now in the national park of Cilento – great rolling hills with rocky slopes. We wiggled our way up to the Pass of Sentinella, crossing at 1,283 metres. Walnuts and olives grow on the lower slopes. The olive nets were out, ready for the fruit fall. A sign read 'Welcome to the Land of Wine and Olive Oil'. We could not resist going on to Paestum and one more visit to Amalfi before finishing our 2004 exploration on 4 October, the same date Lear finished his wanderings in the Kingdom of Naples.

26
Dogo; dighi, doghi, daghi, da

Cowes to Calabria had a ring about it. Lear, as explained, had come from Sicily, which we had made a dash for in 2000. Lear explored Calabria, Ulteriore Prima and then the states to the north, Principato, Basilicata, etc., all in 1847. We looked at the latter first in 2004 and then went south to Calabria in 2005.

Strangely, it is still quicker to fly to Palermo in Sicily and cross over from Messina to Reggio than any other way from the United Kingdom. Edward Lear and his companion, John Proby, went by hired boat from Messina to Reggio on 25 July 1847. Gilly and I took our hire car on Tuesday 25 October 2005 on the rail and car ferry, crossing the straits in a half hour.

Edward Lear rose early on 26 July:

> If you wish for milk at breakfast time in these parts of the world, you ought to sit in the middle of the road with a jug at early dawn, for unless you seize the critical moment of the goats passing through the town, you may wish in vain.

There was an Old Man of Messina, whose daughter was named Opsibeena;
She wore a small Wig, and rode out on a Pig,
To the perfect delight of Messina.

He was up early to try to find the best views of Reggio. The town impressed him. 'One vast garden, and doubtless one of the loveliest spots to be seen on earth.' To him, the vegetation was becoming as important as the view. He went on to describe how:

> A half-ruined castle, beautiful in colour and picturesque in form, overlooks all the long city, the wide straits and snow-topped mongibello beyond.

'Mongibello,' Lear explains in his book, is 'a Saracenic name for Mt. Etna.'

> Below the castle walls are spread wide groves of orange, lemon, citron, bergamot, and all kinds of such fruits as are called by the Italians agrumi [citrus fruits].

Reggio. Lithograph by Edward Lear, from Journals of a Landscape Painter in Southern Calabria, etc, 1852.
Private collection

Our search for Lear's view of Reggio was undertaken, on the advice of the hall porter of the Palace Hotel, by taxi. The driver, a lady with a ponytail, whisked us up the hill deftly, sometimes darting the wrong way down a conveniently

empty one-way street, when the right one was jammed with traffic. We came to a park with a good view of the city, but Lear's capture was blocked by flat-topped apartment blocks. We could not see Etna either, as the haze was too thick, though the intervening strait sparkled in the sun, ruffled by a gentle breeze.

On 19 July 1847, Lear and Proby hired a horse and a guide, Ciccio, short for Francesco. He explained that:

Our plan was to do always just as we pleased – going straight ahead or stopping to sketch, without reference to any law but our own pleasure; to all which he replied by a short sentence ending with – dógo; dighi, dóghi, dághi, dà – a collection of sounds of frequent recurrence in Calabrese lingo, and the only definite portion of that speech we could ever perfectly master.

The three of them and the horse went on to Motta San Giovanni. They had letters of introduction to Don Francesco Maropoti. A knot of neighbours gathered in their host's house most evenings to discuss what had happened during the day.

Don Francesco also explained the position and attributes of England to the rest of the society, assuring them that we had no fruit of any sort, and that all our bread came from Egypt and India; and as for our race, with a broad contempt for minute distinctions, he said in a word, you are a sort of Frenchman; it's all the same.

We followed Lear to Bagaladi, which Don Francesco had dismissed with the words 'What should there be to see in Bagaladi?' However, the three had gone there. We left the E90 at Melito and started our climb to the hills, eventually reaching Bagaladi. We rather agreed with Don Francesco Maropoti and went back on our tracks to turn left and wind our way up to San Lorenzo. There, a very large tree that we could not identify had been planted in front of the church of Santa Maria La Neve. There were certainly spectacular views of the surrounding country from the edge of the square.

The two painters and their guide spent the night at Bagaladi, making use of their letters of introduction. Lear said that 'it is always a great amusement to us to speculate on the reception we are likely to meet with from our unknown hosts on arriving at any new place.' In this case, they had reached the family Panutti, who were in bed enjoying a siesta when they arrived. Signor Panutti was the head of the rural police and he pressed them to stay. They could see San Lorenzo high up in the hills. Don Peppino Panutti had come from Livorno but had to leave because of 'a little accident; that is to say, he killed someone.'

Condofuri is across the valley from San Lorenzo and can only be reached directly by walking, which, of course, is what Lear and his party did. They wished to rest at Condofuri but they had no luck with their introductions. They lunched and rested in a hut:

It was as dark as Erebus; so in the palpable obscure I sat down on a large live pig, who slid away, to my disgust, from under me, and made a portentous squeaking, to the disquiet of a horde of fowls, perched on every available spot above and below.

Still, they enjoyed roasted eggs and made their way toward Bova, again across a great river valley.

Our road to Bova Superior was bordered with the broad, fleshy-eared prickly pear. At the 'ear tip' was an orangey-red fruit. We passed a dark donkey minding his own business and sharing our road. Just within the hill town of Bova, 820 metres,

(Above) Maldwin Drummond and Mesiano Domenico outside the Palazzo Marzano. (Above right) The Palazzo, where Lear stayed.
Photos: Gilly Drummond

believe it or not was the black bulk of an old steam locomotive. How on earth did it get there? We parked in the little square and asked for the Marzano Palazzo. A resident in the tabaccheria responded to Gilly's questions, pointing out the Mayor's house across the square, saying that was formerly the Palazzo Marzano. Lear had recorded that:

> The Marzano Palazzo is among the most prominent of the houses here, and, homely and unornamented as it is, stands on its brown crag, looking over worlds of blue wood, and Sicily floating on the horizon's edge, with a most imposing grandeur – and just where a painter would have put it.

Lear stayed with Don Antonio Marzano, and Gilly photographed me with Mesiano Domenico, our new acquaintance whom Gilly had met in the tobacconist's shop.

Lear and Proby spent 1 August quietly in Bova, the time split between lionising and drawing. Lionising was being shown the sights by your host. Lear recalled how:

> At sunset we sauntered in what they termed 'il Giardino', one of those weed-full disarranged spots of ground, so delightful to the 'dolce far niente' of Italian life, and so inducive of 'lotus-eating', quiet and idleness.

Bova. Lithograph by Edward Lear, from *Journals of a Landscape Painter in Southern Calabria, etc*, 1852.
Private collection

The old castle perched on top of the hill, crowning the view of the Palazzo Marzano as seen from the cobbled square, is above the church. The twin bell towers can be seen in Edward Lear's print of Bova.

Lear left Bova on 3 August. Their host, Don Antonio, wrote a sonnet in honour of one of his drawings. The party made southwest across another valley and up to the dramatic small town of Palizzi. When they reached the town, they found

it 'swarming with perfectly naked, berry-brown children'. He found it difficult 'to make my way through the gathering crowd of astonished mahogany Cupids'.

Palizzi. Lithograph by Edward Lear, from *Journals of a Landscape Painter in Southern Calabria, etc*, 1852. *Private collection*

> The taverna was but a single dark room, its walls hung with portraits of little saints, and its furniture a very filthy bed with a crimson velvet gold-fringed canopy, containing an unclothed ophthalmic baby, an old cat, and a pointer dog; all the rest of the chamber being loaded with rolls of linen, guns, gourds, pears, hats, glass tumblers, puppies, jugs, sieves, etc.; still it was a better resting place than the hut at Condofuri, in as much as it was free from many intruders.

While Lear and his party arrived from the top of Palizzi, we came from the coast road. A huge rock dominates the town. This large stone tooth may be the reason for building there in the first place, for the Calabrians seem to like perching their houses on outsized stones. Although our arrival was a little before Ave Maria, or dusk, and the shadows were lengthening, the great molar stood before us, looking as if it had chewed the town around it. Gilly and I went down to the river. The bridge appeared to be the one Lear's pen and pencil describes so well. Lear had sketched from the track below the bridge. The evening was closing in, so we were unable to find the exact spot.

Few of the little mountain towns seem to have hotels today. These are congregated on the coast. Lear and Proby kept away from the sea, wandering along the hill paths. They made for Staiti. We pushed on to Bovalino. The Aphrodite Palace Hotel could not have been further removed from Palizzi's one-room tavern. The rounded entrance looked like a Hollywood interpretation of a classical building, with added Moorish overtones. Even so, in this autumn season, it was just bed and breakfast. We were sent to a restaurant bar, dominated by a large television screen. Roma was playing Inter Milan. The commentary and rushing players seemed to be in the restaurant, as if the screen was folded around the diners.

We drove northeastward along the shore road. The sandy beach was fringed with bamboo, interspersed with eucalyptus, a foreign import. The railway runs between the road and beach. There are few distinguished buildings and concrete is the universal vernacular with flat or modern disconnected sloping roofs. Few old buildings of any quality relieve the scene.

Lear had noted the Tower of Gerace, just west of the River Nerico. He turned inland there for Gerace itself. 'Very pretty is that gray tower, standing all alone on a rock by the blue waves, with a background of the graceful hill of Gerace, and many lines of more distant and loftier mountains.' This must have been the one

Gerace. Lithograph by Edward Lear, from Journals of a Landscape Painter in Southern Calabria, etc, 1852. Private collection

time he ventured onto the beach. We could not find it, glancing through the trees and over the railway line. Perhaps the sea has claimed it, but it is marked on a modern map.

Siderno was noted by Edward Lear as 'a thriving place among the ports of this coast'. We crossed the railway line to have a look. There were a few boats pulled up on the beach but there was no one about and the only sign of sea activity was a number of lobster pots piled against a fence. There are, of course, many definitions of 'a port'. A good sloping beach was a useful port for those whose shelter was gained by pulling their boats out of the reach of the waves.

The church at Gioiosa

We took the long way round to Gioiosa, climbing through rolling hills and cascading valleys. A large farmhouse was being renovated, which was unusual. Nearby a cottage had had the same treatment. Both buildings owed their foundations to huge rocks, which gave them a defensive air.

Lear had passed this way, but went on from Gerace, which we were to visit later, to Roccella and to Stilo, the furthest northeast he was to travel. He then returned cross-country to Gioiosa, now in our sights. Gilly and I parked our Ford in a square in front of a yellow and white painted church. Exploring downhill by the left-hand of the two roads, we paused by an old important building, the Palazzo Amaduri, now given over to public purpose, part a library and the other the Bureau of Europe. Sitting at a desk below the old, curved ceiling was a pretty dark-haired girl dressed in jeans. She was working at a modern desk, on top of which sat a flat-screened computer and telephone. Raffaella Rinaldis was busy with both, tapping a key, talking into the phone and staring, large-eyed, at the screen. Gilly asked her about the town and the memorials we had seen on the walls of the building in the square by the church. Under the five names was written '*Apostoli di Libertà Fecero Sventolare le Tricolore d'Italia*'. The five had died on 6 September 1847, a few months after Lear had been in Gioiosa and at the beginning of the *Risorgimento*, which was to be put down savagely by the Austrians. For more information, we would have to talk to the Professor Eldo Naymo, who knew everything about the history of the town. We tried to telephone the Professor, but he was out. During lunch in a little café in the Piazza Veneto, the waiter, after having been shown Edward Lear's drawing of Gioiosa, said the river had been covered over to extend the square. The River Romano, therefore, had disappeared, at least in the middle of the town. Gilly and I went to the place where the river, now dry, dived under. We thought we could make out an arch that is shown in a building by the river, before the great sheer rock face, in Lear's drawing. The great wall of rock rose above us, supporting lines of houses.

We had moved the car out of the square in our search for the river. This proved

Gioiosa. Lithograph by Edward Lear, from *Journals of a Landscape Painter in Southern Calabria, etc*, 1852. *Private collection*

an unusual blessing, for we were standing near, trying to make out the church that appears on the right of Lear's drawing. Our puzzling was interrupted by a well-built man of medium height who asked, to our astonishment, if we were looking for Edward Lear. Our surprise increased as he continued, 'I will show you how to reach Baron Rivettini's house. You walk up this street,' he said, pointing out the other route to the church square. 'You will then see a building whose walls stick out. That's his house.'

Lear had described the house as large and imposing, 'but the Baron was not within, and the servants, with none of that stranger-helping alacrity of hospitality, so remarkable in more northern provinces of the Kingdom of Naples, appeared too much amazed at the sudden arrival of strangers.' Their letter of introduction merely invited them to sleep where they were, without any refreshment. Lear did not think much of this and demanded to see the Baron. After a while, he was taken to a saloon on the first floor where there was a party playing cards. 'One of them, a minute gentleman, with a form more resembling that of a sphere than any person I ever remember to have seen was pointed out to me as the Baron by the shrinking domestic who had thus far piloted me.' Without interrupting the game, Lear and Proby were invited to stay, and coffee was brought and a large room assigned for their use. They dined with the Baron and his friends and survived his incessant phrase, 'Why, what for?' to anything they might say. They long remembered him as 'Baron Wherefore'. Lear wrote, 'There was left on my mind a distinct impression of some supposed or anticipated evil. Coming events cast their shadows before.' Their unease, of course, was caused by the events to be carved in marble by the church. Edward Lear was perhaps to experience 'coming events casting their shadows before', when his two brothers and his nephews fought on opposite sides in the American Civil War, 1861–65 (see Appendix 2).

Talking of plaques, there was one on the wall of the Palazzo Rivettini in the Via Cairoli, which records that Edward Lear had stayed there with the Baron in 1847. I wonder which of the two would have been more surprised at this stone memory.

Our new-found friend, Giovanni Sfara, offered to drive us to the place where Lear had sat to record this town. The view was dramatic. The church we had pondered over had had its top removed. Otherwise, it was the same. The town has not changed that much either, though the river has partially disappeared.

A plaque in Gioiosa commemorating Lear's stay at the house of Baron Rivettini on 18 and 19 August 1847

Our friend then offered to drive us out along the hairpin road on the opposite side of the river to give us a different angle. All the way he was on the phone to his mother, either calling her or she telephoning him. The question was always the same, 'Where are you?' Giovanni wanted to show us the dry river bed, so down we went and after a telephone call or two from mother, we scraped and bumped over the rough gravel track and arrived at the bed of the river. 'There were ten water mills in this stretch,' he said. 'You can see the remains of the walls that directed the water.' 'Races,' I commented helpfully, but he did not hear, for he was bulldozing out of the dry river bed with the bottom of his car, again reassuring his mother. He dropped us by ours. It was difficult to thank him enough. Gilly observed, 'I can't imagine an Englishman stopping a couple in the street and hazarding a guess that they were on the hunt for an Italian.' However, the experience did show that Lear has made his mark in Italy.

Roccella in 2005

We were soon back on the coast road, heading for Roccella. The castle stands cemented to a large outcrop of rock. It appears to be in two parts, as though the connection has slumped in some earthquake, leaving a tower on another pinnacle connected to the main castle by a ridge. According to Edward Lear, the stronghold had been owned by the Caraffa family.

Lear and Proby had letters of introduction to Don Giuseppe Nanni. We drove our car up the causeway to

Roccella. Lithograph by
Edward Lear, from *Journals of
a Landscape Painter in Southern
Calabria, etc*, 1852.
Private collection

the castle and parked by the gate of this great building, which was being restored. It may well be that Don Giuseppe's buildings were there alongside us, on the right of the road up to the gatehouse.

> Ciccio shouted aloud, but no signs of life were given in the total darkness. We tried this turning – it was blocked up by a dead wall; that way you stumbled among sleeping horses; the next path led you to a precipice.

Eventually a man came out from the dark ruins holding a feeble light, asking what they wanted. Lear, Proby and Ciccio were in the right place. The old palazzo, a collection of tiny rooms, was built against the rock.

The family of Don Giuseppe, Don Aristide, the Canon, and Don Fernando asked them questions as they waited for supper about the proposal to build a tunnel under the Thames, and the produce of England, to which the sleepy Lear replied 'camels, cochineal, sea-horses, or gold dust'. His further assertion that there was fruit in England was received with thinly hidden incredulity.

> You confess you have no wine – no oranges – no olives – no figs; – how, then, can you have apples, pears, or plums? It is a known fact that no fruit does or can grow in England, only potatoes, and nothing else whatever – this is well known. Why, then, do you tell us that which is not true?

Lear replied that England had some fruit that they did not have – currants, gooseberries and greengages, to which their hosts replied, 'There are no such things – this is nonsense.' Don Giuseppe and the others clearly did not realise they were talking to the greatest of all nonsense writers.

> So we ate our supper in quiet, convinced almost that we had been telling lies; that gooseberries were unreal and fictitious; greengages a dream.

I smiled as I looked at the rough walls and then up at the great castle.

On Friday 28 October 2005, another glorious day, we drove on to Stilo. Edward Lear, John Proby and Ciccio left on 14 August 1847 for Stignano. While they took to the hills, we stuck to the coast road and then turned inland. We, therefore, were spared a repeat of Lear's experiences with the Caristo family in Stignano,

> where at dinner there was a most confused assemblage of large dogs under the table who fought for casual crumbs and bones, and when they did not accidentally bite one's extremities, rushed, wildly barking, all about the little room.

The small son climbed onto the table, danced among the dishes and slipped, to sit in the middle of a hot dish of macaroni. Lear observed,

> One sees in valentines Cupids on beds of roses, or on birds nests; but a slightly-clothed Calabrese infant sitting in the midst of a hot dish of maccaroni appears to me a perfectly novel idea.

Stilo is a jewel. Lear thought it promisingly picturesque as he approached on the mule track. We expected to come across the gateway he drew as we penetrated

Stilo. Lithograph by Edward Lear, from Journals of a Landscape Painter in Southern Calabria, etc, 1852. Private collection

the suburbs. Gilly and I walked from the Piazza Vittoria Emanuel along a narrow street to this, the San Stefano Gate. The church warden, who had been instructed by his wife that we wanted to see the inside of the church, appeared

Stilo in 2005: the San Stefano gate.

and let us in. The Romanesque building was a place of unornamented peace. The gateway and church are on a raised platform, with the approach to the gate on one side. One of the towers Lear showed in his drawing has been demolished, perhaps to allow an extension to the church of San Stefano. Above the town is the Byzantine gem of a church, Cattolica, built in the tenth century with five cylindrical domes.

We returned by the coast road and climbed to Gerace from the coastal town of Locri. Lear's party had come across country from Stilo to Placanica, through Gioiosa, where we had been, to Agnano and Canolo, on the summit of which stands the Palazzo of Don Giovanni Rosa, where they stayed. The three wandered the town and its extraordinary environs, 'where masses of Titan rock threaten to crush the atom of life that nestle beneath.' The party 'feasted on a dish of roasted squirrels and funghi of wonderful shapes and colours' with their eighty-two-year-old friend. A great festival was taking place, but the dancing was rather a failure, as the Bishop of Gerace had published an edict prohibiting the practice by any of the fairer sex, so there were only male dancers.

Gilly and I did not stay in the town. Perhaps Lear's interpretation was right – 'the powdery state of the architecture of Gerace is not agreeable when under the influence of the winds usually prevailing around the isolated rock.' The town is certainly imposing today, but the price of overcoming its inaccessibility has been high. The winding crisscross of elevated roads dulls the senses and encourages travellers to leave before they arrive.

Our car took us west, climbing the Aspromonte Range to the Pass of Mercante. The turning leaves of the sycamore contrasted with the green of the ilex and the slower yellowing of the beech trees, making the woods on either side of the road naturally painted cathedrals, with wild cyclamen decorating the shaded ground on the roadside.

As we approached Cittanova, we passed old olive groves with lawn-like grass in between the trees. There were no nets to collect the olives. The grass was cut short to aid the harvest. Lear had come this way and captured the same view of the Gulf of Gioia. His party had tarried on the front slope of the mountain, but we hastened on. Edward Lear reported that Gioia is 'one of the most mournful of places'. He went on,

> There is no drinkable water in the place, and a few poor wretches who are left in charge of the warehouses are melancholy and horrible objects – malaria-fever being written on every line of their face and form. Ciccio said, 'if you sleep, you are dead men, dighi, doghi, da!'

This was all in the past, for the marshes have now been drained and the place has a bustle about it, working happily in the principal trade of then and now, olive oil.

The old town of Palmi sits under a great bluff, a headland, Monte Sant' Elia, which rises 579 metres and careers to the sea in two slumps. In Lear's day there was a wide open space before the town, a rocky platform with a wall on the edge of the cliff.

Below the cliff is the little fishing port, and the sandy strand is one of the beauties of Palmi – both escaped Lear's attention. On the other hand, he noticed the Lipari Isles, 'which, in shape somewhat like a row of inverted cups and saucers,

here adorn the horizon.' One of these cups could have been Stromboli, an active volcano that rises to 925 metres and has been nicknamed 'the Lighthouse of the Mediterranean'.

Palmi. Lithograph by Edward Lear, from *Journals of a Landscape Painter in Southern Calabria, etc*, 1852. *Private collection*

When it came to spending the night at Palmi on 25 August, Edward Lear and his companions were rather put off by the appearance of the inn keeper – 'the most Brobdingnagian of living landladies':

> True, the thermometer was at the highest, and the lady might be suffering from the great heat; but the apparition of her dishabille and globe-like form was so remarkable, that we paused at the threshold of so formidable a hostess – the rather that she had evidently been sacrificing earnestly to Bacchus, and was unsteady on her feet as clamorous with her tongue.

As they turned away, bent on finding another inn, the landlady shouted 'Oh, my sons, come in, come in,' but they did not pause. She changed her tune to 'Go to the black devil', throwing a large broom down the staircase. They followed Ciccio to another place of rest in the town square.

Ciccio took the horse and baggage by road, while Lear and Proby descended to the shore and boarded a boat for Bagnara, the next town south along the coast. The perpendicular crags to the sea reminded Lear of Amalfi or Positano: 'As far as the motion of the boat in a very rough swell would allow me to observe them, I enjoyed these scenes extremely, but I was glad to approach the shore once more.'

Gilly and I drove down to the shore, for the town divides itself into two – the high town and the low town. There is a small fishing and yacht harbour, a bridge and a Moorish house on the point with a fish farm out to sea. We left Bagnara

Bagnara. Lithograph by Edward Lear, from Journals of a Landscape Painter in Southern Calabria, etc, 1852. Private collection

about five in the afternoon, bound for Scilla. It was now the end of October, the weather warm and the sky cloudless.

In a note, Edward Lear remembered that on 5 February 1783 Scilla was struck by an earthquake. The Prince of Scilla and four thousand of the inhabitants of the town gathered on the sand to the south of the castle. A series of after-shocks followed before midnight and part of the mountain above the town was thrown into the straits, creating a tsunami which engulfed in one moment all the four thousand human beings gathered on the shore.

Scilla. Lithograph by
Edward Lear, from *Journals
of a Landscape Painter in
Southern Calabria, etc,* 1852.
Private collection

Unknown to Lear, the quake also smoothed the shape of the sea bottom. The old irregularity caused whirlpools, revolving patches created by the denser water sinking and the bottom layers welling upwards from below.[7] The two dangers in entering the Straits of Messina were, in ancient times, the seven-headed monster Scilla, who issued from her cave to pluck sailors from the decks of passing vessels, and Charybdis, a whirlpool, close by the Sicilian shore. Virgil celebrates all this in the *Aeneid.* The whirlpools are now much less and an earthquake seems to have fixed Scilla too.

Lear and Proby visited the Rocks of Scilla off the Point:

> We took a boat to the rocks of Scilla, and very magnificent did they appear, rising above the boiling current of dark blue foamy water. But it was too rough for so bad a sailor as I am to allow of making any drawings, so we returned to our inn.

These rocks were tumbled by the violent earthquake of 1908. The shore road now goes through a protective tunnel at the base of the castle headland. While drawing the castle at Scilla, before embarking on the boat trip to the Rocks of Scilla, the travellers again experienced hostility. Locals were uncomfortable with artists drawing features, particularly military ones, in case they were spies. Lear understood this and wrote:

> This was not quite so absurd as it may seem, if we reflect that the conquest of many countries by others has been proceeded by individual observation and research.

The three left Scilla on 28 August 1847. They were nearing the end of their landscape-painting tour of Calabria. They wandered to Villa San Giovanni, the ferry port, though it was not quite goodbye. Lear paid off Ciccio, rewarding him generously and adding a tip, which caused their guide to burst into tears. 'Dighidoghi-da was indeed a most meritorious fellow.' They accompanied Ciccio as far as Gallico, his native village, and met his wife and family. John Proby had to spend three days in Messina and Lear accompanied him and then returned to Reggio, doing a little tour on the mainland, with Ciccio again accompanying him. He was anxious to see the mountain town of Pentedatilo, spending a night in the house of Don Pietro Tropaea, to whom he had been given an introduction by his friend Consigliere da Nava, who had helped him with previous introductions.

> Don Pietro gave me a most friendly welcome, it is not to be disguised that his casino was of the dirtiest; and when I contemplated the ten dogs and a very unpleasant huge tame sheep, which animated his rooms, I congratulated myself that I was not to abide long with them. Moreover, it appeared to me that some evil, general or particular, was brooding over the household, which consisted of a wife, haggard and dirty in appearance, and agitated in a very painful degree; an only son, wild and terrified in every look; and a brother and nephew from Montebello, strange, gloomy and mysterious in aspect and manner.

The atmosphere was not improved by two or three guns being fired, which caused Donna Lucia Tropaea to burst into tears. Things got worse during dinner and Don Pietro shrieked aloud that the 'Revolution has already begun.' With coolness, Lear recognised that he was in Italy all alone and he must find his way out of it 'as best I may'. He wrapped himself in his plaid and lay down on the bed allotted to him in the front room. He was awoken by a strange noise, which was repeated, coming from underneath his bed – 'a hideous gurgling sob four or five times reiterated'. Just as he was about to strike a light, his bed was suddenly lifted up to the accompaniment of more puffing and sobs, mingled with the tinkle of a bell. Lear jumped off the bed, grabbed his stick, only to find that the intruder was the huge, tame sheep.

In Pentedatilo Lear and Ciccio met the same hostility as at Scilla. Even Ciccio was now nervous. They made their way back to Reggio, where the 'quiet town was brilliantly lighted up, and every house illuminated; no women or children were visible, but troops of men, by twenties and thirties, all armed, and preceded by bands of music and banners.' Lear could not collect his baggage from the hotel. The porter shouted, 'There are no more keys – there are no more passports, no more kings, no more lords, no more judges, no more nothing! Nothing but love and liberty, friendship and the constitution.' Lear did not dispute love, liberty, friendship or constitution. He saw things were getting out of order and went to Cavaliere da Nava's house, where he found him confined. Eventually Lear reached Villa San Giovanni, where he persuaded a reluctant boatman to take him over the water to Messina, where he rejoined Proby, who was as worried as Lear – probably more so, as fourteen or fifteen people had been killed in the revolt there.

On 5 September a steamer arrived from Malta and Lear and Proby jumped aboard, getting off in Naples, where they embarked on the tour that included Basilicata, already described.

Edward Lear's reaction to all this disturbance was to display courage and coolness. In pursuit of his work as a topographical artist, he had to put up with curiosity, which could easily develop into verbal and physical harassment. Giorgio and those whom he took with him, under instruction, provided some defence, but it was usually more sensible to move on.

Determination and courage are linked, and Lear had good helpings of both. His determination to overcome epilepsy is an illustration of this. He used this combination to achieve his long expeditions in search of just the right view.

Edward Lear encouraged our pursuit with his pictures, his diary, his letters and, of course, his friendship with my grandfather. The ability to make lasting friends with those he met was another of his strengths. He had the power to amuse. It was not only his nonsense, but the illustrations that he added to his limericks, poems and songs, almost as an afterthought, which had an immediacy about them that proved irresistible to children and adults alike. His purpose was to amuse. There was no requirement to change people's view on life, beloved of some poets, but just to trigger a creasing around the eyes, a smile and a laugh. Remember his Mrs Jaypher:

> Mrs Jaypher said it's safer,
> If you've lemons in your head
> First to eat a pound of meat
> And then to go at once to bed.

Tigerlillia Terribilis.

Lear's topographical paintings had serious purpose. He wrote to Lady Waldegrave from Cannes on 9 January 1868 about this:

> By degrees I want to topographize, and topographize all the journeyings of my life, so that I shall have been of some use after all to my fellow critters besides leaving the drawings and pictures which they may sell when I'm dead.[8]

Lear could not stop humour creeping into his pencil drawings 'from nature'. In order to remind himself of objects and colour in his landscapes, he used such words as 'rox' for rocks, 'bloo ski' for blue sky. His sketches, with these annotations, were later decorated with washes and then penned out in ink. These sketches were not for sale, but a record for worked-up pictures to be completed at a later date. In *Gang Warily*'s voyage, we landed and stood with a reproduction, shuffling backward and forward, to see for ourselves the accuracy of his work. Even though time has wrought change, the outline and some of the buildings were very recognisable. Though Lear liked the description 'the painter of poetical topography', his poetical and romantic self did not allow for flights of fancy.

By following Lear's journey inland to the Kingdom of Naples and Calabria, we found that his words and pictures, compared with today's scene, were windows on his ways. This included not only his art but his power of observation, his understanding of the people he wrote about, and, above all, his sense of humour and the ridiculous.

Lear's published words in his *Journals* gave pause for thought. Occasionally, they encouraged forensic interpretation. Remember when he was with John Proby and Ciccio in Palizzi, southern Calabria. They were ushered into a single, dark room in the inn in which, among a list of other objects, was 'an unclothed ophthalmic baby'. There was only a dim light, yet Lear was able to describe the eyes of the little one as ophthalmic. Ophthalmia is an infection of the eye, or the membrane that surrounds it, and ophthalmia of the newborn is a very severe form caused by the sexually transmitted disease gonorrhoea. His recognition may have come through his own early acquaintance with syphilitic disease. In Lear's diary of 8 August 1881, he wrote, 'Considering that I myself in 1833 had every sort of syphilitic disease, who am I to blame others, who have had less education and more temptation.'[9] It should be remembered that gonorrhoea was not differentiated from syphilis until the first part of the nineteenth century. Lear, a keen observer, was able to spot such a condition in poor light.

Lear's *Journals of a Landscape Painter* described his wanderings in Calabria. Its sister publications were devoted to his travels in Albania (1851)[10] and Corsica (1870).[11] These give an insight into not only his pictures and his way of working, but also of the man himself.

Lear the artist and author, incorporating his nonsense writings, his zoological and topographical works and his books, is now appreciated for all his talents. It was not always so. We have seen how he pressed his friends to buy, and we have seen his efforts to produce and sell a mass of watercolours, which he called 'the tyrants'. Selection was another of his faults, for Lear put his sketches in with his very best pictures on show at Stratford Place or in the galleries of his two succeeding houses in San Remo. These actions tended to suppress his sales and his reputation as an artist. However, in the last century two Americans, William Osgood Field and Philip Hofer, collected and studied his pictures. These are now housed in the Houghton Library at Harvard University, together with other Lear material, which has been the object of research, much assisted by the friendly encouragement of the Library's staff. The world of Edward Lear has been illuminated by Vivien Noakes, his biographer, whose efforts and scholarly ways have done so much to create an understanding of the artist. This was greatly helped by the exhibition devoted to Edward Lear held at the Royal Academy of Arts in 1985, for which Mrs Noakes edited the catalogue. The exhibition reawakened interest in Lear and his pictures.[12] Lear's reputation as a polymath is now secure, and the value of his pictures has grown beyond his wildest expectations.

In Italy, where Lear chose to live for a third of his life, he was lionised by his home town of San Remo in a definitive exhibition in the city in 1997,[13] but Lear's Italian reputation did not end with the close of that event, as Gilly and I discovered when wandering in his footsteps around Calabria. There, Edward Lear is seen as the symbol of 'green tourism'. Walking and painting are very welcome examples of how visitors, as they would have been called in Lear's day, described as tourists today, should enjoy and be a part of the countryside. Our two new friends, Mesiano Domenico, whom we met in Bova, and Giovanni Sfara in Gioiosa, were keen to promote Lear as a green tourist. The former gave us a booklet extolling the artist's virtues in this direction and the latter pointed out the trail that had been marked in his honour in Gioiosa.

When we started on our great adventure, sailing from Osborne House on the Isle of Wight and ending up at the 'heel of Italy', I produced some writing paper with a drawing of Lear, Foss (his cat) and myself following on behind. I did not realise then, as we dropped the mooring buoy over the side in Cowes Harbour, what an enormous pleasure and understanding the journey was to bring, in following **after you, Mr Lear**.

Appendix 1

A brief chronology of the life of Edward Lear

1812	Edward Lear born at Bowman's Lodge, Highgate, London.
1816	Ann Lear, Edward's eldest sister, takes responsibility for his upbringing.
1827	Bowman's Lodge sold.
1830	Two volumes of Lear's *Illustrations of the Family of Psittacidae, or Parrots* published by E Lear and R Ackerman. Becomes an Associate Fellow of the Linnean Society. Meets Lord Stanley, later 13th Earl of Derby.
1831–32	Meets John Gould and goes on a European tour with him.
1832–36	Starts work at Knowsley for Lord Stanley.
1835	Tours Ireland with Edward Stanley, Bishop of Norwich, and his son Arthur Penrhyn Stanley.
1836	Walking tour of the Lake District. Failing eyesight and the beauty of the place foster the idea of becoming a topographical landscape painter.
1837	Travels to Rome, second Continental visit, via Belgium, Germany, Switzerland and Rome.
1838–48	Lives in Rome, returning occasionally to England.
1838	Naples and Amalfi. Experiments with oil paints.
1842	Sicily and the Abruzzi.
1843	The Abruzzi.
1845	Makes friends with Chichester Fortescue, later Lord Carlingford.

1846   Lear's Golden Year. Publication of *Illustrated Excursions in Italy*, Vols. 1 & 2 (Thomas McLean). First edition of *A Book of Nonsense*, under the name of Derry Down Derry, published by Thomas McLean. Publication of *Gleanings from the Menagerie and Aviary at Knowsley Hall* (written by J E Gray, with illustrations by Lear). Gives a series of drawing lessons to Queen Victoria at Osborne House, Isle of Wight.

1847   Tour of Sicily, Calabria, Compania and Basilicata with John Proby. Revolution in Reggio. Italy becomes unsettled and nervous.

1848   Goes to Malta and on to the Ionian Islands and Corfu. Athens and a tour of Greece, to Constantinople, Greece again and Albania before returning to Malta. Meets Thomas Baring, later Lord Northbrook, and Franklin Lushington, judge in the Ionian Islands.

1849–53   Lives in England.

1849   Egypt, Malta and southern Greece, accompanied by Lushington. Attends Sass's Drawing Academy as a precursor to entry to the Royal Academy Schools.

1850   Lear accepted first as a probationer, then as a full student of the Royal Academy Schools, but does not stay long.

1851   Publication of *Journals of a Landscape Painter in Albania* (Richard Bentley). Meets the Poet Laureate, Alfred Tennyson, and his wife Emily at the Lushingtons'. Tour of Devon and Cornwall. Death of Edward, 13th Earl of Derby, Edward Lear's patron.

Edward Lear (seated in the centre of the group), photographed on a visit to Egypt.
By Courtesy of Henry Sotheran Ltd

1852   Meets the Pre-Raphaelite Brotherhood's co-founder William Holman Hunt, who became a valued friend and teacher in the art of oil painting. Publication of *Journals of a Landscape Painter in Southern Calabria* (Richard Bentley).

1853   England, winters in Egypt.

1854   Travels up the Nile. Visits Philae and goes to Malta and England before going on to Switzerland.

1855–58   Lives in Corfu.

1855	Second edition of *A Book of Nonsense* (Thomas McLean).
1856	Giorgio Kokali works for Lear for the first time. Albania. Travels to Mount Athos. Visits the Dardanelles, the site of Troy and Smyrna.
1857	Albania, London, returning to Corfu.
1858–60	Lives in Rome.
1858	Bethlehem, Petra, Jerusalem and the Lebanon. Back to England but winters in Rome.
1859	Meets Edgar Atheling Drummond of Cadland, Lear's banker. Become friends. England and St Leonards, then back to Rome.
1860	Back in England working on the oil painting *Cedars of Lebanon* at Oatlands Park Hotel.
1861–64	Lives in Corfu.
1861	Sister Ann dies. The *Cedars* well received by critics. Tours Italy, Switzerland, winters again in Corfu. Third edition of *A Book of Nonsense* published by Routledge, Warne & Routledge.
1862	Malta and on to England and then Corfu. Starts on the 'Tyrants'.
1863	Ionian Islands. Publishes *Views in the Seven Ionian Islands* (E. Lear).
1864	Leaves Corfu as British rule is ended. Visits Athens and Crete, returns to England. Travels to Nice. More Tyrants. Walks from Nice to Genoa and back. Lear's 'Corniche Walk' was to have been the basis for a book that was never published. Stays in Nice.
1865	Nice, back to England and then to Venice to complete a picture for Lady Waldegrave. First of Lear's nonsense stories, *The History of the Seven Families of the Lake Pipple-Popple*. Spends winter in Malta.
1866	Returns to England bent on asking Gussie Bethell, Lord Chancellor Westbury's daughter, to marry him, but does not. Travels to Egypt.
1867–70	Lives in Cannes.
1867	Visits Jerusalem, returns to England, winters in Cannes. Composes *The Owl and the Pussy Cat*, his first nonsense song, for Janet Symonds, who was ill in bed.
1868	Tours Corsica, back to England, wintering again in Cannes.

1869   Cannes, Paris, England, Cannes. *Journal of a Landscape Painter in Corsica* published by Robert Bush. Edward Geoffrey, 14th Earl of Derby, dies.

1870   Purchases land in San Remo to build the Villa Emily.

1871–81   Lives in San Remo at the Villa Emily.

1871   Villa Emily completed. Edward Lear and Giorgio Kokali move in. *Nonsense Songs, Stories, Botany & Alphabets* published by Robert Bush.

1872   *More Nonsense, Pictures, Rhymes, Botany, Etc.* published by Robert Bush. England. Sets off for India but only reaches Suez. The cat Foss arrives at the Villa Emily.

1873–75   Tours India and Ceylon, returns to England.

1876   *Laughable Lyrics*, last of the nonsense series, published at end of the year by Robert Bush.

1877   Returns to Corfu to visit the sick Giorgio.

1878   Visits Monte Generoso in Switzerland. Villa Emily blighted by the building of a house in Edward Lear's view and light.

1879   Monte Generoso again.

1880   Purchases land for the new Villa Tennyson, San Remo. Spends autumn at Monte Generoso.

1881–88   Lives in San Remo at the Villa Tennyson.

1881   Monte Generoso. Moves from Villa Emily into Villa Tennyson.

1882   Villa Tennyson, Monte Generoso.

1883   Villa Tennyson, Monte Generoso. Giorgio Kokali dies there. Italian 'walk' to Perugia, Florence, Pisa, Spezia, Genoa.

1884   Villa Tennyson, Recoaro (northeast of Verona) and Milan.

1885   Villa Tennyson, Brianza (Lombardy, north of Milan).

1886   Villa Tennyson, Brianza.

1887   Villa Tennyson. Foss the cat dies. Andorno (northeast of Turin).

1888   Edward Lear dies 29 January, buried in the English Cemetery, San Remo.

Appendix 2
Edward Lear's family

Edward Lear was fond of tracing his origins back to the Danes and to the name of Lør. His interest in his background was coloured by his feeling of rejection by his parents, ameliorated by the love and care of his eldest sister Ann (b. 1791), the third of Jeremiah and Ann's family. He was the twentieth of twenty-one children, and this made his own immediate family of great concern. His fondness for a quick turn of phrase and his romantic disposition would have favoured a musty Viking ancestor. Research by Mark Fisher has pushed the family tree back a generation or two.

Edward Lear's ancestors

Humphrey (Umfery) Leare
died 1606, Tisbury, Motcombe (Shaftesbury)
Yeoman farmer

Edward Leare
died ?1692

George (I) Leare
born c.1633
Butcher, Gillingham

George (II) Leare
born c.1666, Gillingham; died 1745, London
Freeman & Fruiterer, 'the Gingerbread Baker'

Henry Lear

(1709–1763)
married Margaret Lester (c.1710–1795)
Whitechapel, Stepney, London

Jeremiah Lear

(1757–1833)
married Ann Clark Skerritt (1766–1844)
Freeman & Fruiterer, sugar refiner and stockbroker

Jeremiah and Ann (Edward's parents) had twenty-one children, of whom only twelve survived beyond their twenties. Only Charles Lear, missionary (child number sixteen), and our Edward (number twenty) made it to the year 1888.

Four of Lear's brothers and sisters married and had issue. The first of these was Sarah Lear (number six, born in 1794), who married Charles Street. Two children were the result, Charles Henry and Frederick William, both born in Arundel, 1824 and 1827. The family emigrated to the South Island of New Zealand. Sarah died in Dunedin in 1873. Charles Henry passed away around 1885 but the younger son returned to England and died in 1864, three years before his father in New Zealand.

Henry Lear (number eight, born 1798) married a person unnamed. They had two daughters, Caroline and Fanny, and four sons who enlisted in the American Union Army. They lived in Brooklyn, New York.

Eleanor Lear (number nine, born 1799) married a William Newsom. He was elected to the Bank of England in 1816, when he was seventeen, living in London at 279 High Street, Southwark. He must have been clever, for the Bank records show that he did the writing test in twenty-five minutes and took eight minutes to finish the maths exam. Eight minutes was below other recorded times in those days. He became Head of the Issues Department and retired in 1848 to live in Leatherhead.

Frederick Lear (number fourteen) was born in 1805. His wife Rosa Annie Smyth was eight years his junior. Frederick was a mining engineer. The couple emigrated, first to the West Indies (Cuba and Jamaica) and then to Missouri, where he obtained land in Jefferson County. Their first child, Francis Frederick Lear (1832–1889), was born in Jamaica and Rosa (1840–19??) in Cuba. The next child, a girl born in 1842, began life in Missouri. Francis enlisted and rose to the rank of Second Lieutenant in the Missouri Light Artillery, and saw action at the Battle of Springfield on 8 January 1863 on the Union side.

Another Francis Lear (Francis M Lear) was originally a corporal in the Union Army, but became a Confederate and was captured with nine others. He was caught up in the Palmyra Massacre of 18 October 1862 in Missouri, where ten prisoners of the Confederate Army were shot in retaliation for the murder of a local man, Andrew Allsman. General John McNeil, who ordered the executions, became known as the Butcher of Palmyra. However, that Francis Lear may not have been one of Frederick's sons.

Edward Lear's two brothers left England under a cloud. One had been in trouble for forgery, the other having deserted from the Army. Edward Lear recorded this recollection in his diary of 27 April 1881: '2 of my brothers suffered for deserting the Army, & for Forgery.' It is not possible to discover which brother deserted without knowing his regiment(s). The two sons appear to have gone astray after their father became financially embarrassed in 1816, when Henry was eighteen and Frederick eleven.

Notes

Part I

1. Arthur Benson and Viscount Esher, *Letters of Queen Victoria, 1837–61*, Vol. II. John Murray, London, 1908

2. Michael Turner, *Osborne House*. English Heritage Guide, 2000.

3. Marina Warner, *Queen Victoria's Sketchbook*. Macmillan, London, 1979.

4. Vivien Noakes, *Edward Lear: the Life of a Wanderer* (revised edition). Sutton Publishing, Stroud, 2004.

5. Vivien Noakes, *Edward Lear: the Life of a Wanderer*.

6. Montagu Guest and William Boulton, *The Royal Yacht Squadron*. John Murray, London, 1903.

7. Vivien Noakes, *Edward Lear, 1812–88*. Royal Academy of Arts in association with Weidenfeld & Nicholson, London, 1985.

8. Edward Lear, Diary, 17 January 1865 (Houghton Library, Harvard University).

9. Vivien Noakes, *Edward Lear: the Life of a Wanderer*.

10. Edward Lear, Diary, 9 October 1882 (Houghton Library, Harvard University).

11. Edward Lear, Diary, 4 February 1871, 12 April 1871, 30 March 1872 (Houghton Library, Harvard University).

12. Edward Lear, Diary, 31 July 1882 (Houghton Library, Harvard University).

13. Bertha C Slade, *Edward Lear on My Shelves*, collected for William B Osgood Field. New York, 1933.

14. Epilepsy Foundation, *General Information on Epilepsy*. Fact Sheet No. 6 (FS6), 1997.

15. Roger Dobson, 'Illness: the pathway to creative genius'. *Times Online*, 31 December 2005, quoting references from St Louis University School of Medicine.

16. Dr E H Reynolds, Chairman of the Fund for Epilepsy, in a letter to Maldwin Drummond, 28 February 2003.

17. Edward Lear, Diary, 7 November 1862 (Houghton Library, Harvard University).

18. Notes taken at the Houghton Library, Harvard University.

19. Thomas Nash, *The Life of Richard, Lord Westbury*. Richard Bentley & Son, London, 1888.

20. Sylvia Pagan Westphal, 'Glad to be asexual'. *New Scientist*, 16 October 2004.

21. Edward Lear, Diary, 19 June 1871 (Houghton Library, Harvard University).

22. William Laird Clowes, *The Royal Navy: a History*. Sampson, Low, Marston & Company, London, 1897.

23. Grant Uden and Richard Cooper, *A Dictionary of British Ships and Seamen*. Allen Lane, Kestrel Books, London, 1980.

24. William Laird Clowes, *The Royal Navy: a History*.

25. Henry Wemyss, *Sotheby's Sale Catalogue*, April 1997.

26. Peter Levi, *Edward Lear: a Biography*. Macmillan, London, 1995.

27. Scott Wilcox, *Edward Lear and the Art of Travel*. Yale Centre for British Art, New Haven, Connecticut, 2000.

28. Peter Levi, *Edward Lear: a Biography*.

29. Peter Levi, *Edward Lear: a Biography*.

30. William Laird Clowes, *The Royal Navy: a History*.

31. H Wheeler and A Broadley, *Napoleon and the Invasion of England* (Vol. 1). John Lane, London, 1898.

Part II

1. Edward Lear, *Selected Letters* (ed. Vivien Noakes). Clarendon Press, Oxford, 1988.

2. Edward Lear, *Selected Letters* (ed. Vivien Noakes).

3. Edward Lear to Fanny Coombes, 3 March 1837. In Vivien Noakes, *Edward Lear: the Life of a Wanderer* (revised edition). Sutton Publishing, Stroud, 2004.

4. Patrick Delaforce, *The Grand Tour*. Robertson McCarta, London, 1990.

5. M B Huish, *The Seine and the Loire*. J S Virtue, London, 1895.

6. Sir Edward Thorpe, *The Seine from Havre to Paris*. Macmillan, London, 1913.

7. Edward Lear, *Letters of Edward Lear to Chichester Fortescue ...* (ed. Lady Strachey). Fisher Unwin, London, 1907.

8. Richard Rogers and Mark Fisher, *A New London*. Penguin, London, 1992.

9. Edward Lear to Chichester Fortescue, 13 December 1858. *Letters of Edward Lear to Chichester Fortescue ...* (ed. Lady Strachey).

10. André Parinaud, *Barbizon: the Origins of Impressionism*. Bonfini, Bergamo, Italy, 1994.

11. John Ruskin, *Library Edition of the Works of John Ruskin* (ed. E T Cook and Alexander Wedderburn), Vol. 35. George Allen, London, 1903–12.

12. Lawrence Campbell, *Introduction to John Ruskin's The Elements of Drawing (1857)*. Dover Books, New York, 1971.

13. Bernard Denvir (ed.), *The Impressionists at First Hand*. Thames & Hudson, London, reprinted 1995.

14. Clemency Fisher (ed.), *A Passion for Natural History: the Life and Legacy of the 13th Earl of Derby*. National Museums and Galleries of Merseyside, Liverpool, 2002.

15. Philip Hofer, *Edward Lear as a Landscape Draughtsman*. Belknap Press, Cambridge, Massachusetts, 1967.

16. Jean-Baptiste Gresset, Poem quoted in *Michelin Green Tourist Guide, Burgundy–Jura*.

17. Philip Gilbert Hamerton, *The Saone: a Summer Voyage*. Seeley & Co., London, 1887.

18. Edward Lear, Letter to Edgar Drummond of Cadland, 29 September 1865.

19. Philip Gilbert Hamerton, *The Saone: a Summer Voyage*.

20. Vivien Noakes, *Edward Lear, 1812–88*. Royal Academy of Arts in association with Weidenfeld & Nicholson, London, 1985.

21. Philip Gilbert Hamerton, *The Saone: a Summer Voyage*.

22. Philip Gilbert Hamerton, *The Saone: a Summer Voyage*.

Part III

1. John Sugden, *Nelson: a Dream of Glory*. Jonathan Cape, Random House, London, 2004.

2. Edward Lear, *Later Letters of Edward Lear to Chichester Fortescue (Lord Carlingford), Frances, Countess Waldegrave & Others ...* (ed. Lady Strachey). Fisher Unwin, London, 1911.

3. Eric Partridge, *A Dictionary of Slang and Unconventional English*. Routledge & Kegan Paul, London, 1982.

4. John Ruskin, *Library Edition of the Works of John Ruskin* (ed. E T Cook and Alexander Wedderburn). George Allen, London, 1903–12.

5. Edward Lear, *Later Letters*.

6. Edward Lear, *The Complete Verse & Other Nonsense* (ed. Vivien Noakes). Allen Lane, London, 2001. Shorter edition omitting some editorial matter, Penguin Books, 2002.

7. Le Corbusier, *The City of Tomorrow and Its Planning* (1925) and *The Radiant City* (1933); also Alain de Botton, *Why architects get it wrong* (book extract, Sunday Telegraph, 2 April 2006).

8. Edward Lear, Diary for 1864 (with microfilmed copies of all his diaries), held by the Houghton Library, Harvard University.

9. Edward Lear to Emily Tennyson, 16 February 1880.

10. Rodolfo Falchi and Valerie Wadsworth, *Edward Lear: Holloway 1812 – Sanremo 1888*. Lalli Editore, Comune di Sanremo, 1997.

11. John Munday, *E W Cooke, 1811–1880*. Antique Collectors Club, Woodbridge, 1996.

12. Edward Lear, *Letters of Edward Lear to Chichester Fortescue ...* (ed. Lady Strachey). Fisher Unwin, London, 1907.

13. Edward Lear, Diary for 1864 (Houghton Library, Harvard University).

14. Edward Lear, Diary, 23 May 1860 (Houghton Library, Harvard University).

15. Edward Lear, Diary, 22 May 1860 (Houghton Library, Harvard University).

16. Edward Lear, Diary, 23 May 1860 (Houghton Library, Harvard University).

17. Edmund Howard, *Genoa: History and Art in an Old Seaport*. Sagep, Genoa, 1978.

18. Edward Lear, Diary, 21 May 1860 (Houghton Library, Harvard University).

19. Edmund Howard, *Genoa: History and Art in an Old Seaport*.

20. Edward Lear, Diary, 19 May 1860 (Houghton Library, Harvard University).

Part IV

1. Edmund Howard, *Genoa: History and Art in an Old Seaport*. Sagep, Genoa, 1978.

2. Angelo Landi and Giuseppe Marcenaro, *Il Porto della Luna*. Sagep Editrice della Luna, Genoa, 1993.

3. Edward Lear, Diary, 15 May 1860 (Houghton Library, Harvard University).

4. Guido Biagi, *The Last Days of Percy Bysshe Shelley*. Fisher Unwin, London, 1898.

5. *In the Wind's Eye: Byron's Letters and Journals* (ed. Leslie A Marchand), Vol. 9, 1821–22. John Murray, London, 1979.

6. *In the Winds Eye*, Vol. 9, 1821–22.

7. Edward Lear, Diary, 18 September 1861 (Houghton Library, Harvard University).

8. John Rousmaniere, *The Luxury Yachts*. Time Life Books, Alexandria, Virginia, 1981.

9. Augustus Hare, *Cities of Northern & Central Italy*, Vol. 2. Daldy, Isbister & Co., London, 1876.

10. Paul Gruyer, *Napoleon, King of Elba*. Heinemann, London, 1906.

11. Henry Denham, *The Tyrrhenian Sea*. John Murray, London, 1969.

12. Chichester Fortescue (later Lord Carlingford), Diary, 1845, quoted in *Letters of Edward Lear* (ed. Lady Strachey), Fisher Unwin, London, 1907.

Part V

1. Edward Lear to Ann Lear, 14 December 1837, from 39 Via del Babuino. *Selected Letters* (ed. Vivien Noakes). Clarendon Press, Oxford, 1988.

2. Edward Lear, Diary, 22 September 1861 (Houghton Library, Harvard University).

3. Clemency Fisher (ed.), *A Passion for Natural History: the Life and Legacy of the 13th Earl of Derby*. National Museums and Galleries of Merseyside, Liverpool, 2002.

4. Edward Lear, *Selected Letters* (ed. Vivien Noakes).

5. Edward Lear, *Later Letters of Edward Lear to Chichester Fortescue (Lord Carlingford), Frances, Countess Waldegrave & Others ...* (ed. Lady Strachey). Fisher Unwin, London, 1911.

6. Edward Lear, *Later Letters*.

7. Edward Lear, *Journals of a Landscape Painter in Albania, Illyria* (2nd edition). Richard Bentley, London, 1852.

8. Edward Lear to Edgar Drummond, 5 August 1859 (Cadland Archives).

9. Edward Lear to Edgar Drummond, 1 October 1859 (Cadland Archives).

10. Edward Lear to Edgar Drummond, 4 November 1859 (Cadland Archives).

11. Edward Lear to Edgar Drummond, 21 December 1859 (Cadland Archives).

12. Cyril Drummond, EAD, Vol. 1 (Cadland Archives).

13. Baron Muncaster, *Ransom and Murder in Greece* (ed. Crosby Stevens). Lutterworth Press, Cambridge, 1989.

14. Edward Lear to Edgar Drummond, 4 November 1859 (Cadland Archives).

15. Edgar Drummond, Muncaster papers (Cadland Archives).

16. Edward Lear, Account, The Royal Bank of Scotland Group archives, Drummonds Bank customer account ledgers GB1502/DR/427.

17. Baron Carlingford, ... *And Mr Fortescue: a selection from the diaries from 1851 to 1862 of Chichester Fortescue, Lord Carlingford* (ed. Osbert Wyndham Hewett). John Murray, London, 1935.

18. Edward Lear to Edgar Drummond, 22 October 1863 (Cadland Archives).

19. Edward Lear to Edgar Drummond, 26 October 1863 (Cadland Archives).

20. Edward Lear to Ann Lear, 28 May 1838. Vivien Noakes, *Edward Lear: the Life of a Wanderer* (revised edition). Sutton Publishing, Stroud, 2004.

21. Edward Lear to John Gould, 17 October 1839. *Selected Letters* (ed. Vivien Noakes). Clarendon Press, Oxford, 1988.

22. Antonella Basilico Pisaturo, *Painters on Capri 1850–1950*. Edizioni la Conchiglia, Capri, 1998.

23. Homer, *The Odyssey*, Book 12.

24. Edward Lear, Diary, 10 May 1862 (Houghton Library, Harvard University).

25. Dieter Richter, *Turner's Amalfi Sketchbook: In Search of the South*. La Nuova Italia, Florence, 1989.

26. Edward Lear to Ann Lear, 10 June 1838.

27. Edward Lear to Chichester Fortescue, 12 February 1848. *Letters of Edward Lear to Chichester Fortescue ...* (ed. Lady Strachey). Fisher Unwin, London, 1907.

28. Edward Lear to Hubert Congreve, 1883. *Later Letters of Edward Lear ...* (ed. Lady Strachey).

Part VI

1. Edward Lear to the 13th Earl of Derby, 5 June 1842. *Selected Letters* (ed. Vivien Noakes). Clarendon Press, Oxford, 1988.

2. Edward Lear to Lady Waldegrave, 15 March 1863.

3. Edward Lear to Edgar Drummond, 12 April 1867, written from Hotel Damascus, Jerusalem (Cadland Archives).

4. Except where otherwise indicated, the quotations from Edward Lear in Chapters 24–26 are all taken from both parts of this book: *Edward Lear, Journals of a Landscape Painter in Southern Calabria, Etc*. Richard Bentley, London, 1852.

5. Edward Lear, *Viaggio in Basilicata* (1847). 2nd edition, Edizioni Osanna, Venosa, 1990

6. Edward Lear to Chichester Fortescue, 16 October 1847. *Letters of Edward Lear to Chichester Fortescue ...* (ed. Lady Strachey). Fisher Unwin, London, 1907.

7. Henry Denham, *The Tyrrhenian Sea*. John Murray, London, 1969.

8. Edward Lear to Lady Waldegrave, 9 January 1868. *Later Letters of Edward Lear ...* (ed. Lady Strachey).

9. Edward Lear, Diary, 8 August 1881 (Houghton Library, Harvard University).

10. Edward Lear, *Journals of a Landscape Painter in Albania, Etc.* London, 1851. 2nd edition: Richard Bentley, London, 1852.

11. Edward Lear, *Journal of a Landscape Painter in Corsica*. London, 1870.

12. Vivien Noakes, *Edward Lear, 1812–88*. Royal Academy of Arts in association with Weidenfeld & Nicholson, London, 1985.

13. Rodolfo Falchi and Valerie Wadsworth, *Edward Lear: Holloway 1812 – Sanremo 1888*. Lalli Editore, Comune di Sanremo, 1997.

Select bibliography

Travel works by Edward Lear

Views in Rome and its Environs. Thomas McLean, London, 1841.

Illustrated Excursions in Italy. Thomas McLean, London, 1846.

Viaggio in Basilicata (1847). Edizioni Ossana, Venosa, 1990.

Journals of a Landscape Painter in Albania, &c. Richard Bentley, London, 1851. 2nd edition, 1852.

Journals of a Landscape Painter in Southern Calabria &c. Richard Bentley, London, 1852.

Views in the Seven Ionian Islands. Edward Lear, London, 1863.

Journal of a Landscape Painter in Corsica. Robert Bush, London, 1870.

Lear's works, with commentary by other authors

Durrell, Lawrence. Introduction, in *Lear's Corfu: an Anthology Drawn From the Painter's Letters.* Corfu Travel, Corfu, 1965.

Murphy, Ray (ed). *Edward Lear's Indian Journal.* Jarrolds, London, 1953.

Proby, Granville (ed). *Lear in Sicily.* Duckworth, London, 1938.

Quennell, Peter. Introduction, in *Edward Lear in Southern Italy.* William Kimber, London, 1964.

Quennell, Peter. Introduction, in *Edward Lear in Greece.* William Kimber, London, 1965.

Quennell, Peter. Introduction, in *Edward Lear in Corsica.* William Kimber, London, 1966.

Slade, Bertha C. *Edward Lear on My Shelves,* Collected for William B Osgood Field. New York, 1933.

van Tal, H (ed). *Journals: a Selection.* Arthur Barker, London, 1952.

Biography

Chitty, Susan. *That Singular Person Called Lear.* Weidenfeld and Nicholson, London, 1998.

Davidson, Angus. *Edward Lear, Landscape Painter and Nonsense Poet (1812–1888).* John Murray, London, 1938.

Levi, Peter. *Edward Lear: a Biography.* Macmillan, London, 1995.

Montgomery, Michael. *Lear's Italy: in the Footsteps of Edward Lear.* Cadogan Guides, London, 2005.

Noakes, Vivien. *Edward Lear: the Life of a Wanderer.* Collins, London, 1968. Revised and enlarged edition, Sutton Publishing, Stroud, 2004.

Published letters of Edward Lear

Noakes, Vivien (ed). *Edward Lear: Selected Letters.* Clarendon Press, Oxford, 1988.

Strachey, Lady (ed). *Letters of Edward Lear to Chichester Fortescue (Lord Carlingford) and Frances, Countess Waldegrave.* T Fisher Unwin, London, 1907.

Strachey, Lady (ed). *Later Letters of Edward Lear to Chichester Fortescue (Lord Carlingford) and Frances, Countess Waldegrave and Others.* T Fisher Unwin, London, 1911.

Lear the artist

Falchi, Rodolfo & Wadsworth, Valerie. *Edward Lear: Holloway 1812 – Sanremo 1888.* Lalli Editore, Comune di Sanremo, 1997.

Hofer, Philip. *Edward Lear as a Landscape Draughtsman.* Belknap Press of Harvard University Press, Cambridge, Massachusetts, 1967.

Noakes, Vivien. *Edward Lear, 1812–88.* Royal Academy of Arts in association with Weidenfeld & Nicholson, London, 1985.

Wilcox, Scott. *Edward Lear and the Art of Travel.* Yale Center for British Art, New Haven, Connecticut, 2000.

Nonsense books by Edward Lear

A Book of Nonsense (by Derry Down Derry). Thomas McLean, London, 1846, in two parts.

A Book of Nonsense, third edition, with many new pictures and verses. Routledge, London, 1861.

Nonsense Songs, Stories, Botany and Alphabets. Robert Bush, London, 1871.

More Nonsense, Pictures, Rhymes and Botany, Etc. Robert Bush, London, 1872.

Laughable Lyrics. Robert Bush, London, 1877.

Nonsense books published after Edward Lear's death

Strachey, Edward (ed). *Nonsense Songs and Stories.* F Warne, London, 1895.

Strachey, Lady (ed). *Queery Leary Nonsense.* Mills and Boon, London, 1911.

Strachey, John St Loe (ed). *The Lear Coloured Bird Book for Children.* Mills and Boon, London, 1912.

Facsimile of a Nonsense Alphabet Drawn & Written by Edward Lear. F Warne, London, 1926.

Megroz, R L (ed). *A Book of Lear.* Penguin, London, 1939.

Edward Lear's *Nonsense Omnibus.* F Warne, London, 1943.

The Collected Nonsense Songs of Edward Lear. Grey Walls Press, London, 1947.

The Complete Nonsense of Edward Lear. Faber & Faber, London, 1947.

A Nonsense Alphabet. Victoria & Albert Museum, HMSO, London, 1952.

Davidson, Angus & Hofer, Philip (eds). *Teapots & Quails.* Constable Young Books, London, 1965.

Alderson, Brian (ed). *A Book of Bosh.* Penguin, Harmondsworth, 1975.

Liebert, Herman W (ed). *Lear in the Original.* H P Kraus, New York, 1975.

The Nonsense Verse of Edward Lear. Illustrated by John Vernon Lord. Harmony Books, New York, 1984.

Hyman, Susan (ed). *A New Nonsense Alphabet.* Bloomsbury, London, 1988.

Noakes, Vivien (ed). *The Complete Verse and Other Nonsense.* Penguin, London, 2001.

Natural history by Edward Lear

Beechey, F W. *The Zoology of Captain Beechey's Voyage.* London, 1839.

Darwin, Charles (ed). *The Zoology of the Voyage of HMS Beagle.* London, 1841. Drawings attributed to John & Elizabeth Gould, painted by Edward Lear.

Fisher, Clemency (ed). *A Passion for Natural History: the Life and Legacy of the 13th Earl of Derby.* National Museums & Galleries, Merseyside, 2002.

Gould, John. *The Birds of Europe.* Published by the author, printed by Richard & John Taylor, London, 1837. 5 volumes.

Gray, J E (ed). *Edward Lear, Gleanings from the Menagerie & Aviary at Knowsley Hall.* Privately printed, Knowsley, 1846.

Lear, Edward. *Illustrations of the Family of the Psittacidae, or Parrots.* R Ackermann & E Lear, London, 1832.

Natural history: some illustrations by Lear

Tree, Isabella. *The Ruling Passion of John Gould: a Biography of the Bird Man.* Barrie & Jenkins, London, 1991.

Art

Brown, David Blaney. *The Art of J M W Turner.* Headline, London, 1990.

Campbell, Lawrence. *Introduction to John Ruskin's The Elements of Drawing (1857).* Dover Books, New York, 1971.

Cook, E T & Wedderburn, Alexander (eds). *Library Edition of the Works of John Ruskin.* George Allen, London, 1903–12.

Cumming, Robert. *Art.* Dorling Kindersley, London, 2005.

Munday, John. *E W Cooke, 1811–1880.* Antique Collectors Club, Woodbridge, 1996.

Pisaturo, Antonella Basilico. *Painters on Capri 1850–1950.* Edizioni la Conchiglia, Capri, 1998.

Richter, Dieter. *Turner's Amalfi Sketchbook: in Search of the South.* La Nuova Italia, Florence, 1989.

Richter, Dieter. *Alla Ricerca del Sud: Tre Secoli di Viaggi ad Amalfi nell' immaginario europeo.* La Nuova Italia, Florence, 1989.

Warner, Marina. *Queen Victoria's Sketchbook.* Macmillan, London, 1979.

Wilcox, Timothy. *Francis Towne.* Tate Gallery Publishing, London, 1997.

Wilcox, Timothy. *The Triumph of Watercolour: the Early Years of the Royal Watercolour Society 1805–55*. Philip Wilson, London, 2005.

The Barbizon School and Impressionism

Charles, Daniel. *Le Mystère Caillebotte*. Editions Glénat, Grenoble, 1994.

Denvir, Bernard. *Encyclopaedia of Impressionism*. Thames & Hudson, London, 1990.

Jurzak, Ingrid & others. *Inspirations de bords de Seine: Maximilien Luce et les peintres de son époque*. Somogy Editions d'art, Paris, 2004.

Parinaud, André. *Barbizon: the Origins of Impressionism*. Bonfini, Bergamo, Italy, 1994.

History and travel

Delaforce, Patrick. *The Grand Tour*. Robertson McCarta, London, 1990.

Hardy, Robert Gathorne. *Amalfi: Aspects of the City and her Ancient Territories*. Faber & Faber, London, 1968.

Hare, Augustus. *Cities of Northern & Central Italy*. Daldy, Isbister & Co, London, 1876. 2 volumes.

Hewett, Osbert Wyndham (ed). *And Mr Fortescue: a Selection from the Diaries from 1851 to 1862 of Chichester Fortescue, Lord Carlingford*. John Murray, London, 1935.

Howard, Edmund. *Genoa: History and Art in an Old Seaport*. Sagep, Genoa, 1978.

Landi, Angelo & Marcenaro, Giuseppe. *Il Porto della Luna*. Sagep, Genoa, 1993.

Muncaster, Baron Josslyn. *Ransom and Murder in Greece: Lord Muncaster's Journal, 1870*. Lutterworth Press, Cambridge, 1989.

Wheeler, H & Broadley, A. *Napoleon and the Invasion of England*. John Lane, London, 1898.

General biography

Benson, Arthur & Esher, Viscount. *Letters of Queen Victoria 1837–61*. John Murray, London, 1908.

Biagi, Guido. *The Last Days of Percy Bysshe Shelley*, T Fisher Unwin, London, 1898.

Bolitho, Hector & Peel, Derek. *The Drummonds of Charing Cross*. George Allen & Unwin, London, 1967.

Gruyer, Paul. *Napoleon, King of Elba*. Heinemann, London, 1906.

Marchand, Leslie A (ed). *In the Wind's Eye: Byron's Letters & Journals*. John Murray, London, 1979.

Nash, Thomas. *The Life of Richard, Lord Westbury*. Richard Bentley, London, 1888.

Sailing, naval and nautical

Clowes, William Laird. *The Royal Navy: a History*. Sampson, Low, Marston & Company, London, 1897. 7 volumes.

Guest, Montagu & Boulton, William. *The Royal Yacht Squadron*. John Murray, London, 1903.

Rousmaniere, John. *The Luxury Yachts*. Time Life Books, Alexandria, Virginia, 1981.

Shelley-Rolls, Sir John. *Yachts of the Royal Yacht Squadron 1815–1932*. Zaehnsdorf, London, 1933.

Sugden, John. *Nelson: a Dream of Glory*. Jonathan Cape, Random House, London, 2004.

Uden, Grant & Cooper, Richard. *A Dictionary of British Ships and Seamen*. Allen Lane, Kestrel Books, London, 1980.

Navigation and voyaging

Bowskill, Derek. *The Channel to the Med: a Guide to the Main Routes Through the French Canals*. Opus, Wadhurst, 1995.

Denham, Henry. *The Tyrrhenian Sea*. John Murray, London, 1969.

Hamerton, Philip Gilbert. *The Saone: a Summer Voyage*. Seeley & Co, London, 1887.

Heikell, Rod. *Italian Waters Pilot*, 4th edition. Imray, Laurie, Norie & Wilson, St Ives, 1995.

Huish, M B. *The Seine & The Loire, Illustrated ... after Drawings by J M W Turner*. J S Virtue, London, 1895.

McKnight, Hugh. *Cruising the French Waterways*. Stanford Maritime, London, 1984.

Morgan-Grenville, Gerard. *Barging into Burgundy*. David & Charles, Newton Abbot, 1975.

Roberts, J & Morgan-Grenville, G. *No Ordinary Tourist: the Travels of an Errant Duke*. Milton Mill Publishing Ltd, Bridport. 2006.

Thorpe, Sir Edward. *The Seine From Havre to Paris*. Macmillan, London, 1913.

Other

Partridge, Eric. *A Dictionary of Slang & Unconventional English*. Single-volume edition. Routledge, London, 1982.

Rogers, Richard & Fisher, Mark. *A New London*. Penguin, London, 1992.

Maldwin Drummond

Maldwin Drummond has three consuming interests – sailing and wondering about the sea, Britain's maritime heritage, and the New Forest, where he farms.

In his early days on the water, yacht racing provided good training. Maldwin shared a Flying 15 with his brother, crewed in six-metres with his stepfather and was part of the crew of the *Gladeye*, a hundred-square-metre 'windfall' that won one or two minor prizes in the Fastnet race of 1955.

While in the Rifle Brigade in Germany and a member of the British Kiel Yacht Club, he cruised in a converted German Olympic six-metre without an engine around the Baltic. Cruising became a passion, but it had to be with a purpose. Expeditions were organised to discover if there was any relationship between the Viking crosses on the west coast of Norway and those to be found on Scotland's Highland fringe. Maldwin was also fascinated by the Baltic end of the Crimean

Maldwin Drummond aboard *Gloriana* RYS, rounding Cape Horn, 1 March 2006. *Photo: Gilly Drummond*

War, and looked for the graves of British seamen in the Åland Islands, part of the Finnish archipelago. He owned a number of yachts during this time, including the first *Gang Warily*, a Scottish fishing vessel that he persuaded to sail. The second *Gang Warily* was a cutter, one of the heroines of this book, and has a few paragraphs of her own in Chapter 2.

Cruising under sail persuaded Maldwin Drummond of the value of sail training. He became the chairman of the design committee for the *Sir Winston Churchill*, and was then chairman of the Sail Training Association for five years. This led to a great interest in Britain's maritime heritage, and eventually to chairmanship of the Maritime and *Cutty Sark* Trusts as well as the *Warrior* Preservation Trust, which conserved and restored HMS *Warrior* (1860) and brought her to Portsmouth. An interest in the natural environment, both land and sea, resulted in the book *The Yachtsman's Naturalist*, which endeavoured to introduce the amateur sailor to creatures that live above, below and on the surface of the sea.

Cruising in his own boat, Maldwin reached north to the Lofoten Islands off the coast of Norway and south to the heel of Italy. As a crew member on yachts of friends, he and Gilly have sailed along the southwest coast of Chile, through the Horn Archipelago and around the Horn on plant-hunting expeditions, as well as from Phuket to the Maldives and from New Zealand's South Island along the east coast to the northern tip of Cape Reinga. The oceans have their charm, but it is the challenge of the wild coast that stirs him most. Erskine Childers, whom he followed when writing his literary detective story *The Riddle*, had a favourite quotation from Tennyson's *Ulysses*: 'Come my friends, 'tis not too late to seek a newer world.' In a letter to his sister Dulcie, Childers added '– on from island unto island, to the gateways of the day.' Maldwin feels like that too.

Also by Maldwin Drummond

Conflicts in an Estuary, 1973

Secrets of George Smith, Fisherman (editor & illustrator), 1973

Tall Ships (illustrated by Mike Willoughby), 1976

Salt-Water Palaces, 1979

The Yachtsman's Naturalist (with Paul Rodhouse), 1980

New Forest (with Philip Allinson), 1980

The Riddle, 1985

West Highland Shores, 1990

John Bute, an Informal Portrait (editor), 1996

The Book of the Solent (editor, with Robin McInnes), 2001

Index

Page numbers in **bold** refer to illustrations

235

Also from
SEAFARER BOOKS and SHERIDAN HOUSE
www.seafarerbooks.com www.sheridanhouse.com

JOSEPH CONRAD: MASTER MARINER

PETER VILLIERS

Before he published his first novel in 1895, Joseph Conrad spent 20 years in the merchant navy, eventually obtaining his master's ticket and commanding the barque

Otago. This book, superbly illustrated with paintings by Mark Myers, traces his sea-career and shows how Konrad Korzeniowski, master mariner, became Joseph Conrad, master novelist. Alan Villiers, world-renowned author and master mariner under sail, was uniquely qualified to comment on Conrad's life at sea, and the study he began has been completed by his son, Peter Villiers.

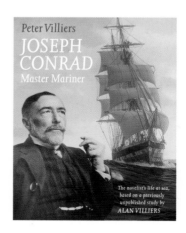

'A book that finally does justice to Conrad's time at sea'
Traditional Boats and Tall Ships

Illustrated with 12 paintings in full colour by Mark Myers RSMA F/ASMA

UK ISBN 0-9547062-9-3 USA ISBN 1-57409-244-8

CRUISE OF THE CONRAD

A Journal of a Voyage round the World, undertaken and carried out in the Ship JOSEPH CONRAD, 212 Tons, in the Years 1934, 1935, and 1936 by way of Good Hope, the South Seas, the East Indies, and Cape Horn

ALAN VILLIERS

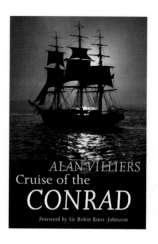

In 1934 the Australian sailor and writer Alan Villiers set out to fulfil his life's ambition – to obtain, equip and sail a full-rigged ship around the world, and enthuse others with his own love of sail before the opportunity was lost for ever. He was successful. His record of that extraordinary journey, more odyssey than voyage, was first published in 1937. In this new edition, complete with a short biography of Alan Villiers and richly illustrated with his own photographs, it will inspire a new generation of sailors and sea-enthusiasts.

'No other book like this will ever be written'
The Sunday Times

With a foreword by Sir Robin Knox-Johnston • Illustrated with photographs

UK ISBN 0-9547062-8-5 USA ISBN 1-57409-241-3

THE WAPPING GROUP OF ARTISTS

Sixty years of painting by the Thames

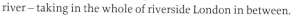
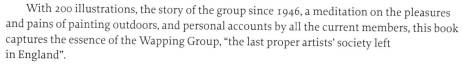

For sixty years, members of the Wapping Group have met to paint by the River Thames en plein air. Outdoors and undaunted in all weathers, come rain or shine, they have set up their easels from the broad tideways of the estuary to the willow-fringed backwaters up-river – taking in the whole of riverside London in between.

With 200 illustrations, the story of the group since 1946, a meditation on the pleasures and pains of painting outdoors, and personal accounts by all the current members, this book captures the essence of the Wapping Group, "the last proper artists' society left in England".

'... a delight to the senses and an essential new addition for any bookshelf'
E14 Magazine

'Sixty years after it was created, the Wapping Group is still flourishing and has won itself a secure niche in the artistic life of the capital ...'
Classic Boat

UK ISBN 0-9547062-5-0   USA ISBN 1-57409-218-9

WITH A PINCH OF SALT

A collection of nautical expressions and other stories as interpreted by

CAPTAIN NICK BATES

Are you **clewed-up** about all those expressions that so enrich the language of sailors – not to mention the landlubbers who have **Shanghaied** their vocabulary? Do you know **Captain Setab's Second Law of Dynamics**, or why **timbers shiver**, even in **horse latitudes**, where a **brass monkey** has nothing to fear? This little book, **chock-a-block** with the wit and wisdom of a Captain who **came up through the hawse pipe** to command one of the most famous vessels afloat, gives you **the whole nine yards**.

'... a nice piece of work ... remember it when Christmas comes'
Telegraph [NUMAST magazine]

UK ISBN 0-9547062-3-4   USA ISBN 1-57409-227-8

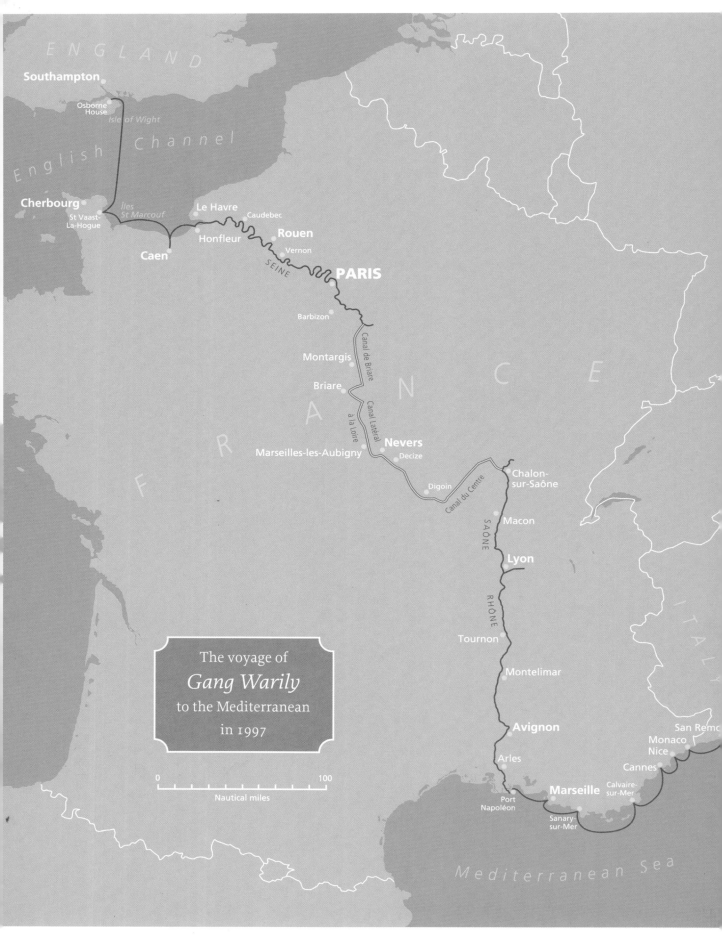

ENGLAND

Southampton

Osborne
House
Isle of Wight

E n g l i s h   C h a n n e l

Cherbourg
St Vaast-
La-Hogue
*Iles
St Marcouf*
Le Havre
Caudebec
Honfleur
Rouen
Vernon
Caen
SEINE
PARIS

Barbizon

Montargis

Briare

Canal de Briare

Canal Lateral
a la Loire

Canal Lateral
a la Loire

Marseilles-les-Aubigny
Nevers
Decize

Digoin
Canal du Centre
Chalon-
sur-Saône

Macon

SAÔNE

Lyon

RHÔNE

Tournon

Montelimar

Avignon
San Remo
Monaco
Nice
Arles
Cannes
Marseille
Calvaire-
sur-Mer
Port
Napoléon
Sanary-
sur-Mer

F R A N C E

I T A L Y

The voyage of
Gang Warily
to the Mediterranean
in 1997

0   100

Nautical miles

M e d i t e r r a n e a n   S e a